LOYAL PROTESTANTS *and* DANGEROUS PAPISTS

EARLY AMERICAN HISTORIES

Douglas Bradburn, John C. Coombs, and S. Max Edelson, Editors

LOYAL PROTESTANTS *and* DANGEROUS PAPISTS

Maryland and the Politics of Religion in the English Atlantic, 1630–1690

ANTOINETTE SUTTO

UNIVERSITY OF VIRGINIA PRESS

Charlottesville and London

University of Virginia Press

Printed in the United States of America on acid-free paper

First published 2015

ISBN 978-0-8139-3747-2 (cloth)
ISBN 978-0-8139-3748-9 (e-book)

1 3 5 7 9 8 6 4 2

Library of Congress Cataloging-in-Publication Data
is available from the Library of Congress.

For J.

CONTENTS

Acknowledgments / ix

Introduction / 1

PART I. CONFESSIONAL POLITICS

1. The Early Chesapeake and the Politics of Jacobean England / 13

2. The Personal Rule of Lord Baltimore / 26

3. Anarchy and Allegiance / 47

4. Pamphlets, Polemic, and the Revolutionary State / 58

PART II. COLONY AND EMPIRE

5. Conflicts of Interest / 81

6. War and Peace in the Chesapeake / 92

7. The Proprietary Regime and the Machinery of Empire / 104

PART III. CRISIS

8. Rumor and Politics / 129

9. News, Rumor, and Rebellion / 142

10. Glorious Revolutions / 159

Epilogue / 175

Notes / 181

Bibliography / 223

Index / 247

ACKNOWLEDGMENTS

This book would not be what it is without the support of numerous colleagues and friends. Peter Lake, Peter Silver, and John Murrin read interminable early drafts of the project and offered a wealth of criticism and insight. Sara Brooks, Rupali Mishra, and a long list of other Princeton friends and acquaintances provided moral support. The book in its current form was created during my fellowship at Vanderbilt University and my first years at the University of Mississippi, where the friendship and historical expertise of my colleagues were invaluable.

LOYAL PROTESTANTS *and* DANGEROUS PAPISTS

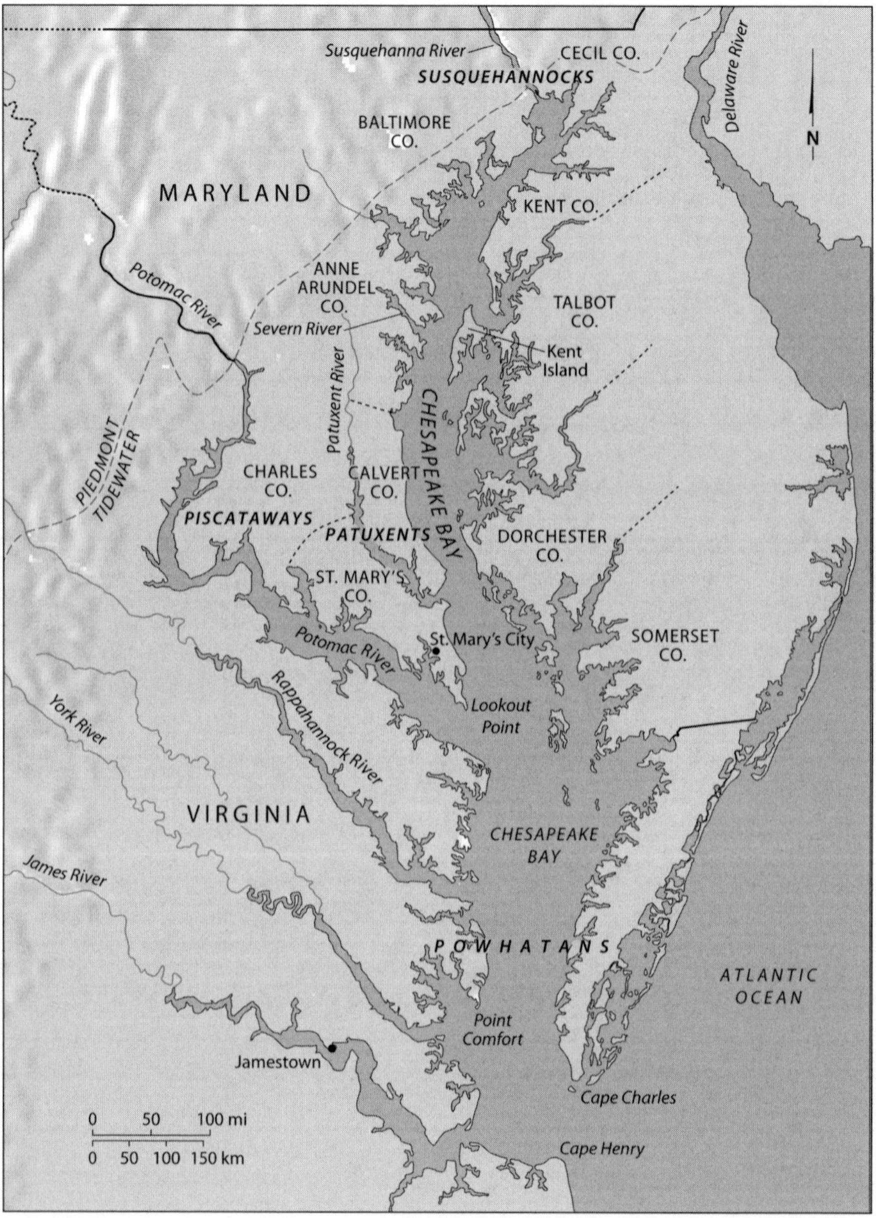

Maryland in the 1600s

INTRODUCTION

A characteristic early Stuart colonial project—which, uncharacteristically, survived—seventeenth-century Maryland is both familiar and foreign. Seen, as it often has been, through the lens of its land, workers, and staple commodity, Maryland's seventeenth century appears as an uneasy coalescence of social, economic, and political structures that by the early 1700s brought wealth and status to a few, a modest competency to others, and far more limited prospects to many more. The colony grew from a scattering of farms and trading posts in the 1630s to a land of modest opportunity for free migrants by the 1650s.[1] The price of its economic mainstay, tobacco, fell over the course of the century, and the amount that Chesapeake workers produced rose, creating wealth for landowners and lifetimes of hard labor for many others. Land and the freedom it could bring were increasingly hard to come by. Maryland in 1700 was more stable, demographically and politically, than it had been in the 1640s or 1650s, but it was also more starkly hierarchical. For those on the bottom looking up at century's end—servants, slaves, landless laborers—the gulf between their circumstances and those of the colony's elite would have seemed vast. Such distinctions were rendered ever more visible by the transformations in material culture wrought by the eighteenth-century imperial economy.[2] For the Piscataways, Susquehannocks and other Native residents of the area, the English in Maryland brought new goods and occasionally military or political support, but they also brought disease, violence, and dispossession.

From this perspective, Maryland was an English colony like many others. It shared a tobacco economy and much of its social structure with Virginia; the two Chesapeake colonies, in turn, shared the challenges of warfare, trade, diplomacy, religious conflict, and political order with other colonies, nations, and empires of early America, even as the specific circumstances of their histories and geographies rendered each of them distinct. But Maryland was peculiar. Its anomalous politics of religion, specifically the Catholic proprietors' policy of toleration and the colony's lack of an established church, have drawn the attention of generations of American historians. It was a colony of a Protestant kingdom, governed by Catholics and populated mainly by Protestants, including those who did not conform to the Church of England—in the eyes of many seventeenth-century people, its church affairs were dangerously unmoored from its official structures of authority. Over and over again, colonists, polemicists, and administrators commented on this disquieting state of affairs. Maryland was repeatedly wracked by political disorder in the seventeenth century, never without reference to the subversive qualities of papists, the malice of Protestant nonconformists, or the danger posed by religious diversity in general. That toleration in Maryland proved controversial is surprising only if one sees it through modern eyes: in the seventeenth century, what this sort of confessional arrangement meant and what (if anything) to do about it were questions central to conflicts over authority, legitimacy, and allegiance that brought revolution to the seventeenth-century Anglophone world twice over. The long, awkward negotiation between the needs of an expanding English state, early modern confessional politics, and the peculiarities of a little Chesapeake colony are the core of the story this book tells. It is a story about the violent and colorful political world of early Maryland, but it is also a story about the English state, and ultimately about the British empire.

Maryland offered its Catholic proprietors, the Calvert family, the prospect of New World wealth; it also offered them an opportunity to revise the uneasy relationship between English Catholics and the state. Such a revision was not merely of interest to Catholics. The Maryland proprietors' Catholicism led them to avoid a religious establishment in their colony. All Trinitarian Christians might worship as they chose.[3] But to argue for toleration in the early 1600s was not a principled withdrawal from a long and bloody confessional fray.[4] It was a profoundly political and profoundly controversial move. To suggest that subjects need not share a religion with their monarch overturned an entire edifice of assumptions about loyalty, law, and political order. In the 1630s, England's King Charles I was receptive to such an idea, but his willingness to patronize Catholics was intertwined with a view of the law, royal power, and the nature of the English state that ultimately placed him on the losing side of a civil war. Religious toleration in Lord Baltimore's colony was significant on its own terms and central to the experience of the English colonists there. At the same time, it was merely one element of the political matrix in which the colony operated. Maryland was launched into the middle of a long argument about religion, loyalty, and the state, and it remained entangled in that argument until the final years of the century.

This argument about religion and the state was in turn embedded in related questions about English expansion abroad and the Anglophone Atlantic—a history of Maryland is necessarily also a history of the seventeenth-century English empire. Voyages to the Americas, Africa, and Asia in the sixteenth and early seventeenth centuries presented a dizzying array of ways in which the English might engage with the wider world.[5] Chartered trading companies sought to establish footholds in India, Russia and the Middle East. Mariners—or pirates—such as Francis Drake or John Hawkins raided Spanish shipping for treasure and slaves. Groups of investors attempted settlement colonies on the North American coast but met with small success. The English connected the discovery of the Americas (and Americans) with the great confessional divisions of their day; the desire to make money was mingled with a sense of Protestant mission.[6] The earliest decades of sustained English enterprise abroad overlapped with the slow conversion of England into a Protestant nation—though the content of that Protestantism and how it ought to shape English government and policy proved difficult to define.[7]

How all this transatlantic, cosmopolitan activity was formally connected to the state posed an additional puzzle. Familiar legal structures such as trading monopolies, letters patent, or, in the case of Maryland, the Durham palatinate offered jumping-off points.[8] But old legal mechanisms in new places could breed controversy.[9] The crown and various committees of the Privy Council, not Parliament, governed the English colonial world in the seventeenth century. The nature of colonial government depended on the nature of royal power and the ties that bound subjects to monarchs. As historians of the English Civil Wars and the Revolution of 1688 have noted, the nature of royal power under the Stuarts was—at the risk of understatement—disputed. Arguments about law, religion, and kingly prerogative that drove interconnected rebellions in England, Ireland, and Scotland were not limited to the British Isles. Chesapeake colonists assumed that they had liberties as English people that did not derive from the prerogative powers of the crown, a claim that rarely meshed seamlessly with the Maryland proprietors' assumptions about their royally granted charter powers.[10]

This expanding state was nominally Protestant, yet the connection between the crown and the Church of England, too, was less straightforward than it seemed. Was uniformity of religion the tie that bound subjects to the king, or that held the polity together—and did Protestant uniformity require complete conformity to the Church of England? If the tie was via the Church of England alone, of which the king was supreme head, Protestant nonconformists could be both Protestant and disloyal. But if it was more important simply not to be Catholic, was there a space within the polity for Catholics at all? Could the crown grant a colonial charter to such persons? By the 1680s, some inhabitants of Maryland argued—persuasively, in the end—that it could not. The process of extending English authority across the Atlantic was necessarily bound up in arguments about law, loyalty, and confessional difference, and placed stress on some of the most tender points of the English political system.[11]

The slipperiness of the connection between confessional identity and political allegiance in the seventeenth century produced both conflict and opportunity in the English Atlantic. Charles I's views on religion and loyalty made it an eminently reasonable move to grant a colonial proprietorship to a Catholic in 1632.[12] But the fact that he did so proved enormously contentious—the same political moment that allowed for Maryland's creation also ensured its proprietors would be plagued by attempts to alter or overturn their charter. For this reason, the Glorious Revolution proved the end of an era in Maryland. The religious settlements after 1688 offered formal toleration for Protestant dissenters in England. The nature of the post-Revolutionary empire took years to work out fully, but one essential question was answered. It was more important not to be Catholic than to be in complete conformity to the Church of England. The eighteenth-century empire rested on this broad-bottomed definition of Protestantism.[13] Earlier, the nature of the state's Protestantism—or rather, the nature of the relation between "Protestantism" and the state—had been up for grabs, which inadvertently created a space for Catholics. If nonconforming Protestants could reveal lack of loyalty to the crown by dissenting from the Church of England, their disloyalty could outweigh the fact of their Protestantism. And perhaps Catholics might demonstrate loyalty sufficiently that their lack of Protestantism did not matter. This was the position of Charles I. It was certainly the position of James II, who dispensed with the Protestantism part of the formula altogether. The Revolution of 1688 ended the

Catholic Calverts' reign in Maryland because the possibilities opened up for Catholics by Charles I and his heirs were tied to a style of monarchy that the English ultimately rejected.

The internal politics of the English state were not the only force shaping the ideological landscape of the English Atlantic. The relationship between crown and colonies changed dramatically over the course of the seventeenth century. As the empire grew in wealth, population, and importance, specially appointed commissions and committees of the Privy Council were no longer sufficient to meet its administrative needs. The English had always needed to assert their claims to New World land and people against competing claims by other European powers.[14] There was also an internal process of negotiation, through which the precise relationship between colonies and state was worked out. Creating an empire and creating the early modern state were mutually constitutive and often controversial processes—the state and the empire were created by the people at the "peripheries" as well as those in the imperial center.[15]

As the state grew, however, two problems became ever more difficult to avoid. Part of the process by which early modern states and their overseas empires were created involved negotiation with localities. Local sources of authority were recognized or created as a way of drawing new people or new territory into the orbit of the state, but in the process, new privileges and potential claims on the state were created. States later had to reckon with their own creations—sometimes successfully, sometimes not.[16] This process threatened to "unhinge," as contemporaries put it, the English empire between 1660 and 1690, particularly after 1675, when the growth of imperial trade, controversies over religion and loyalty, and the internal politics of the American continent combined to create a deep crisis in American colonial administration.[17]

The second problem was the core meaning of "the state" itself. England was not merely a state; it was (most of the time, at least) a monarchy. In what did "the state" inhere—the body of the king? The unwritten "ancient constitution," or the laws passed by Parliament? Loyalty and lack thereof were at the center of Stuart politics, but so was the question of to what good subjects were loyal. What was the state? As the English polity underwent its seventeenth-century transformation—a process which involved a profound revision of the personal prerogatives of the crown, and for a decade the excision of the crown from the apparatus altogether—the creation of colonial governments via the issuance of charters and letters patent to individuals who might be understood to be of dubious reliability as subjects forced English people to confront this very question. In Maryland, its resolution was at the center of decades of debate over the legitimacy of Lord Baltimore's charter, and without a clear answer to this question in England, there could be none in the Chesapeake.

But this is not merely a story of English or imperial politics. Seventeenth-century America can be envisioned through the ties that bound English colonies to one another and to England; it can also be imagined through the international network of trade, communication, and exchange that linked the Americas, Africa, and Europe; it may be observed yet again from the continental perspective that connected the world of the tidewater Chesapeake via economic networks, political allegiances, and the circulation of people and information to places deep in the American interior.[18] The Atlantic perspective calls into question interpretive frameworks that privilege narrowly English or British concerns. The "periphery" that grew in tandem with the center was not a periphery for everyone, and not everyone in it—or in the center, either—was English.[19] It is tempting to split the difference between the English empire and the international Atlantic—were there "national Atlantics"? The challenge of Atlantic history writ large is the concept's occasional shapelessness.[20] The appeal of a specifically English Atlantic lies in its capacity to tease out previously unrecognized dimensions of problems historians have examined most often through a national or imperial lens—it presupposes we are interested primarily in the history of the Anglophone world, but offers a way of writing this history that encourages a wider view than more traditional national or imperial histories.[21]

This book is an English Atlantic history of seventeenth-century Maryland. But it is English Atlantic history of a specific kind. The Atlantic history of English activity abroad in the sixteenth and seventeenth centuries illuminates several problems crucial to understanding this particular colony, particularly the intertwined evolution of English encounters with "others," the growth of the Atlantic economy, and the expansion of the authority of the English state into the Americas. But to explain Maryland's tumultuous and unpredictable politics, the insights of the Atlantic model must be drawn together with the more insular concerns of seventeenth-century English politics. Maryland was an unusual creation, a colony in the hands of Catholics within a polity run by Protestants. It was subject to persistent and sometimes violent disputes over the relative power and place of Catholics and Protestants within its government and within the English world as a whole. It was also subject to persistent and sometimes violent disputes about things that seem not religiously motivated at all, the primary example of this being the long-running controversy between Cecil Calvert, 2nd Lord Baltimore, and Virginia trader and councilor William Claiborne over Claiborne's claims to a trading post on Kent Island, in the northern part of the Chesapeake. Even the "religious" nature of some of its ostensibly confessional controversies is called into question by the participants' seemingly mixed motives—several of the most virulently anti-papist revolutionaries in 1689, for example, were married to Catholics.[22] How should we tell this story?

Religion offers a way to integrate the disjointed events of Maryland's seventeenth-century history, but the mode of explanation requires a detour through the politics of religion in Stuart England—specifically, the politics of other people's religion in Stuart England. This seemingly narrow aperture offers a view of early Maryland that places the colony in the center of a far larger matrix of early modern conflicts over the nature of the state. This matrix included questions of colonial administration but was centered around early modern English arguments over the meaning of confessional difference, the sources of political conflict, and the origins and nature of political power. These conflicts tore England and Britain apart repeatedly in the seventeenth century, and their seeming intractability offered little hope for their resolution in Maryland. But Maryland's troubles were as American as they were English. The Catholic proprietary regime was brought down not only by events in England, but by the slow convergence of the ever weightier demands of the empire's administrative machinery and a politics of religion recognizably English but transformed by the American world.

* * *

The book is divided into three sections. Part I places the origins of the Maryland proprietorship amid the tangled legal and confessional politics of the late sixteenth and early seventeenth centuries. The decades of England's first overseas ventures were decades of conflict over the character of the Church of England and what conformity to it did or did not mean, the nature of the powers of the crown and its relation to those wielded by Parliament, and the relationship between the king's prerogative and the many other sources of law within the realm. England's earliest American settlement colonies were shaped by these debates in ways both obvious and subtle.

As important to the political world as the content of these controversies were their very presence and strange persistence. Early Stuart English people did not accept sustained and bitter conflict as a normal part of the political process. To them conflict signaled not politics as usual, but the presence of faction: malicious, self-interested persons out for their own gain rather than the kingdom's good. Who the factious persons were depended on one's point of view. James I and his son Charles were liable to blame Puritans—subversive, hypocritical malcontents who bleated about Protestant piety all the while trying to grasp power for themselves through specious appeals to liberty. Many of James's and Charles's critics, on the other hand, suspected not "blood-sucking sectaries"[23] but rather scheming papists, who wormed their way into the polity, even into the king's council chamber, and subtly undermined order, good government, and true piety on every conceivable level. The demise of the Virginia Company was shaped by the language of anti-Puritanism and "popularity" under James I, and ten years later the slightly different anti-Puritanism of Charles I would create an unprecedented opportunity for the Catholic Calvert family. Anti-Puritanism, like its better-known obverse anti-popery, was a coherent and instantly recognizable language of politics in the seventeenth century, one that was central to the political successes of people like Cecil Calvert and without which the torturous politics of the 1620s and 1630s make little sense.

These decades, which saw vitriolic disputes over the meaning of loyalty, the extent of royal power, and what criticism or limitation of that power might mean, are crucial for understanding the later history of the Chesapeake. Some Virginia Company diehards perceived the Maryland charter as an infringement of their liberties as English subjects—but whether this was the case or not depended on one's view of the limits of royal power and the prerogatives of the English crown. The presence of a Catholic proprietorship raised equally tricky questions about loyalty, the meaning of religious nonconformity, and the nature of the tie between subject and king. Lord Baltimore's understanding of his own royally granted charter powers proved productive of violent conflict over the status of English subjects in America, the likely sources of subversion, and the legal ties that bound colony and crown. These conflicts made and unmade government in the Chesapeake several times over in the 1640s and 1650s, just as they did in England. What was the state? If one was loyal, to what or whom was one loyal?

Lord Baltimore emerged from the 1650s relatively unscathed. England's overseas possessions were small and scattered in the early part of the century. The politics of the 1620s and 1630s had created a space in which colonies like his might develop, and while they raised disturbing questions, the empire was not yet large enough or valuable enough to require elaborate administrative oversight: such questions could linger unanswered. Or, at least for a time, they could be answered with the claim that a loyal subject had a legal charter, and that ought to suffice. The politics of the 1630s had offered Baltimore a way to assert loyalty to Charles I and argue for the disloyalty of those who might oppose his charter. He could make a case for his identity as a good subject to Charles, and even (with a bit of mild ideological revision) to the Commonwealth. In the context of England's loosely organized early Stuart empire, this was enough.

Part II begins with a point of both continuity and change. In the 1660s, Lord Baltimore and the governor and council of Virginia argued over a plan to revive the faltering tobacco trade. The problem grew out of the need to manage the increasingly valuable Chesapeake tobacco economy, but it was argued in shrill terms of loyalty and subversion that evoked the early Stuart past. The growing empire had added a new dimension to loyalty: the need to make the administration of empire work in the interest of the crown. Over the course of the 1660s and 1670s, Cecil Calvert and his son and successor Charles negotiated a rapidly shifting politics of empire in which defense of proprietary privilege could no longer rest on a mere reiteration that the king had granted them the charter. Cecil Calvert may have regarded his privileges as written in stone, but Charles II and James II did not—what the king might give, the king might take away, especially when old delegations of authority to colonial proprietors or companies created colonies whose people and products now needed to be controlled more firmly in order to operate in the crown's interest. Prerogative power had offered opportunity in the 1630s—it threatened the opposite forty years later.

The later seventeenth century also saw the beginning of a particularly American version of familiar confessional politics. The links many English clerics and administrators wished to draw between religious conformity and political loyalty added to the pressure the new administrative apparatus placed on the Calverts, but it was in the American context that the proprietors' religion made them particularly vulnerable. English encroachment on Native American land and the complex internal politics of the American continent convinced the English by the 1670s that "the Indians" were likely to kill them at any moment. The proprietary regime seemed to do a great deal of talking to Indians, but no results emerged—perhaps Catholics' true loyalties lay not with their fellow English people, but with the Catholic French and the Iroquois.

Part III describes how ordinary settlers created a specifically American variety of anti-popery that combined a variety of provincial grievances into a terrifying whole. In the late 1670s and early 1680s, disorder in the Chesapeake and transatlantic fears of Catholic conspiracy seemed on the brink of toppling the proprietary regime. Two men, Josias Fendall and John Coode, were believed to be about to raise a rebellion—but in the end, they did not. The incident revealed both the power and limitations of anti-popery alone. Without direct word from England, or some event that offered obvious justification for action, the potential uprising evaporated. Even those who were skeptical of the papist-French-Indian conspiracy story fell into confessional language when describing what had happened, however. Anti-Puritanism (or anti-popularity) and articulations of what caused subversion from below had also taken on a particularly American form in the Chesapeake thanks to Nathaniel Bacon, but complaints of "Baconists" did not have the same universal resonance as the old papist/Protestant divide. In 1689, the proprietary regime's failure to proclaim William and Mary offered John Coode and the Protestant Associators the chance to overthrow Baltimore's government. This seemed a triumph of anti-popery, and it was, but only up to a point. Coode and his associates were never fully recognized as the legitimate government of Maryland. It was less a victory for the Associators than a defeat for Lord Baltimore, who had been caught between an ideological rock and an administrative hard place. Coode and the Associators were reliably pro-William, anti-Catholic, and anti-French. Particularly in light of the evidence of lapses in the enforcement of monarchical power in Baltimore's colony, there was no positive reason why his proprietorship ought to continue. He might well be the most loyal and obedient of subjects, but a changed imperial and ideological context had shifted how attachment to the monarch was demonstrated—the Catholic proprietors' best defense of their regime had been pulled out from under their feet.

PART I
Confessional Politics

I

The EARLY CHESAPEAKE *and the* POLITICS *of* JACOBEAN ENGLAND

The "merging and emerging worlds" of the early Chesapeake seemed to promise vast profits and marvelous vistas of adventure and abundance.[1] What form that profit might take remained as uncertain as English knowledge of Chesapeake people and geography. Elizabethan experience offered an array of models for English people seeking wealth or power through overseas activity—it is only with hindsight that we can smile at the Virginia Company's skepticism of "that weed," tobacco, that some of their colonists began to cultivate by the late 1610s.[2] Even in the 1620s, investors imagined Virginia as a source of silk, glass, and other elegant consumer goods or even as a base for piracy against the Spanish. Across the Atlantic, Jamestown colonists soon learned that they had stepped not into a timeless Eden but rather into a place its first settlers called Tsenacommacah.[3] The historical and political landscapes of the Powhatans, Susquehannocks, and others were useful to the English at some times, often in ways the newcomers never fully appreciated, and less so in others. The native residents of the Chesapeake found the English occasionally friendly but more often troublesome. What form the relationship between natives and newcomers would take was hard to know.[4] In 1616 Matoaka or Pocahontas, the daughter of the chief of the Powhatan, visited England and met its monarch. Just a few years later, in 1622, the Powhatans struck a blow against Jamestown that left the English terrified.

English people were eager to grasp the riches and marvels of the New World. But they feared that travel and knowledge had a price. Sixteenth- and early seventeenth-century travelers, whether to the New World, the Mediterranean, or elsewhere, brought home information useful to the commonwealth, but in doing so they risked their own cultural and spiritual integrity—widened horizons could invite corruption and degeneracy.[5]

Contact with American people led the English to ask whether Native Americans represented a past stage of civilization that the English themselves had left behind—or perhaps their vaunted European civility was merely another name for luxury?[6] Travel might corrupt—or it might offer a mirror of corruption that already existed. Perhaps as they gained civility, the English had lost the virtues of primitive simplicity. Both John Smith and William Strachey, for example, writing about Virginia in times of political tension in England, were interested in the question of the common people's obedience to political rulers, a sign of order and virtue, and both found reason to admire the Americans they met. Smith noted that "[they have] among them such government, as that their magistrates for good commanding and their people for due subjection, and obeying, excel many places that would be counted very civil," and Strachey attributed the English colonists' own admiration of Powhatan to an innate sense of the majesty of kingship.[7] Although the framing of the problem would take on different forms as the century progressed, English people were already using new world encounters and experiences to articulate questions, even fears, about what made them English and what that meant.

English people anticipated opportunities for commerce and Protestant evangelism, but such opportunities had a way of raising uncomfortable questions. What were colonies for, and how were they to be governed? What was their place within the realm, if indeed they were in it? How might they change those English people who lived there, or even those who did not? Colonial possessions and people might even transform the English state, both in terms of simple wealth—the Spanish provided an example of that—and perhaps also in other ways that were as yet difficult to imagine.

Late Elizabethan and early Jacobean colonial ventures had a way of failing, sometimes spectacularly so. In other cases they merely vanished without a trace.[8] The survival of Virginia through the 1610s and the hugely profitable tobacco boom of the 1620s pushed the crown and the king's advisors—not to mention investors, company directors, and colonists—to articulate the place of colonies and their inhabitants within the English polity.[9] But the timing of the question shaped the answer. The 1610s and 1620s brought deepening political conflict as the English argued over whether and how they would enter the Thirty Years' War in Europe. A series of financial weaknesses, confessional fractures, and legal gray areas within the English state became ever more difficult to avoid.[10] Disagreements over finance, church policy, and foreign affairs took shape within a political culture strikingly different from our own, one that valued harmony and unanimity and understood persistent conflict not as a sign that compromise among various interests was necessary, but rather as an indicator of deeper troubles: extended conflict revealed that corruption, malice, and faction were at work.

Who the malicious or factious persons might be depended on one's religious views. English people saw political conflict in confessional terms.[11] Conflict might be caused by the popularity-seeking Puritans that so annoyed James I—or by the creeping poison of popery that so alarmed the subjects of his son, Charles. In a political world in which it was impossible to declare oneself for anything but loyalty to the crown, the law, and the public good, it was necessary to say what one was against—was the problem the influence of Catholic or crypto-Catholic advisors who respected neither law nor right religion, or was it more important to challenge those who would use the language of liberty and Protestant patriotism to undermine the power of royal prerogative for their own selfish ends?[12] This tangle of policy and ideology became intertwined with questions of colonial governance; it was within this matrix of ideas that English people articulated and argued questions about what to do with the Virginia Company, which by the early 1620s was in deep trouble.

* * *

By the 1620s, Virginia colonists had discovered that they could make money—in some cases a great deal of money—planting tobacco. The struggling outpost that had been on the verge of collapse over and over since 1607 appeared to have found its economic footing. But not everyone welcomed the prospect of a colony whose only product was a stinking weed. Besides, the journey from tobacco production to profit was a long one, and there was little agreement as to the route. Should the company solicit investments and produce tobacco under its own auspices, or was it preferable to allow migrants and adventurers to cultivate their own "particular" plantations while the company focused simply on supplying the colonists and securing a monopoly on marketing the tobacco? The issue was important to the colony's directors and investors, but may not have meant much to those in the colony itself. Without adequate food or peaceful relations with Native Americans the effects of logistical rearrangements were limited.[13] For most migrants, the Powhatans' devastating strike against the English in

1622, followed by famine, loomed much larger than the vicissitudes of the Company.[14]

Problems of diplomacy, supply and logistics bled into issues of personal and professional rivalry within the Company itself. The relationship between these "cross agitations," as one contemporary put it, the politics of the 1620s, and events in the Chesapeake were complex.[15] The faction within the Company associated with the prominent London merchant Thomas Smythe and that attached to the investor and politician Edwin Sandys had different visions of the company's future and the most appropriate relationship between investors and colonists, but these did not always map easily onto the great and growing ideological divergences of the early 1620s. National policy questions did occasionally intrude. By 1626, for example, after the dissolution of the Company, Charles I's desperate need for nonparliamentary sources of money suggested the possibility of a royal tobacco monopoly that would comprehend all tobacco imported into the kingdom, including that from the Chesapeake.[16] Earlier, under Company rule, the Rich family wished to use the colony as a privateering base against the Spanish, a risky policy in the early 1620s as James I felt out a potential match (ultimately unsuccessful) between his son Charles and the daughter of the king of Spain.[17]

Some key events of the Company's last years were matters more of luck and opportunism than a working out of deep questions of principle. The goal of those Company investors who opposed then-treasurer Edwin Sandys was less ideological than practical: they wanted to break up the Company so as to gain control of it when it was rechartered. And they did believe it would be—James seems to have promised as much.[18] But he died in 1625 with the Company still officially dissolved, although a mistake had prevented the charter's annulment from being officially entered in the records. This combination of royal assurance and technical error would prove the core of a long and rancorous Virginia Company grudge against the Maryland charter of 1632, which granted Lord Baltimore land that the ex-Company adventurers believed ought to belong to their colony.[19] Some of the administrative changes enacted while Sandys was treasurer, including the creation of a representative assembly in the colony, make it tempting to wonder if efforts to quash company's charter were not a subtle argument about the power and place of legislatures in America or elsewhere. The many practical reasons for dissolving the Company—most notably its failure to make money and the alarming death rate of the colonists—were far more important than the presence or absence of an assembly, however.[20] Virginia's little legislature was well below the royal radar.

This does not mean that the Company's demise was divorced from political considerations, however. By 1624, when the Company's charter was vacated, James I had become increasingly edgy about "popularity," or subversion from below by malcontents, often Protestant nonconformists, who used appeals to the people in order to gain power for themselves and undermine the power of the crown. This set of associations went back to his youth. As the king of Scotland, he had supported the bishops of Scotland's episcopal church as natural props of monarchy. He had tangled with powerful Presbyterian churchmen in Scotland long before he became king of England, and the link in his mind between Protestants of the Puritan variety and threats to his authority never weakened. In England, he feared "new Puritanical strains, that makes [sic] all things popular" as well as malcontents who courted the people and promised them liberty so as to aggrandize themselves.[21] In England, the agitation in the 1570s and 1580s for a Presbyterian church settlement had been linked by the more conservative to a popular conspiracy; the Presbyterian style of church government was seen as a threat to the authority of the crown. The potential power of public opinion and the threat to the state of those who might court it were amply demonstrated by the career of the Earl of Essex in the 1590s and early 1600s.[22]

Events after 1618 only sharpened the king's views on such matters. The question of whether, and how, England would enter the Thirty Years' War in Europe created tension between the king and a vocal subsection of Parliament. Despite dynastic ties to the embattled Frederick, the Protestant Elector Palatine, James was reluctant to wage war; certainly he did not want the type of all-out confessional war being argued for in the House of Commons. James saw himself as an ecumenical peacemaker—the so-called "Protestant Cause" left him cold. Moreover, aside from the question of entry into the war itself, the vocal role some members of Parliament were attempting to play in the decision angered the king. To him, this was an infringement on his prerogative because the power to declare war was a matter of state outside the purview of Parliament. The confessional coloring of the dispute only reinforced his suspicion of a strong connection between enthusiastic Protestantism and threats to monarchy.[23]

There was no necessary connection between the plight of the Elector Palatine and the fate of Virginia, but the coincidence offered the enemies of Sir Edwin Sandys too good an opportunity to pass up. Sandys's various colonial commitments and his occasionally misplaced assertiveness in defending them had earned him bitter enemies in some fairly high places.[24] Neither was he a particular favorite of the king. During the controversy in the early 1620s over England's entry into the war in Europe, there was a brief period during which James's son and heir Charles allied with James's favorite, the Duke of Buckingham, and a number of MPs in an effort to push James into precisely the sort of expensive, naval war against the Spanish that James did not want, leaving James beset—as he saw it—on all sides by a conspiracy of popularity. Among those MPs was Sir Edwin Sandys. This conflict reached its peak in 1623–24, just as the fate of the Virginia Company was being decided.[25]

Some of Sandys's opponents in the struggle over the future of the Virginia Company took the obvious path and used James's dislike of "popularity" to discredit him. First, they claimed with some justice that he was manipulating the voting system within the Company. Moreover, the voting system itself had troublesome popular elements, since an investment of any size entitled the holder to a vote. Small adventurers, or adventurers who divided their shares among kinsmen or friends, could thus outvote more substantial and experienced investors.[26] More specific indications of an attempt to paint Sandys as a Puritan populist come from a conversation between Nathaniel Rich and the trader Captain John Bargrave. Rich wrote down an account of their talk, and said Bargrave claimed he had known Sandys for a long time and thought "that there was not any man in the world that carried a more malicious heart to the government of a monarchy than Sir Edwin Sandys did." Bargrave, again according to Rich, "had heard him say that if our God from heaven did constitute and direct a form of government, it was that of Geneva . . . his intent was to erect a free state in Virginia." This was one of the earlier gestures made by English controversialists toward linking colonial governments and the presumed political proclivities and loyalties (or lack thereof) of the governors; it would not be the last. Sandys, according to Bargrave, had also pressed Archbishop George Abbot to allow Puritan sectaries to settle there.[27] Rich recorded that his conversation with Bargrave occurred in May 1623. By this time, the first of several royally appointed commissions to investigate Virginia affairs was already active. Those who opposed Sandys were trying hard to push the investigation in the direction of action against Sandys and his group rather than action against the Company as a whole. No decision had as yet been made concerning the Company's future, and had he wished to, there would still have been time for Rich to try to tar Sandys with Bargrave's words.

The challenge with using the popularity charge against Sandys in particular was that fault lines within the Virginia Company did not align perfectly with other lines of political conflict. Some of the men who opposed Sandys on matters Virginian were, like him, among those "noble Patriots" drawn into the Duke of Buckingham's "patriot coalition" during the winter of 1623–24 or had favored the war even earlier.[28] Among these was the Earl of Warwick, who, along with his cousin Nathaniel Rich, wanted to use Virginia as a base for privateering against the Spanish.[29] This could have made using the Bargrave conversation more trouble than it was worth, since an attempt to use the popularity argument against Sandys might have backfired in the faces of men who approved a policy against Spain that the king considered tied to that very same problem of Puritanism and popular agitation.

But such a powerful language of denunciation was hard to resist. An account written by a partisan of the Virginia Company several decades later states that the anti-Sandys group in the Company faction cleverly managed to convince King James that "the form of the company's government, as consisting of an excessive number of counselors and a confused popularity," was "a nurse of parliamentary spirits and obnoxious to monarchical government."[30] James may have heard about the Bargrave conversation. In 1623, the Virginia Company and the related Somers Isles Company defended themselves to the king against accusations that "the government as it now stands is democratical and tumultuous," a charge they termed "a slander."[31] The language of democracy and popularity reappeared again in James's July 1624 commission to settle a new government for Virginia, which noted that the colony's government had devolved into "so popular a course . . . which caused much contention and confusion."[32] Years later, prominent inhabitants of Virginia who feared a rechartering of the Company would use the same language in an address to Charles, describing the dreaded Company as a "popular and tumultuary government."[33]

James may also have been pressured on this point from other directions. According to a later account of the life of the prominent merchant Nicholas Ferrar, the Conde de Gondomar, who was Spain's ambassador to England, wanted the Virginia Company quashed. Gondomar told James that he ought to "look to" the meetings of the Virginia Company, where "too many of his nobility and gentry resorted to accompany the popular Lord Southampton and the dangerous Sandys." Even though the Company "might have a fair pretense for their meetings, yet he would find in the end that court would prove a seminary for a seditious parliament." Gondomar also apparently suggested that the problem was one for kings, not subjects, to manage.[34] A "Discourse of the Old Company" addressed to the council in April 1625 noted that "it hath been said by many" that the overthrow of Virginia was "part of the Count of Gondomar's instructions." They doubted Gondomar had deliberately set out to undermine the colony but noted that "in bringing about his own ends, he could create here instruments of ourselves against ourselves."[35] If the general story of Gondomar's opposition to the Company was true, Gondomar's suggestions of popularity and potential sedition were well calculated to resonate with James, who had spent his last two parliaments attempting to convince some of his pushier subjects that there were *arcana imperii,* secrets of state, with which they must not meddle.

George Calvert was among the participants in the debate over popularity, foreign policy, and the Virginia Company in the early 1620s. Like Sandys, Calvert's career entangled him in both controversies over foreign policy and prerogative and troubles with the chartering and administration of American colonies. He was from a Yorkshire family that had a long history of brushes with the law over Catholicism and absence from the state church. His early upbringing and education were Catholic, but from his early teens until his conversion to Catholicism in 1625 he conformed to the Church of England. A protégé of the prominent and controversial royal advisor Sir Robert Cecil, Calvert served as an MP for the first time in 1609, acting primarily as a yes-man for Cecil.

By the early 1620s Calvert had been appointed to the Privy Council, and he sat in the Parliaments of both 1621 and 1624.[36] Here he seems to have been a reliable mouthpiece for the crown. In December 1621 he was tasked by the king to order the House of Commons not to waste time on matters that were not their responsibility; James also indicated that he could not "with patience endure" the "antimonarchical words" he had been hearing from that quarter.[37] Months earlier, when Sandys was imprisoned for being, as Calvert himself put it, "too busy and industrious to trouble his majesty's service and affairs," Calvert had tried to explain to Parliament that Sandys had not been arrested for too great a freedom of speech in the House of Commons.[38] As Secretary of State in the early 1620s, he helped to manage the controversial and ultimately failed negotiations to arrange a marriage between Charles and the Spanish infanta. Calvert was so closely associated with the Spanish marriage negotiations that when he converted to Catholicism in 1625, some assumed that he had done so under foreign influence. George Abbot, the Archbishop of Canterbury, reported that "Mr. Secretary Calvert hath never looked merrily since the prince his coming out of Spain: it was thought, that he was much interested in Spanish affairs: a course was taken to rid him of all employment and negotiations. This made him discontented; and, as the saying is, *desparatio facit monachum,* so he apparently did turn papist, which he now professeth, this being the third time that he hath been to blame that way."[39] The bishop and court chaplain Godfrey Goodman claimed that Calvert was "infinitely addicted to the Roman Catholic faith, having been converted thereunto by [the Spanish ambassador] Count Gondomar and Count Arundell, whose daughter Secretary Calvert's son had married."[40] Calvert's official position also brought him into the controversy over the Virginia Company. In addition to being a private investor in the Company, he was involved as Secretary of State in various negotiations between crown and Company, and in 1624 he was appointed to the commission that was set up to investigate how the colony was being run.[41]

In the course of his parliamentary and official career, Calvert brushed up against questions of loyalty and allegiance at every turn. James feared and resented "popularity," and, as his councilor, Calvert echoed the king's pronouncements to Parliament about loyalty and the danger of "antimonarchical" sentiment. Even if his family's history of recusancy had not brought him into firsthand contact with the late Elizabethan and early Stuart politics of religion, his official employments would certainly have done so, particularly the drawn-out negotiations with Spain. Questions of loyalty were inextricable from questions of religion. James disliked Puritans—they had a tendency to criticize monarchs—but he was willing to tolerate Catholics, at least up to a point. During the Spanish marriage negotiations, it became clear that an alliance with Spain would require adjustment of some English rules concerning church attendance. In 1622, Calvert passed on news that circuit judges were advised to "carry themselves towards Catholics temperately considering his Majesty's alliance now at this present negotiated with a prince of that religion." James wanted to set an example of "mercy and grace." But if any Catholics presumed too much and "carrie[d] themselves . . . insolently and scandalously" they would discover the limits of the king's tolerance.[42] The possibility of a Catholic alliance suggested "favor intended to the Catholics."[43] From James's perspective, this meant merely an extension of his royal grace that ought to be deferentially acknowledged and repaid with grateful obedience.

For others, toleration of Catholics suggested darker forces at work. Thomas Scott, who was precisely the sort of Protestant nonconformist James disliked, linked toleration of Catholics to the threat of universal monarchy under the twin headship of the Pope and the king of Spain. Scott also revealed the potential links between English colonies in America and the great confessional conflicts that agitated Europe and the British Isles. The international Catholic conspiracy he described opposed English activity in Virginia because the English there might "raise another England to withstand our [Scott wrote in the voice of the Catholics] new Spain in America, as this old England opposeth our present state."[44] Scott presented Virginia as a Protestant mirror of England, there to counter the Catholic colonies attached to Spain. He was not the last to assume that English colonies should—perhaps must—be seen as a part of this cosmic battle.

George Calvert converted to Catholicism in 1625 amid this vitriolic argument over who represented the greater threat to monarchy, order, and true religion. By this time James had been succeeded by his son Charles I, and Calvert's conversion raised what would be one of the signal questions of Charles's reign—what was the relationship between confessional identity and political allegiance? Charles's response to Calvert's resignation was revealing. He was willing to keep Calvert on the council; there is evidence to suggest he was even willing to let him evade the oath of supremacy in order to retain him.[45] For Charles, Calvert's loyalty and service to the king were more important than the presence of a Catholic on the Privy Council. Bonds to the monarch, not confessional alignments, held the polity together. Charles would never waver from this position, even as accusations mounted in the 1630s and early 1640s that he was too close to too many Catholics, to the peril of his kingdom. But in 1625, the political maelstrom that would eventually overtake Charles was still twenty years away. He accepted Calvert's resignation, and in recompense for the loss of office and for past service, gave him the title of Baron of Baltimore.[46]

Calvert spent the later 1620s engaged in a colonial project in Newfoundland, a project that like so many of its early seventeenth-century contemporaries did not work out as well as expected. In this Calvert was no different from the many other Elizabethan and Jacobean projectors whose plans for profit proved miscalculations. The trouble in Newfoundland was mainly the cold climate, but the experience also highlighted a problem that Calvert's son Cecil would encounter more powerfully in Maryland. A minister named Erasmus Stourton accused him of having the children of Protestants in the colony forcibly baptized as Catholics.[47] Stourton's accusation appears both silly and predictable, but it highlighted a troublesome point. Colonies were an extension in some form—precisely what form was as yet a tricky question—of the English state. Stourton's accusation was a claim about baptisms, but it was also a claim about politics. Calvert had usurped the authority of (Protestant) parents to have their children baptized in their own faith—he had interfered with the structure of the family and attempted to draw Protestants away from their "native" religion. The household was an important part of the structures of order that held society together. In accusing him of tampering with it, Stourton was accusing Calvert of the type of crimes typical of papists—subversion of order and right religion on every level.[48]

Calvert abandoned the colony in 1629. His voyage home took him first to Virginia, where he found a warmer climate but a decidedly colder reception. The Virginia council got the impression that he intended to settle there and this provoked a disagreement that revealed in condensed form the problems presented by a Catholic in a Protestant colony. The council of Virginia was uneasy about his religion. As they reported later to the Privy Council, Calvert and "some of his followers," all Catholics, "utterly refused" to take the oaths of allegiance and supremacy. The oath of supremacy was an affirmation that the monarch of England was the head of both the kingdom and the church and a promise to reject all foreign power or jurisdictions of any kind. The oath of allegiance had been created by statute in 1606, the year after the Gunpowder Plot. It required the oath taker to swear allegiance to the king and deny that the Pope had any power to depose princes. Jacobean Catholics differed over whether the oath of allegiance was intended as a straightforward loyalty test or a more devious attempt to serve up the oath of supremacy in a different form. Some took it, but most prominent clerical and lay Catholics refused.[49] In theory, refusal of the oaths was treason.

Calvert proposed a different oath that he and the Catholics with him could take instead, but the Virginia council objected. They did not think they were permitted the "latitude . . . to decline from the prescribed form." Indeed, they had always been very "happy . . . in the freedom of our religion which we have enjoyed, and that no papists have been suffered to settle their abode amongst us."[50] Freedom of religion here meant the harmony ensured by religious uniformity. The council's words pointed to a question that they assumed was closed, but which the Lords Baltimore would demonstrate was not. The Virginians indicated that they thought the link between Protestantism and loyalty to the crown obtained even in the American world. Calvert should have taken the oaths in Virginia as he ought to have in England. But Calvert's presence and his Newfoundland colony, however unsuccessful, undermined that assumption. George Calvert had demonstrated his soundness as a subject to the satisfaction of King James, who had issued the original letters patent for the Newfoundland colony. Calvert's conversion had not caused the charter to be revoked, and Charles had not indicated that he had any objection to Catholics with colonial charters. Lord Baltimore's errand in the Americas was entirely above-board, and yet he would not swear the oaths that were understood to legally demonstrate one's loyalty to the crown and the realm. Perhaps the rules in America were different, and all that mattered was the charter—but as the long history of controversy about Cecil Calvert's Maryland colony would demonstrate, to make that claim was to argue for a version of the English state that made many English subjects profoundly uneasy.

* * *

In 1629, when George Calvert refused the oaths of allegiance and supremacy in Virginia, the relationship between English colonists resident in the New World and the authority of the crown was relatively untested. English trading corporations abroad in the early Stuart period tended to govern their own according to internal rules.[51] In general, the legal map of the New World from a European perspective was "variegated." The status of people there was unstable, and terms like "loyal subject" or "traitor" could be hard to pin down.[52] Whether a company, corporation, or other entity acted lawfully or not could be difficult to determine. For example, Sir Thomas Gates and Sir Thomas Dale imposed martial law in Virginia in 1611 in order to prevent disaster. Gates, Dale, and others thought this necessary, but some colonists were outraged, and the incident fed into the lengthening litany of Virginia Company abuses.[53] Even twenty-some years later in Maryland, a dispute between assembly and proprietor over how to adopt laws and whether the ones Lord Baltimore had sent were suitable led one assemblyman to suggest that martial law was applicable and the charge of mutiny might do for a variety of crimes until they got the matter sorted out.[54] English inhabitants of colonies did not occupy the same legal space as their compatriots in England, but what legal space or spaces they did inhabit was difficult to determine.

This question grew more urgent over the 1610s, 1620s, and 1630s as more English people crossed the Atlantic. What worked for trading factories and military bases did not necessarily work for settlement colonies. But the question of how this relationship was to operate was not worked out in a political vacuum. Just a few months before George Calvert's visit to Virginia in 1629, Charles I had angrily dismissed Parliament, frustrated at his subjects' failure to act as he thought loyal subjects ought and suspicious that a Puritan faction in the House of Commons was out to undermine his authority.[55] Parliament would not meet again for over ten years.

In the 1620s, increasingly sharp debates over religion, loyalty, and monarchical power mingled with matters of colonial administration. Edwin Sandys was tarred with "popularity." George Calvert was accused of having Protestants' children forcibly baptized as Catholics. After 1632, when a second Chesapeake colony was created out of land that some claimed still belonged to the first, the politics of loyalty and the languages of popularity, anti-Puritanism, and anti-popery created a conflict over the nature of colonial governments and the English state that would rage for decades.

2

The PERSONAL RULE *of* LORD BALTIMORE

Charles I dismissed Parliament in early 1629 and did not summon it again until 1640, when the demands of war with Scotland made it unavoidable. He had come to believe that a faction of anti-monarchical conspirators, most of them Puritans, were working to undermine his authority and alienate him from the loyal majority of his subjects. These twin ideas, loyalty and subversion—devotion to the king and derogation of his powers—would shape both his "personal rule" of the 1630s and the fortunes of Maryland, whose Catholic proprietor was perfectly poised to take advantage of the politics of these years.

As far as the king was concerned, the problem had begun under his father with the controversy over how to enter the war in Europe—James had consistently rebuffed the suggestion that England fight a war on confessional terms.[1] Charles was willing to engage England in the conflict, but he did so more out of a perceived need to defend family and national honor than any desire to join an apocalyptic Protestant battle against the Catholic anti-Christ. Despite a vast outlay of funds, his efforts ended in defeat and embarrassment. For this the House of Commons blamed his favorite, the Duke of Buckingham, and attempted to impeach him several times. The king considered the attempts to impeach Buckingham a personal attack on himself. Moreover, as the country's failures to alter the course of the European war became more evident, the House of Commons was increasingly wary of providing Charles with money for the war, or for anything else—they did not know what he was going to do with it, and he consistently rebuffed their attempts to exchange supply of funds for redress of their grievances about both Buckingham and the conduct of the war.[2] Charles understood this as an attempt by subjects to determine his policy and limit his power, which to him again appeared evidence of disloyalty and a lack of trust. Although sometimes willing to attempt negotiation, fundamentally he did not believe he was obligated to explain himself to Parliament or justify his actions.[3]

By 1629 members of the House of Commons who wished to fight the "Protestant cause" in Europe, guard liberty and property at home, and prevent the encroachment of popery were baffled and rebuffed again and again by a king who appeared to want to do none of these things and refused to explain why. That Charles might be a budding tyrant was not merely the idle speculation of a few malcontents. In 1629, a manuscript tract purported to be written by the king's council described a plan to "bridle" Parliament, increase the royal revenue, and reframe English government so as to make Charles "an absolute tyrant." The alleged plot drew considerable attention.[4] The accusations may have been wild, but contemporaries' assumption of their plausibility is telling. Charles, for his part, wanted to be trusted and obeyed by his subjects, who seemed perversely keen on attacking him without justification, impeaching his favorite, making demands about foreign policy that he did not think were within their authority to make, and demanding recognition of rights he did not recognize.

Increasingly Charles believed the greatest threat to his authority came not from Catholics in England or popery abroad, but from "factious spirits" or hard-line Protestants in Parliament itself, who were courting "popularity" in order to gain power for themselves.[5] These men (not all of whom were actually Protestant nonconformists) often used arguments about the nature and antiquity of the English common law and the "ancient constitution" to curb what they saw as unlawful excesses of monarchical power. Charles believed that his prerogative preceded and limited the common law, not—as his political opponents would have it—the other way around.[6] To criticize his power was to undermine monarchical authority and was ipso facto evidence of disloyalty. However much early Stuart political culture might value harmony and consensus, there was a significant division over what they would all have agreed was center of the system: the powers of the crown.

During his so-called personal rule of the 1630s, Charles became ever more preoccupied with personal loyalty to the king as a means of signifying loyalty. The culture of the Caroline court emphasized the beauty of order, peace, and virtue, revolving harmoniously around the "sacral figure of the king."[7] More than his predecessors, Charles emphasized formality, ceremony and reverence for the king's person. The king's famed domestic felicity was not merely personal happiness—it represented the natural harmony of a man governing his family and a king his kingdom. The core of monarchy lay in the person of the monarch.[8]

Charles Stuart's understanding of kingship created an opportunity for English Catholics in the 1630s. The politics of the personal rule offered a potentially different set of terms on which English Catholics might engage with the state—a relationship that had had a fraught history since the religious revolutions of midcentury. All of Elizabeth's subjects, like those of her Stuart successors, were required to attend the services of the Church of England. The experiences of those who did not, whether Catholics or nonconforming Protestants, varied. Whether lay or clerical, humble or powerful, Catholics were connected to the English state not by relationships of simple persecution on one hand and straightforward endurance, resistance, or complicity on the other. Rather, the place of Catholics within the English polity and even the boundaries of Catholicism itself were subject to constant negotiation and revision.[9] Under Elizabeth, the execution of Jesuit priests for what the regime labeled treason and what the Jesuits themselves claimed was for the sake of conscience opened up an argument about the nature of the Elizabethan state and the limits of its powers—not to mention what fell under the category of "religion" and what religion had to do with political allegiance.[10]

Even questions that might appear internal to the Catholic community were shaped by political context. The approbation controversy of the 1620s revealed the many-layered relationships between religious affiliation, personal interest, and loyalty to the English state. The dispute's name derived from the requirements laid on regular clergy by Richard Smith, who was appointed Bishop of Chalcedon in 1624—England's first Catholic bishop in some time. Smith assumed that this office gave him conventional episcopal authority over clerics and Catholic laypeople in England, and in accordance with church law he required that clergy have his approbation before they heard confessions. But England was not a Catholic country. Regular clergy had developed their own structures of administration and discipline over the years and were reluctant to submit to Smith; prominent lay Catholics feared episcopal taxes and visitations of household chapels. They also feared that if they submitted to the formal ecclesiastical jurisdiction Smith was set on, they would be guilty of praemunire under English law.

This was a serious matter. Praemunire was originally a charge of pursuing a suit abroad that was cognizable in English courts. After the Reformation, it came to refer specifically to any assertion of papal jurisdiction within England. Punishment for praemunire was severe, and could include forfeiture of property. Opposing Smith was a way to demonstrate loyalty to the English state and avoid such a terrifying prospect. The laity could evade the bishop's meddlesome demands and in rejecting this imposition of Catholic authority they could also show that their primary loyalties were to crown and state, not Rome.

Regular clergy and many lay Catholics, then, had reason to make common cause against Smith and had political reasons to do so that lay beyond the immediate issue of approbation. Among the laity, George Calvert was well known as a partisan of the Jesuits, who were among Smith's primary opponents on this issue. Smith, for his part, played the same political game as Calvert and the Jesuits, attempting to place his attempts to control the regular clergy in parallel to Archbishop Laud's efforts to impose internal uniformity on the Church of England. Like Puritans, he argued, Jesuits were disorderly and subversive, with a persistent tendency to undermine duly constituted structures of authority. In this version, Smith and his adherents were the true loyal English subjects and ought to have Charles I's support.[11] The categories of "good Catholic" and "loyal subject" and the nature of the connection between them were subject to dispute; this dispute itself was shaped by the complex politics of loyalty and allegiance during the reigns of James I and Charles I.

Catholicism as experienced by Catholics was subject to revision and dispute, but the Protestant view of Catholicism became increasingly brittle during the last decades of the sixteenth century. As Protestantism and Englishness were bound together, Catholicism became the bogey against which allegiance to the English church and crown was defined. Catholics were not Catholics but papists—servants of the Pope, not the crown. As English Protestants understood it, the ultimate goal of popery was universal papal tyranny, the destruction of Protestantism, and the damnation of souls. To this end, papists put the interests of their religion before all else. In return, the church promised its followers wealth, luxury, power, and other earthly rewards. Papists were at once greedy, wicked, and deluded. To achieve papal domination of the world, papists aimed to overturn Protestantism, particularly Protestantism in England. They were a threat to the English government, legal system, and established Protestant church. Papists worked by intrigue and insinuation. They wormed their way into the service of the king and provided him with evil counsel; they attempted to divide king from Parliament; and, some feared, they had infiltrated the English church. Popery was associated with cloak-and-dagger operations, poisoning, magic, and sexual transgression. Women were imagined to be particularly vulnerable to popish persuasion, and papists were said to target influential women for conversion. Finally, many people linked papists to the threat of foreign domination, especially by the Spanish and, later, the French. When in power, or when backed by powerful foreigners, papists moved from secret machinations to horrific violence. Here Protestants often instanced the St. Bartholomew's massacre in Paris in 1572, or the Irish rebellion of 1641.[12] Popery was, to put it simply, the inverse of all that was good, just, English and Protestant.[13] Anti-popery was a political language—like the anti-Puritanism so dear to the hearts of James I and Charles I, it was not merely a static collection of prejudices, but a narrative that identified villains, explained conflicts, and synthesized grievances. As a political weapon, it could be wielded judiciously or indiscriminately, sloppily or with precision—or perhaps not used at all, depending on the circumstances.

The connection between Protestantism and Englishness shaped English overseas ventures in the late sixteenth and early seventeenth centuries. Like other Europeans, the English connected the "discovery" of the Americas to the religious fractures within Europe and the great eschatological sweep of Christian history.[14] The justification for the English presence in North America initially depended on their responsibility to evangelize the Native Americans and make Protestants out of them before they were taken into bodily and spiritual slavery by the Spanish—the "virgin soil" of America was in danger of being "polluted with" the "lust" of the Catholic Spanish.[15] But not every English person anticipated a Protestant empire. The New World might instead serve as a dumping ground for the confessionally undesirable. One Elizabethan Catholic leader, Cardinal William Allen, expressed dismay at a rumor that English Catholics were going to be dispatched to the New World "to have freedom of conscience" there, a move he considered "a strange cozenage and craft, to be rid of the poor gentlemen" while pretending to favor and advance them. Allen suggested that it would be better to send the Puritans there instead, to "purge" the realm of such persons.[16] Allen was apparently uninspired by the idea of English Catholics evangelizing Native Americans. But whether the transportation of Protestants or Catholics to the New World was an opportunity or a punishment, the question of the Protestantism (or not) of England and the New World activity of the English was impossible to separate.

While English Catholics negotiated the fraught politics of the late sixteenth and early seventeenth centuries and faced an ever-clearer articulation, in the form of anti-popery, of the threat they were believed to pose, the Church of England underwent a parallel transformation. Between 1590 and the 1620s, the doctrinal consensus that had obtained since early in Elizabeth's reign broke down. A vocal minority of churchmen who wished to equate Calvinism with Puritanism, and both with subversion, used the politics of the 1620s to gain ascendency.[17] Charles I drew a sharp distinction between "Puritans" and "loyal Protestant subjects," and this view was congenial to men like William Laud, who had long tried to make an equation between Calvinism and Puritanism that would cast both as threats to established order.[18] Both Laud—whom Charles appointed Archbishop of Canterbury in 1633—and Charles favored a style of piety that emphasized beauty, ritual, and order. Under Laud, Communion tables were positioned to look more like altars, church members were asked to take Communion at the often newly installed altar rails, and Sabbatarianism was discouraged. The Laudian style also emphasized uniformity. Laud's predecessor, George Abbot, had worked to keep moderate Puritans within the national church—in his view, popery was the threat, not nonconformity. Under Laud, the middle ground between nonconformists and the hierarchy eroded. Sacramental changes were paralleled by scholarly arguments that not only equated Calvinism with Puritanism and excoriated both but also suggested that Catholicism, rather than condemning its adherents to hell as most Protestants believed, might even offer Christian salvation.[19]

Charles was interested less in the subtleties of doctrine than he was in the beauty of order and obedience. As head of the church, he connected ritual respect for things divine with respect for the sacred character of monarchy. Communion tables turned to resemble altars were not just an element of piety, but a visual reminder of the great deference due to both the church and the king who ultimately governed it.[20] Protestant nonconformists who resisted such alterations were not objecting to mere ceremonies—they were attempting to undermine the power of the crown. Despite the resemblances between the heavily ritualized, formal style of piety Charles favored and

Catholicism, Charles did not see himself as countenancing popery. He was, as he understood it, merely encouraging the proper form of Protestantism, which was episcopal and monarchical.

But Charles had never been one to explain himself, and many people, both Protestant and Catholic, misread his intentions. He expressed little animus toward Catholics—he was, after all, married to one. His French wife maintained a large Catholic entourage, with many connections between the court and the various Catholic ambassadorial chapels. Moreover, during the 1630s the king considered negotiations with first the Spanish and then the French about the possibility of England reentering the war in Europe. Beyond matters of altar rails and vestments, Charles also did precisely what Protestants expected a Catholic monarch to do: he violated their liberties, and the sanctity of property, by imposing nonparliamentary prerogative taxation in the form of ship money. Ship money was a long-familiar form of prerogative taxation historically levied during war on coastal areas for naval protection. Charles attempted to impose it during peace and extend it to inland counties. Though the tax was collected, it was a logistical and financial rather than a political success. This came on the heels of the closely related controversies of the late 1620s over the Forced Loan, the Five Knights' case, and the Petition of Right, all of which involved the exercise of royal power to imprison subjects or collect money in ways that many of Charles's subjects considered to be abuses of the king's prerogative or even violations of English law. To many Protestants, this looked like creeping popery in the highest places.[21]

To some Catholics it looked like an opportunity. Charles's conversion to Catholicism was rumored at several points during the 1630s.[22] The Laudian changes to doctrine and practice within the English church were perpetually misconstrued by Catholic observers, and Laud himself was assumed to be ripe for conversion.[23] Grigorio Panzani, the papal envoy to the English court in the 1630s, misapprehended Cecil Calvert's efforts to write a loyalty oath for his Maryland colonists and concluded that Lord Baltimore was working on revisions to the English oaths of allegiance and supremacy that would allow Catholics in England to take them.[24] Hope was widespread that negotiations with Rome, or with Spain or France as part of a treaty, would result in toleration for the king's Catholic subjects.

The confessionally ambiguous policies of the Caroline regime created an opportunity to redefine the relationship between English Catholics and the state. A number of Catholic gentlemen took up the loyalty rhetoric surrounding the Forced Loan of the 1620s and endeavored to demonstrate their loyalty and reliability as subjects by assisting in its collection.[25] Charles himself noted several years later that some of his Catholic subjects were more loyal to him than certain sorts of Protestants.[26] This moment of opportunity coincided with the expansion of the state abroad and—for the Calvert family—with the patronage opportunity created by George Calvert's royal service. The Maryland charter granted by Charles I to Calvert in 1632 expressed the possibilities—whether terrifying or exhilarating—of confessional realignment that opened up in the 1630s.

In this context, George Calvert's conversation with Charles over what to name the prospective colony is telling. Charles suggested Mariana after his wife, Henrietta Maria, but Calvert noted that Mariana was the name of a Jesuit who had written against monarchy and suggested Maryland instead, a name both loyal and royal.[27] If Charles was willing to acknowledge George and Cecil Calvert as loyal subjects and appropriate vehicles for the expansion of English power and influence in the New World, perhaps this meant that the innovations of the 1630s were the new normal—a welcome prospect. But the Maryland charter placed the Calvert project on a collision course with investors in the now-defunct Virginia Company, who argued that their original charter had encompassed all of the Chesapeake and that the issue of these new letters patent to Lord Baltimore amounted to an unfair and possibly illegal confiscation by the king of their property.

George Calvert knew that the Company interest opposed his patent. In 1632 he wrote to Lionel Cranfield for advice, asking the erstwhile Lord Treasurer to "assist me with your memory what the course was which was taken with the old Virginia Company for taking in their patent which I learn they pretend still to be in force." Calvert thought that James had meant the patent to be "damned forever," but needed more evidence in support of this point, since the land for which he sought a charter lay "once within their old patent" although "not near their plantation." As far as Calvert knew, the area was "in his majesty's power to grant."[28]

The Virginia Company disagreed. They battled the Maryland patent with a mixture of confessional insinuation and claims that Lord Baltimore and his patent were a danger to the state. In a letter to Charles's councilor Thomas Wentworth, Cecil Calvert complained that Virginia partisans attempting to "overthrow" his patent had told members of the Privy Council that Baltimore "intended to carry over nuns into Spain, and soldiers to serve that king." This accusation had not been taken seriously, but it had been further alleged that the two ships bound for Maryland "departed from Gravesend without any [paperwork] from the Custom House, and in contempt of all authority, my people abusing the king's officers and refusing to take the oath of allegiance." The Privy Council believed this and held Baltimore's ships in port until the proprietor was able to convince them that they had been "abused and misinformed."[29] The Jesuit presence in Maryland caused rumors to circulate that Baltimore, "professing an establishment of the Romish religion only" had created a "nursery of Jesuits."[30] In America, some communities of Indians around St. Mary's were told, probably by Virginia councilor William Claiborne, that the Maryland settlers were Spanish, and therefore dangerous.[31]

As erstwhile Virginia Company investors explained, Baltimore's religion was a danger to the state. His loyalty was unreliable, and given the extent of the power that had been delegated to him, there was no telling what might occur. Baltimore could distribute land as he pleased, even to "aliens, savages or enemies of the kingdom." His power to offer "honors, lands" and "privileges" to anyone he wished would "dispeople" Virginia and attract dubious "persons of all sorts whatsoever different from the other colonies in religion, affection or otherwise." The proprietor could build what amounted to a private and not necessarily Protestant kingdom of his own in America. He had "royal and imperial power" over his domains, and it was a dangerous thing for such power "to be granted to any person in fee simple in places so remote . . . free from all dependency on others," an argument against the Maryland charter that would return with greater force later in the century. What the Virginia magistrates of the 1630s feared was that with this power, which included that "to make peace or entertain war," Baltimore might "engag[e] all the rest of the English colonies" in who knew what sort of conflicts and as a result, the "utter ruin or essential safety of the whole English plantation in all that country of America" would depend on him.[32] The threat from Maryland was that Baltimore as a Catholic would feel stronger ties to foreign co-religionists, particularly Spaniards, and these foreign enemies would use Baltimore's colony as a door through which to infiltrate and undermine the English polity and the interests of the English king and his subjects. His powers were too vast for a mere subject, and as a Catholic he could not be trusted to wield them in the interest of his own country.

Knowing the power of such claims, Cecil Calvert, who took over the project when his father, George, died in 1632, was aware of the trouble that accusations of popish subversion could cause. In the 1630s, the stars seemed aligned in his favor. Between 1624 and 1631, Virginia affairs were overseen by a committee of the Privy Council, but in 1631 the king appointed a new commission for Virginia headed by the Earl of Dorset. This new commission included many of those who favored a restoration of the Company's charter. They managed to convince the attorney general to issue an order that no more American land grants be passed that threatened the Virginia Company interest. These men also tendered to the king a report strongly recommending that the Company receive a new charter, and negotiations as to the details of the proposed letters patent began. Agreement between the king and the Virginia Company interest, however, broke down over questions of local governance. The first question was the extent of local autonomy to be offered to the colonial governor and council. The members of the Dorset commission, perhaps aware that Charles was unlikely to approve anything that hinted of popularity, proposed a system in which the king had a great deal of direct control. This was rejected by the Virginia adventurers. The second point was the Maryland patent. It had been issued by the king in early 1632 despite the order the Dorset commission had coaxed out of the attorney general. The members of the company refused to consider a new version of their patent which recognized the Maryland grant. Thus the arrangements broke down, and no further official action was taken with regard to Virginia until 1634, when the Dorset commission was replaced by one headed by Archbishop Laud. Laud's group found no difficulty in approving the Maryland patent.[33]

Yet Lord Baltimore could not feel entirely secure. The very process by which he had gained his own patent suggested the problem: what the king gave, the king might take away. If the crown could annul the Virginia charter and grant land that had fallen under those letters patent to Baltimore as a new colony, there was nothing legally to prevent the king from visiting the same misfortune on Cecil Calvert. And kings could be swayed by reports of disloyalty or disobedience. It is not surprising, then, that Calvert's concern for the reputation of his colony occasionally edged toward paranoia. In the letter to Thomas Wentworth in which he had complained of the stay placed on his ships and the accusations of disloyalty, he added darkly that he was sure his enemies had "corrupted and seduced my mariners" and "defamed the business all they could by their scandalous reports, to discourage men from it."[34] His instructions to his brother Leonard in 1633 reveal a proprietor both concerned with not offending Protestants and jumpy about threats to his own authority. He instructed Leonard, appointed as governor, and councilors Jerome Hawley and Thomas Cornwallis to identify "the private plots of his lordship's adversaries in England" using whichever "instruments" among the passengers and crew seemed most apt for the task. Further interrogations were to take place once the party had landed in the Chesapeake. Baltimore also ordered that no one "in any case or for any respect whatsoever [was] to go to James Town."[35]

The Maryland proprietor's concerns with misrepresentation of his enterprise were also evident in the changes made to some of the promotional material. The Jesuit Andrew White wrote an account of the initial voyage in 1634 that was published in England as advertising for the colony. But whoever put together this printed text made some telling changes from White's original. White's narrative included a description of the first Catholic Mass and the conversion of an abandoned Indian house to a Catholic chapel. The revised version described the colonists' celebratory Mass on their arrival as "certain prayers" to solemnize the "taking possession of this country for our savior, and for our sovereign lord the king of England." A similar elision occurred with regard to the chapel.[36] White's original account mentioned that the Indian inhabitants of the Chesapeake had been told, probably by an English person, that six Spanish ships would soon arrive to claim the area for Spain. The Indians had armed themselves in preparation.[37] The English printed version of White's account mentioned the Indians being armed and fearful at the expedition's arrival, but not that anyone had been told the Spanish were coming.[38] Lord Baltimore's political position in the 1630s was strong, but not so strong that it could not be undermined.

The proprietor's best defense of his privileges was to lean heavily on his loyalty to the king and the power of the prerogative. As the 1630s wore on, the equation of criticism of the king with disloyalty or "popularity" became increasingly rigid.[39] Such an equation provided an excellent defense against those who might attack the Maryland project: Charles had granted the Calverts their charter, and therefore criticism of the charter (or what it provided to the proprietor) was criticism of the king, and hence evidence of disloyalty. This argument via loyalty also justified the religious liberty offered in the colony. The king had given Cecil and his father a charter that did not require the establishment of the Church of England or any other denomination. What the king did was ipso facto legal, and to question the charter or any of its clauses was to question the king's authority. The implied argument about liberty of conscience for Catholics was that the king was well within his rights to give extensive privileges to Catholics, and this in no way could be construed as a threat to public order. Those who opposed the charter on these grounds were therefore seditious. The fact that Baltimore had this charter, which allowed him to take up this particular policy with regard to his co-religionists, indicated that Catholics were perfectly loyal subjects and it was really those who would oppose the charter—or the proprietor's authority—who threatened order and stability.

This stance vis-à-vis the prerogative highlights the significance of the proprietor's long controversy with the Society of Jesus. The Calvert family had been cozy with the Society since the 1620s. The Jesuits were invited to found a mission to the Indians in Maryland and to minister to English Catholics there. Trouble arose when the Jesuits insisted on the ecclesiastical privileges and tax exemptions that they would have received in a Catholic country in Europe. As the Jesuits understood it, church law was universal, and as a Catholic Calvert was bound to respect it. Calvert saw things differently. He insisted that the power of the crown gave him his charter, and thus law in Maryland stemmed from that charter and ultimately the prerogative of the English king. The Jesuits could not expect him to subvert the crown's power. Such an argument was in Calvert's interest in several different ways. It cemented his own personal authority in Maryland—and it demonstrated that he was precisely the sort of subject that Charles I might want. Catholic, yes, but one who put the interests of the crown before the claims of his own religion. It was precisely what Charles wanted to hear in the 1630s, as he pondered alliances with Catholic powers on the continent—that loyalty to the king trumped confessional difference.[40]

There were also more specific levers the proprietor might pull, some of which came within his reach alongside a more specific instance of the Virginia Company problem. Among the Virginia councilors who had given his father the brush-off in 1629 was a man named William Claiborne. A member of the Virginia Council since 1624,[41] Claiborne had set up a trading post on Kent Island, which lay in the northern part of Chesapeake Bay, seemingly within the boundaries of the Maryland patent. His claims to Kent Island predated Baltimore's patent by several years, however. George

Yeardley, then-governor of Virginia, had given him a trading permit in April 1627, and by 1631 Claiborne had a trading commission from the king.[42] Baltimore's patent also had a small proviso about previous settlement. The patent specified the bounds of the colony, and gave Baltimore all the territory within those bounds that was "hactenus inculta," or as yet unsettled by Europeans. By the time Baltimore's first colonists arrived in the Chesapeake in early 1634, Claiborne was running a trading operation of several years' standing and of sufficient profitability to make it worth defending. As Claiborne saw it, Kent Island was definitely "culta" and thus he was in Virginia, not Maryland. Lord Baltimore thought otherwise.

The prospect of taking over an already lucrative business no doubt figured into the calculations of Lord Baltimore and his family and clients. Several Maryland traders soon learned that absorbing Claiborne's long relationship with the Susquehannocks was easier said than done—the politics of the Chesapeake involved alliances and enmities that could not be manipulated by the English at will.[43] But from the proprietor's perspective the issue was larger than that particular avenue of profit. The dispute over Kent Island reduced to an argument about the validity of the Maryland charter, and, in the end, to an argument about whether there were limits on the prerogative powers of the crown. The process of moving the authority of the English state into the Chesapeake put pressure on one of the sorest issues of early Stuart politics. The debates over the Forced Loan and the Five Knights in the 1620s and ship money in the 1630s had created fierce controversy over the prerogative and its limits. Here was the same problem in a new form. Could the king revoke and regrant New World property on a whim—or could English people in America, like their compatriots in England, argue that property could not be taken without due legal process? Without some solution to the problem of law and prerogative in England, there could be no easy resolution of the dispute over prerogative-derived colonial charters in the Chesapeake.

Lord Baltimore's efforts to neutralize Claiborne took several forms. He offered Claiborne a patent from Maryland for his operation and attempted to drive a wedge between the trader and his business partners in London.[44] Although Baltimore ordered that Claiborne be "let alone" for the first year or so—presumably in order that the proprietor's powers of persuasion might work their magic—Claiborne complained of interference with his trade and harassment by members of the Maryland council.[45]

Baltimore also used the tangled internal politics of the Virginia Company to his advantage. The key to this part of the plan was Virginia governor John Harvey's unhappy relationship with the rest of the Virginia council, including William Claiborne. Harvey had never been popular among the men who held power in Virginia in the 1620s and 1630s.[46] The dissolution of the Virginia Company in 1624 had raised doubts over the security of planters' estates there, particularly if those estates were acquired after the company's charter had been voided.[47] Although efforts to get the Company rechartered were ongoing, they had not produced any results by the mid-1630s. Harvey was aware of the legal difficulties surrounding the Virginia charter, and when he became governor of the colony in 1628 he asked what measures he should take regarding land grants. He was told that the king had made no final decision on the matter, and accordingly when he reached Virginia he suspended all grants of land. His predecessor, George Yeardley, had been willing to issue patents, and Harvey's change in policy was resented. This came on top of an earlier official trip to Virginia during which Harvey appears to have made a poor impression on the Virginia elite. And then there was the arrival early in 1634 of Lord Baltimore's colonists.[48]

Harvey was in a position of both potential influence and potential vulnerability. Two agents for the Virginia Company, William Button and Sir John Zouch, had been dispatched to Virginia in the hope of winning over the governor and council—perhaps evidence could be drawn up in the colony itself that would convince the Laud commission and the Privy Council that the Maryland patent was an infringement on the rights of the adventurers, and that its continued existence was in the interest of no one but Lord Baltimore. But Harvey was not required to play along with Button and Zouch, and he did not want to. By the mid-1630s, he was unpopular with the Virginia elite, politically isolated, and feeling rather beleaguered. As he explained it in a letter to Charles's secretary Francis Windebank late in 1634, his commission as governor did not give him the authority he needed to control the rest of the council, and although he was more than happy to be of service to the king, "at the council table . . . I have almost all against me in whatever I can propose; especially if it concern Maryland." Despite royal commands to assist the new colony, "many are so averse as they cry and make it their familiar talk that they would rather knock their cattle on the heads than sell them to Maryland."[49]

Lord Baltimore was more than aware that that the embattled and embittered governor of Virginia could be of use to him. He made a point of cultivating Harvey from the beginning. His instructions to his brother and the rest of the Maryland council on their first voyage included a command to send "such a one as is conformable to the Church of England" to Jamestown to give Harvey letters from both the king and Baltimore assuring the Virginia governor of Baltimore's friendship and "to present him with a butt of sack from his lordship."[50] The inclusion of the letter from the king with the one from Baltimore was a telling gesture. If Harvey wanted Charles's goodwill, Baltimore implied, supporting the Maryland proprietor was the best way to do it. And Cecil Calvert did make good on his assurance of friendship. Harvey had been requested by the king to render Baltimore and his colony all necessary assistance, and as far as Calvert was concerned Harvey did his best. Late in 1634 he wrote to Secretary of State Francis Windebank to tell him "how readily Sir John Harvey complied with his majesty's commands in assisting, all he could, my plantation" and that he had done so "in a very dutiful manner to the king and a very noble and friendly manner unto me." In acknowledgement of this, Baltimore asked Windebank to "procure [Harvey] a letter of thanks from the king." Baltimore was more than willing to be Harvey's patron and ally against the rest of the Virginia council, including Claiborne. But he was not above a few additional nudges. In the same communication, Baltimore added that his brother-in-law would bring Windebank "some papers which I lately received from those parts concerning one Claiborne's malicious behavior to me and my plantation there." If possible, Baltimore wished for a letter from the king about the Claiborne difficulty "for Sir John Harvey's encouragement in assisting me against Claiborne's unlawful proceedings there." If a royal letter could not be procured in time, Baltimore requested that Windebank himself write to Harvey on the matter, as without the help of "such favorable and lawful protection" as he was now requesting, his colony was "in great danger of being overthrown now in the infancy of it."[51] Windebank did write to Harvey himself a few days later along the lines Baltimore had suggested.[52]

Administrative pressure was accompanied by more direct efforts. In the spring of 1635, skirmishes and episodes of harassment escalated into a miniature naval battle between Thomas Cornwallis, a Maryland councilor who had or would soon have an interest of his own in the Indian trade, and Claiborne.[53] Claiborne soon afterward complained of interference with his trade, as well as the theft of his company's "boats and goods."[54] The

Maryland government seized his enterprise and goods on the island in 1638, and Claiborne himself was attainted for treason by the Maryland assembly. Forty years later, he was still trying to extract compensation from the Maryland government.[55]

Despite the occasional clash in the Chesapeake, however, the dispute was carried out primarily by means of requests and petitions to the Privy Council. This process began even before the first group of Maryland colonists reached the Chesapeake. During the summer of 1633, Baltimore and the Virginia investors petitioned the Privy Council about the problem. The council saw no reason to change the Maryland patent, and opted to "leave . . . the other party to the course of law."[56] What "course of law" they intended Claiborne to follow was not specified. Neither Claiborne nor the Virginia Company ever sued Baltimore over the patent in an English law court. Lawsuits relating to the Maryland-Virginia conflict arose, but only over specific issues of theft, piracy, or violence. Probably Claiborne never sued because there was no appropriate legal venue for such a case other than the Privy Council itself, or the crown, neither of which seemed impatient to bring the matter to a close. In 1634, the council reassured the governor and council of Virginia that that the planters' estates were not at all prejudiced by the revocation of the charter, and that land should be continued to be granted to those in the colony who had claim to it.[57] Given the Laud commission's approval of the Maryland charter at about the same time, as well as some notes for a royal letter to Harvey indicating that the council considered the original Virginia Company charter "dissolved," it seems that what property the Virginians would retain in the Chesapeake was a matter for the king and council alone to determine.[58] This determination did not always place Lord Baltimore in the council's favor—when the proprietor took it upon himself to eject Claiborne from Kent Island in 1638, for example, he received a stiff royal reprimand.[59]

That the king and Privy Council should be the primary court before which the matter was argued made sense—this was, at bottom, a dispute about the nature and limits of the royal prerogative. Baltimore's claim to Kent Island and the validity of his charter in general rested on the assumption that overseas possessions were the king's to dispose of as he pleased via the prerogative, and that the prerogative trumped all other sources of legal claims—this, after all, was the proprietor's answer to the Jesuits' requests for the church privileges customary in Catholic countries. The basis for the Virginia Company's claims was different. Although their assertions of right to the Chesapeake—including Claiborne's claim to Kent Island—ultimately rested on the prerogative, since they originated in the charter given by James I to the Virginia Company in 1606, there was more to it than that. Those who objected to the Maryland patent were stating in effect that once a charter had been granted, once property was legally held, it could not be revoked simply by revoking one set of letters patent and issuing another. The security of colonial property held by English subjects rested on something more than the charter.

The Virginia interest's claims implied that in some way the English common law followed English people to the New World. The prerogative was not the only potential source of legal claims there, otherwise the argument that Claiborne and the others had been wronged made little sense. The argument that the Maryland charter had been granted in error was a difficult one to make in the 1630s, however. Had the Privy Council concluded that Lord Baltimore did not, after all, have legal claims to Kent Island—or even that he did not, after all, have a legal right to the northern half of the Chesapeake—this would be tantamount to stating that in some cases, there were significant limits on the prerogative power of the crown. The New World was distinct from England. And even within the British Isles, English people acknowledged that not all varieties of law were appropriate for all situations.[60] But the distinction between England and its overseas possessions made the problem all the more significant. After all, the issue of whether or not English subjects abroad could make claims that limited the royal prerogative implied something significant about the relationship between crown and subject that was not confined to North America. At stake was not only a piece of New World property but also the nature of the bond between king and subjects.

The nature of this bond was fiercely contested in the 1620s and 1630s. In England, matters of royal power and its limits were argued over via claims about loyalty, confessional difference, and subversion; in the Chesapeake, both the Kent Island dispute and the related ouster of Governor Harvey from his post in 1635 were described by those involved in identical language. Both Baltimore and Harvey used the word "malice" to describe the intentions of Claiborne and the rest of the Virginia council.[61] Harvey's account of the council's forcible ejection of him from office reads like an exaggerated version of the Caroline view of Parliament—a gang of mutinous and disorderly persons who fomented rebellion and made paranoid accusations of subversion by Catholics. He described Samuel Matthews, an ally of Claiborne's on the council, as "the patron of disorder" and suggested that "this faction" was "nourished from England." Harvey described "many letters and secret intelligences he and the rest of the Council have and especially Claiborne, and many meetings and consultations. I doubt not but to find notable combinations."[62] After his ouster, he wrote to Secretary of State Francis Windebank from Plymouth, in England. He apologized for abandoning his post without permission and explained what had happened. The Virginia assembly was "composed of a rude, ignorant and an ill conditioned people [who] were more likely to effect mutiny than good laws and orders, especially whilst the council gave them such examples." The members of the council, "laying violent hands upon me, charged me with treason, for going about (as they said) to betray" them "into the hands of their enemies of Maryland." Harvey suggested that these men were as dangerous to royal authority in Maryland as they were to the same in Virginia. He warned that "they intend no less than the subversion of Maryland" and described how Claiborne and his allies had threatened the government of Maryland that "they intend to supplant them and to send them home as they have done me."[63]

Both Baltimore and Harvey aligned themselves with the power of the crown and described their opponents as malicious, disorderly subversives. In the political climate of the 1630s, this was a more persuasive argument to place before the king and Privy Council than that commanded by Claiborne, Matthews, and the old Virginia interest, who could complain only of confiscated estates and abuse of royal power by royal subordinates. Matthews described Harvey's ouster in a letter to Sir John Wolstenholme, a friend to the Virginia interest and a member of the 1631 Dorset commission. Matthews accused Harvey of usurpation and abuse of power and damaging the estates of Virginians. But his accusations added up to a particular kind of story about government gone wrong. Harvey's government involved an inversion of the principles of proper use of authority—he harmed Virginians in order to help outsiders, thwarting Claiborne's lawful claims and selling grain to Maryland when Virginians desperately needed it. He also "made a dangerous peace . . . with the Indians against the council's and country's advice."[64] With his emphasis on Harvey's unnatural friendship toward Maryland and Lord Baltimore and the implied comparison between improper assistance to Maryland and unwise treaties with Indians, Matthews' words were consistent with the anti-popish categorization of Catholics as dangerous outsiders—but he said little about religion directly, perhaps aware that in 1635 rabid anti-popery was not a strategy likely to extract the desired response from the Privy Council. John West, who the Virginia council had placed in charge after ousting Harvey, sent the king's advisors an account of events that was more conciliatory than what Matthews had sent to Wolstenholme. Countering—whether he knew it or not—Harvey's remarks about disorder, West emphasized the orderliness of the proceedings in Jamestown and the council's desire to keep the peace. West did, though, distinguish between "his majesty's grant to Lord Baltimore" and "the Island of Kent" and Claiborne as its "commander."[65]

Lord Baltimore and John Harvey had the advantage. Between them they could tell a convincing tale of disorder, subversion, and lack of respect for the authority of the crown. Claiborne lost the argument. Baltimore might be reprimanded when his government in Maryland ousted Claiborne from Kent Island, but he was not punished—and Claiborne was not reinstated. Claiborne, Matthews, and the rest of the Virginia Council were not punished for ousting Harvey from power, but Harvey was soon back in office, and Claiborne spent the rest of his career attempting and failing to make good his claims to his former trading post. In the 1630s neither his objections to the Maryland patent nor those of the Virginia interest gained much traction. When the Privy Council received word in the summer of 1635 of what a council memo described as charges of "open contempt of his majesty's authority" by the Virginia council, they directed the attorney general to look into the matter.[66] Memoranda written in December of that year suggest why Harvey was eventually reinstated as governor. A "memorial for Virginia" described the ouster as a "mutiny" and recommended Harvey be given a new commission "with an enlargement of his powers." A second document explicitly tainted Harvey's opponents with Puritanism and all the disloyalty the term implied—it recommended that John Zouch, a Virginia company ally and representative, specifically not be added to the council in Virginia since it was known he was "of a factious disposition of the Puritan sect," and had "consorted himself with Matthews and the rest of the faction." There is reason to think that Lord Baltimore was involved at some level with this series of requests. The "memorial for Virginia" included the proprietor's wish that Windebank would permit all petitions "touching Maryland" to "be examined in the country," i.e., Maryland, where it would be easiest to get to the truth of the matter, before sending them on to England.[67]

The high tide of proprietary fortune in the 1630s was Lord Baltimore's quite serious request that he himself be made governor of Virginia. He wrote several letters to Francis Windebank in which he pressed the secretary to tell the king that he had "take[n] some pains to inform himself of the present state of Virginia, whereof he hath acquired so much knowledge, as he well understands the great prejudice the king suffers, by not receiving so much profit from thence, as he ought to have. . . . [Baltimore] would undertake to improve his majesty's revenue from thence eight thousand pounds yearly . . . without laying any new or other taxes on the planters, than what they now do and most willingly pay." But this plan "cannot be effected unless the Lord Baltimore do repair and reside some time there, which he cannot with his safety well do, except he be authorized and enabled by having the government of that country." Windebank was to make sure he told the king that Baltimore was not grasping or ambitious, but that he could, perhaps, be talked into accepting a salary of £2,000 per annum, paid out of the extensive revenue that his governorship would create for the crown. And if the king cared to speak to Baltimore about it, Baltimore would able "to give him particular and perfect satisfaction of the means and manner, to raise this increase of revenue."[68]

In the end, whether because Windebank never brought the matter to the king's attention, or because the king decided against it, Baltimore was not granted the governorship of Virginia. But the fact that he made the request at all suggests the possibilities opened up to Catholics by the intersection of the politics of the 1630s and the novelty of English expansion abroad. The administration of overseas possessions was still fairly ad hoc, and it was not yet clear how the relationship between metropole and colony was to work, and how law and authority in the New World would be managed. This was a space in which the rules might be tested and changed. The other side of this coin was that the domestic politics that provided Cecil Calvert with the opportunity to take advantage of all this were extremely contentious—the royal claims about Puritans, papists, and prerogative that proved such a boon to the Calverts in the 1630s cost Charles I his head in 1649. Maryland was entangled from the very beginning in the controversies that would shape the politics of the English-speaking world for the better part of a century.

3
ANARCHY *and* ALLEGIANCE

The 1630s offered Cecil Calvert an opportunity unavailable to his Catholic predecessors, for his colonial venture in the Chesapeake offered both a prospect of New World profit and a chance to rearrange old relationships between English Catholics and the state. But although the 1630s suggested a new world in more ways than one, old assumptions about the natural lines of allegiance died hard. Most Protestant English people believed that loyalty and Protestantism went together. They understood the boundary between Maryland and Virginia as a confessional one and assumed that the natural authority for "the Protestants" in Maryland to appeal to in moments of confessional tension was the governor of Virginia. In the 1640s, the set of circumstances that allowed someone like Cecil Calvert to make a realistic bid for the governorship of Virginia in the late 1630s led to the dissolution of Charles I's three kingdoms into civil war. The breakdown of order spread to the Chesapeake in the person of the London trader Richard Ingle; Ingle was not slow to justify his devastating raid on the colony in confessional terms.[1] The idea that Baltimore as a Catholic was a disloyal royalist at war with Parliament who could not be trusted with authority over English people in the Chesapeake had the virtue of both familiarity and a certain amount of truth. The Calverts were royalists, if hardly guilty of the dark crimes with which Ingle charged the proprietary regime. The association of royalism, Catholicism, and abuse of the liberties of English Protestants was so central to the civil wars of the 1640s that Ingle's accusations, however untrue, were impossible to ignore. Made before Parliament, they placed Lord Baltimore on the defensive.

For Maryland's proprietary regime, the 1640s required the decanting of old wine into a new bottle. Arguments for loyalty and legitimacy that had been formulated for the hothouse conditions of the 1630s had to be reengineered for the very different political climate of the 1640s. The revision was not as tidy as the proprietor might have wished. Baltimore attempted to make a case for his loyalty to the new revolutionary regime but enjoyed only limited success. Like Claiborne and the Virginia interest in the 1630s, who had to make a legal case that was essentially uncongenial to the people they were making it to, Cecil Calvert had to show that as a Catholic with royalist connections, he was nevertheless a dependable subject of whatever the English state, post-Charles, turned out to be. He trimmed to the prevailing political winds, but his sense of the source of his authority and how it was meant to operate never changed.[2] Even after Charles's execution in 1649, the politics of the Caroline regime of the 1630s lingered on.

* * *

In 1638, some servants on the Jesuits' plantation, St. Inigo's, revealed the difficulty of reconceiving familiar assumptions about religion and allegiance—not to mention the challenge that Virginia, the Protestant colony right next door, posed to the proprietor's authority.[3] Though they were primarily missionaries and ministers, the Jesuits operated a farm and employed indentured servants like other planters. Not all their servants could or needed to be lay brothers or even Catholics; like other colonists who had access to land, they employed the labor that they could get. But their resemblance to other planters had limits, and their presence was seen by some as anomalous, even threatening. As events at St. Inigo's revealed, English assumptions about authority, Catholics, and confessional difference were not abandoned in the Chesapeake.

The servants drew up a petition complaining of abuse by the Jesuits' Catholic overseer, William Lewis. But rather than going to the individual above Lewis and the Jesuits in the chain of authority that led back to the crown—that is, to Lord Baltimore—they "intended . . . to procure all the Protestants' hands to it" and take it to the Protestant governor of Virginia, John Harvey. These servants probably did not know that Lord Baltimore had instructed his brother and the rest of the council to avoid giving offense to Protestants; they assumed that Catholic authorities would have no interest in addressing confessional tension in the colony, or at least no interest in resolving such tensions in a way that benefitted Protestants. For the abuses they alleged were confessional. According to the petitioners, Lewis "saith our ministers are ministers of the devil, and that our books are made by instruments of the devil" and forbade any Protestant books in his house. Furthermore, whenever anyone had reason to pass by, "the said Lewis taketh occasion to call them into his chamber, and there laboreth with all vehemency, craft and subtlety to delude ignorant persons." Lewis in this version played the part of the typical papist, alternately abusing his authority and working craftily to ensnare innocent Protestants. A narrative so informed by anti-popery was unlikely to resolve itself via the intervention of a Catholic authority—and so the petitioners sought a Protestant one.[4]

Lewis and the Maryland council also assumed that loyalty easily followed religious lines, but they feared faction rather than abuse of the sort the servants described. Other witnesses described a scene that revealed not oppression by Lewis, but rather how he had been needled by his Protestant underlings. Two of Lewis's servants read a book of sermons "aloud, to the end he should hear it, and that the matter being much reproachful to [Lewis's] religion, vizt. that the Pope was Antichrist, and the Jesuits antichristian ministers." Lewis told them the book was false and "he that writ it was an instrument of the devil." His servants assumed that Catholics would necessarily band together; Lewis assumed that the Protestants would. Lewis feared that the point of the servants' petition "was to combine the Protestants together, and to send a petition under all their hands to the governor and council of Virginia, that they would send hither for William Lewis and proceed against him for a traitor."[5] Not for the last time, Virginia served as a kind of confessionally hued counterweight to Maryland. What the Maryland government could not be trusted to do, Virginia might; the activities of the Virginia governor and council—or, in later years, ordinary Virginians themselves—could threaten the stability of Maryland and the security of both the proprietary regime and ordinary Catholics like Lewis.[6]

Like the Jesuits' overseer, the Maryland council was worried about the prospect of persons within the colony "cherishing . . . a faction in religion." They were more than aware of the danger posed by anti-papist stories like that offered by Lewis's servants. Their response to the incident neatly upended the narrative that the petition to Harvey had set up. Rather than punishing the servants, they fined Lewis for "offensive and indiscreet speech" and for forbidding his servants to read a book that was perfectly legal in England.[7] The Maryland government could be counted on to preserve the liberties of Protestants. Defense of political order, including defense of the religion endorsed by the English state, could be safely entrusted to Catholics.

The early 1640s offered the regime several other opportunities to make this point. In March 1641/2, the Maryland assembly received a petition on behalf of the "Protestant Catholics of Maryland," which was abbreviated thereafter as that of "the Protestants."[8] The petitioners complained that the prominent Catholic planter Thomas Gerard had removed books from the small chapel that Catholics and Protestants shared. He had also taken away the key to the building. The assembly fined Gerard 500 pounds of tobacco, as they had William Lewis, and ordered that the fine be used to pay "the first [Church of England] minister as shall arrive."[9] In this case, the assembly acted rather than the council alone. No controversy or dissent over the fine or its future application was recorded—the governor and council had a strong interest in ensuring that peace was maintained and that no one could reasonably claim that Protestants were being disadvantaged. At the same time, the petition was described as the "the Protestant Catholics'" petition or "the Protestants'" petition. The phrase "Protestant Catholics" emphasized that the petitioners were conforming members of the Church of England.[10] Both labels suggested that the petition represented all the colony's Protestants, and that such a body of people were uniform in opinion. The matter was not a dispute between David Wickliff, who presented the petition, and Thomas Gerard, or even between Gerard and some group of specific Protestant individuals. Even if all concerned did their best to mitigate any confessional tension that arose, the assumption remained that religious lines were the natural points of division within Maryland's body politic.

The shared chapel was an opportunity and a liability. If used by both Protestants and Catholics without incident, it could be offered as evidence that placing Catholics in power was not a threat to Protestant liberties.[11] But responsibility for religious edifices was a tricky business. The shared chapel that Gerard locked the Protestants out of seems to have been on his own land.[12] There was no public Protestant church in Maryland in the 1630s—given the lack of a Protestant establishment, it is not clear what "public Protestant church" would even have meant. The history of the religious buildings in St. Mary's City is difficult to trace, but it seems that although Lord Baltimore requested his brother Leonard to build a privately owned chapel on Leonard's own property, this was not done; the Jesuits constructed a new chapel on their land in town in the late 1630s or very early 1640s. This building is referred to in the records as "the Chapel" without further elaboration.[13] This chapel was probably where Catholics in town attended Mass if they did not do so in their own homes.

Such a state of affairs could easily highlight associations that—especially by the early 1640s—the proprietor preferred to leave obscured. The chapel belonged to the Jesuits. By the early 1640s, England was in the midst of civil war; part of the justification for the parliamentary cause was that Charles I was tainted by too close an association with popery. It was at about this time that Baltimore purchased the chapel from the Jesuits—or at least he seems to have tried to.[14] The details of the transaction are murky. An order from Baltimore dated July 14, 1643, noted that his brother Leonard and John Lewgar had purchased the chapel "in my name and to my use." But due to "some mistakes in the business," Baltimore decided not to accept the transaction and ordered Giles Brent, who was acting governor at the time, to "suspend . . . proceedings."[15] The mistakes may have had to do with the land that was apparently purchased along with the building.[16] Given his ongoing controversy with the Society of Jesus, which had not yet reached its end in the 1640s, Baltimore may have regarded some of the land as already his. But the attempt to purchase the building, which would convert it from a Jesuit house of worship to a chapel owned by the colony's royally delegated ruler, may have been an attempt by the proprietor to diminish any official association between his colony and the Society of Jesus.

But by 1643 or 1644, whether such a statement was still worth making was anyone's guess. Fighting between king and Parliament had begun in 1642, rendering the politics of allegiance even more treacherous than they had been in the 1630s. Loyalty to the person of the king—formerly the Calverts' strongest claim to legitimacy—had now become a potential liability. No one could know how the war would end, but geography and tricks of circumstance could render partiality for one side or another very dangerous business. English Catholics were overwhelmingly royalists, and the Calverts were no exception, at least until Charles lost the war. In 1645, their (and their subordinates') presumed loyalty to Charles collided with the longstanding resentment of William Claiborne and a few unhappy accidents to produce a disaster for Maryland that almost destroyed the colony. Maryland survived, but the result was to place the proprietary regime on unsteady ground. Lord Baltimore had to explain to a victorious Parliament why he was *not* a dangerous and disloyal papist. The mixed success of his efforts revealed the strength of the associations between Catholicism, disloyalty, and subversion that he had worked so hard to redraw. Lord Baltimore owed his position to the politics of the 1630s—the very politics that many in Parliament had waged a civil war to undo.

Governor Leonard Calvert left the colony in 1643 for England, where he received a royal commission to take prize any parliamentary ships he encountered in Virginia.[17] The councilor he left in charge in his absence, Giles Brent, was an uncompromising royalist. In early 1643/4 Brent seized the ship of London-based trader Richard Ingle, apparently because of Ingle's political sympathies. According to Maryland court records, Ingle had said "that he was captain of Gravesend for the Parliament against the king." In a separate incident, Ingle had been asked in Virginia to come ashore in the king's name, and "he denied so to do in the Parliament's name, and standing with his curtelaxe drawn, said, he that came aboard he would cut off his head." He was also accused of claiming that "King Charles was no king or words to that purpose" and insulting Charles's nephew Prince Rupert.[18] Members of Ingle's crew also said that Brent had seized the ship for the king because Ingle was a Londoner allied to Parliament.[19]

When he had secured the vessel, Brent set about correcting the politics of the crew, pressing them to swear an oath, variously described as one "to be true to the king without Parliament" or "against the Parliament and rebels." The ship's cooper was sent to fetch beer, and Brent drank a health "to the king without Parliament." He offered double wages to any crewman who would take the ship, without Ingle, back to Bristol for the use of the king, "promising that for the doing they should be well accepted on at Bristol."[20] Ingle escaped with his ship largely due to the intervention of his trading partner, councilor Thomas Cornwallis. This incident was not the last Maryland heard of Richard Ingle—and indeed it was not the first, either.[21] Ingle had been a familiar face in Maryland for several years, carrying a variety of goods for Cornwallis, governor Leonard Calvert, and even at one point conveying two secular priests to replace the Jesuits who at that time were giving Lord Baltimore such trouble.[22] It was likely his long history of trading voyages to the Chesapeake that brought him back the following year after Brent's seizure of his ship.

The details of Ingle's "invasion" of Maryland are well known.[23] Ingle reached the Chesapeake early in 1644/5 on what by all indications was a trading run. But when he arrived he found that a Dutch vessel, the *Spiegel* (the *Looking Glass*) had beaten him to it. This was before the Navigation Acts restricted colonial trade with foreign powers; the Dutch earned a tidy profit dealing with English colonists. Ingle went south to Virginia, where rumor and an encounter with William Claiborne changed his plans.

Maryland colonists had told some of Ingle's crew that Leonard Calvert had forbidden them to pay debts to Ingle that year.[24] Ingle's first mate John Durford heard Argyll Yeardley (son of former Virginia governor Sir George Yeardley), say that Calvert had met with him to compound for all debts that Yeardley owed Ingle, because Calvert had a commission to seize on the debts of all Londoners. Another sailor told a similar story, adding that Yeardley had told Calvert he could not do it because he expected to see Ingle in Virginia very shortly, to which "Calvert replied, that if Ingle or any other should come from London thither he should hang them."[25] Ingle's situation proved attractive to William Claiborne. Ship's surgeon Robert Rawlins said that William Claiborne had told Ingle about Calvert's royal commission and given him a copy of it.[26]

Claiborne had reason to attempt to use Calvert's commission against the proprietary regime. In 1640 he had tried and failed to recover what estate remained to him on Kent Island after the takeover by the Maryland government in the late 1630s.[27] There is evidence that around the same time that Ingle was in Maryland, Claiborne had tried to retake the island by force, justifying himself with an unconvincing royal commission.[28] At about the same time, the Maryland council seems to have planned a stealth mission to the island to gather intelligence and ascertain Claiborne's future intentions.[29] By the time Ingle arrived in Virginia in early 1645, Claiborne may have decided that Ingle and his ship offered an opportunity to recover what he still regarded as his property. Ingle and his crew's subsequent raid on the colony did not return Kent Island to William Claiborne, but Claiborne might have taken some small satisfaction in the sheer amount of destruction the incident wrought.[30]

The significance of Ingle's invasion lies in the extent to which Ingle was able to use the language of religion and loyalty in order to get away with plundering the estates of some of his fellow English subjects. Much like John Coode's coup of 1689, the aftermath of Ingle's invasion demonstrates the power of anti-popery as a political language, leveraged at the right moment and against the right people. Even more importantly, Ingle's disruption of the colony and the necessity for sorting out the legal mess of accusation and counteraccusation that followed forced Baltimore to explain that he was not what Ingle claimed he was: a dangerous Catholic royalist. By forcing the proprietor onto the defensive, Ingle revealed the extent to which the rules of expressing loyalty and legitimacy had changed since the 1630s.

Ingle left Maryland with a significant amount of property that belonged to others as well as several prisoners, including two Jesuit missionaries. His justification for his actions had been developing since his detour from Maryland to Virginia before the attack. Members of Ingle's crew were more than aware of the confessional justification for the raid. They were going to Maryland, as one put it, to "root the papists out from hence."[31] Ingle's parliamentary letters of marque provided both a kind of legal cover and a reason to strike first—Ingle had a commission to seize ships found in hostility to Parliament, but Leonard Calvert also had a commission, albeit for Virginia, to seize the ships and property of those who rebelled against the king, which presumably included Richard Ingle.[32]

When he returned to London, Ingle was sued by several of the people whose property he had stolen. He claimed that those he had captured or plundered were, "in arms, opposition and hostility against the king and parliament"—and indeed, that the entire colony was probably suspect, instancing Calvert's royal commission and adding that "none of the papists at Maryland did oppose" it. The goods he had taken aboard the Dutch ship and elsewhere were not the lawful property of others, but rather supplies intended to be "transported to Bristol, or to the back side of Ireland" for the use of royalist forces.[33] Ingle had harped on the Catholicism-royalism-disloyalty theme very consistently. Not only was his crew more than aware that many of Maryland's richest men were Catholics, but some had heard (erroneously) that most of the settlers were papists.[34] There were also rumors of typical popish abuses involving Catholics arming themselves against Protestants, "such taxations for the king upon the Protestant part there as they were not able to bear," and the confiscation of the Protestants' weapons.[35]

Rumors of links between royalism, abuse, and papists were not limited to those who had been in the pay of Richard Ingle. Leonard Calvert's commission and the "power and trust" from the king it implied had caused a stir in Virginia, where "whisperings and rumors" circulated of the "the king's disaffection to religion." Calvert's commission caused them to "credit . . . the pamphlets" that accused Charles of closet popery.[36] Ingle, then, was swimming with the political tide in 1645. The Jesuits, too, did him a favor by their very presence. He leaned heavily on the associations of Jesuits with malice, deception, and treason, arguing not only that the Jesuit Thomas Copley had, with the Maryland councilor Richard Lewgar, written letters intended to "inveigle and deceive him" but, more sinister still, that Copley had been "practicing to get some of the Indians to go there to cut the throats of the Protestants."[37] Given the Powhatans' recent and devastating strike against Virginia in 1644, this charge was likely to resonate. Indeed, rumors were circulating in Maryland of potential Jesuit complicity with hostile Indians including the statement that Copley approved of the Powhatans' attack.[38] Like the Spanish and French in England, Native Americans in Maryland played the role of untrustworthy and un-Protestant foreigners with whom the Jesuits might be expected to conspire.[39] Ingle even found someone to echo the charges that the Newfoundland minister Erasmus Stourton had made against Lord Baltimore's father in the 1620s. He and one Mary Ford alleged that Thomas Cornwallis, an agent for the "popish faction in Maryland," had stolen two of her children, "seducing them to pop[er]y and divers other foul misdemeanors committed by him." Lord Baltimore's "poisoned purposes" in this, while clearly evident to Ford and Ingle, were not fully articulated in Ford's two petitions to the House of Lords about the matter.[40]

Ingle does not emerge from this series of events as a sympathetic character. But however incredible his charges, he managed to draw a great deal of attention both to the proprietor's religion and to his potential disloyalty to the parliamentary cause. To avoid the long list of lawsuits that were filed against him, Ingle petitioned Parliament. It was at this stage that his allegations of popery and misgovernance threatened Cecil Calvert.

In November 1645, Parliament's committee for foreign plantations heard the petition, which described how Maryland had been settled by "recusants," whose "tyrannical" government had "forced many of his majesty's subjects from their religion." The petition requested a more appropriate government for the colony. Ingle's timing was fortuitous. The lawsuits against him came up in or after July 1645. In June, Parliament won the Battle of Naseby, one of the results of which was the capture of Charles's recent letters to his wife. These letters revealed that the king had been in correspondence with Catholics in Ireland and elsewhere and that he was more than happy to countenance popery in England if assistance from such quarters was forthcoming. The letters also revealed his profound reluctance to trust either his subjects or Parliament.[41] Ingle's court cases were well-timed to capitalize on this information. And, indeed, Parliament was not unsympathetic. They considered the petition, Baltimore's charter, and documents from the Admiralty Court, in which several of the lawsuits against Ingle were filed.

These last showed the court's opinion that Leonard Calvert and Giles Brent were "unfit to be longer continued" in office because of Calvert's commission and Brent's actions against Ingle's ship and crew in 1643/4, when he had offered the oath against Parliament and attempted to send the ship to Bristol. Ingle, who lay under "the trouble of many suits" for his actions was exempted from "undue prosecution" by whatever new government might be supplied for Maryland—and Maryland would need one, because the committee judged that Lord Baltimore had "broken the trust imposed in him" by the charter.[42]

Parliament drew up an ordinance for revoking the Maryland charter, but the ordinance was not acted on, despite a petition in early 1647 from London merchants requesting that Parliament do so. They stressed not only the disruption to trade and the disloyalty to Parliament but also noted that Baltimore and "his agents" had "acted horrid things in that province as papists and enemies."[43] Ingle's—and Claiborne's—mercantile connections had evidently proved useful. This petition was received in March, after Cecil Calvert's own petition dated March 4th. Here the proprietor reminded the lords that the ordinance for suspending his patent was still pending, and he wished to hear the "particulars of the charge to be laid against him," and be given time to prepare his defense.[44] The matter of what to do about Maryland would drag on for another three years.[45]

Ingle had forced Lord Baltimore into an argument about whether he and his officers were loyal subjects of the English state—an argument that was all the more difficult for Baltimore to address, given how significantly the terms of loyalty had changed since the 1630s. In the past he had been able to demonstrate that he was a good subject through personal loyalty to Charles I. Indeed, his demonstrations of loyalty to the king in the 1630s were the root cause of what happened to him and his patent in the 1640s—the very positions that drew Charles I into the civil war placed Cecil Calvert in a position of power, patronage, and influence. The Parliamentarian victory in 1646 pulled the rug out from under this approach. Baltimore had to demonstrate loyalty in a different way; he also had to find a different answer to the question of how a Catholic might be a loyal English subject.

In the late 1640s and early 1650s Baltimore took steps to make the proprietary regime in Maryland more friendly to the parliamentary government and, after 1649, the Commonwealth. In August 1648, he appointed a new governor, William Stone of Virginia, who, unlike previous governors, was neither a Catholic nor a kinsman of the proprietor.[46] But a mere change in personnel was not enough. When Charles I was executed the following year, a deputy of Stone's proclaimed the accession of Charles II in the governor's absence. Baltimore quickly disclaimed the proclamation and removed the deputy, Thomas Green, from office.[47]

The proprietor also leveraged the contrast between Maryland and Virginia to advantage. The governor of Virginia, William Berkeley, was a royalist and no fan of Puritanism. In 1650, a new county, Anne Arundel (the area also called "Providence") was incorporated in Maryland; a significant number of the settlers there were Protestant nonconformists who had come from Maryland to Virginia in the late 1640s to escape Governor Berkeley's insistence on conformity to the Church of England.[48] People of a religious persuasion similar to that of many Parliamentarians lived unmolested in Maryland.[49]

In England, the proprietor continued to defend his patent from the charges that had arisen from the Ingle incident.[50] But neither cosmetic alterations to the proprietary regime in Maryland nor tireless attendance at committee meetings addressed the deeper questions that made Baltimore's authority vulnerable. The civil wars in the British Isles had dismantled the familiar structures of government. Subjects had executed their king for breaking the law and conspiring against them. They were now governing without him as a commonwealth, but on what did the authority of that commonwealth rest? Charles's supposed collusion with Catholics and the danger he and Archbishop William Laud posed to the Protestant religion inspired many a Parliamentarian, but when the war had been won, it was not necessarily clear what to do next. In the 1640s and 1650s the English debated the whether and how of a national church and wrestled with the prospect of religious liberty, at least for Protestants. Some understood the political revolution of the 1640s in apocalyptic terms, expecting the millennium, various earthly and heavenly utopias, or even the end of the world. Others were horrified at the disorder, social, religious, and otherwise that the revolution had unleashed. Still others merely kept their heads down and waited for the storm to blow over.[51] The vexed questions of how to put back together what had been taken apart and on what basis this ought to be done drove the tumultuous politics of the in 1650s, as the English state reinvented itself at least twice, and in the Chesapeake, the old dispute with the Virginia Company reappeared in revolutionary apparel.

4

PAMPHLETS, POLEMIC, *and the* REVOLUTIONARY STATE

The 1650s were a turning point in the history of English overseas expansion. Much of the foundation of the eighteenth-century empire was laid in the revolutionary decades between 1640 and 1660. The English state began to assert its power more directly in its colonial possessions, sometimes by force.[1] At the same time, this decade marked not only the beginning of a shift in how the empire operated—it was also the beginning of a decades-long reckoning with the earlier period of the seventeenth century, one that would not reach its crisis until the 1670s and 1680s. The extension of state power after 1650—and particularly after 1660, as the problem of whether imperial uniformity required religious conformity became ever more pressing—should be understood in relation to the less-regulated empire of the early seventeenth century.[2] The early Stuart legal and confessional ambiguities that had both created proprietorships like Maryland and sustained local conflicts like that between Maryland and Virginia had not vanished by the 1650s. Cromwell's government had resulted from the civil war they produced in England, but the Protectorate did not lay such questions to rest—rather the opposite.

What was the English state—to what were the English subjects of Maryland or Connecticut or Barbados bound, and how did the connection operate? Monarchy was placed on hiatus with the execution of Charles I in January of 1649. The tenure of the Long Parliament, the last Parliament summoned by Charles I and the body that had led the wars against him in the 1640s, lasted until 1653, when Oliver Cromwell and the New Model Army dissolved the remnants of it—the so-called "Rump"—by force, severing the last institutional connection to the prewar regime. The Rump and the Army had long been at odds; the Army resented the Rump's dilatory attitude toward reform, while Parliament feared both Army radicalism and the potentially disastrous outcome of new elections.

Cromwell's justification for dissolution was not that what the Rump was or had been doing was illegal in any technical sense. The grounds for judging the Rump's governance were not the law as it was (or had been) but a different, unwritten standard: the interests of the Army, the nation, and true religion required that the Rump be replaced.[3] For those who subsequently had to make cases for their own loyalty to the Protectorate—or the disloyalty of others—it was a challenge to figure out how the case ought to be put. What did it mean to be a good subject, or a bad one? Entangled with the vicissitudes of the English state and its colonial possessions were longstanding personal and corporate grudges. William Claiborne and the Virginia interest had not lost hope of overturning the Maryland patent, and the politics of the Civil War gave them the perfect opportunity to do so. Virginia's governor, Sir William Berkeley, had remained loyal to Charles, and as a result, Virginia was in need of "reduction" to obedience to the new order in the early 1650s. A trick of wording included Maryland in the Council of State's order to do so. Lord Baltimore was once again required to defend himself and his patent, but this proved a challenge. His arguments had changed little since the 1630s, but the context in which they had to be made rendered them less effective, even less coherent, than they had been twenty years before.

He also had to navigate a new problem, one that would plague him and his son and successor Charles more and more in decades to come: as the reach of the state into the governance of its colonies increased, the prerogatives of the proprietor and the deference owed to the commonwealth or the crown would come into conflict, raising the question of whether or not Baltimore's proprietorship was compatible with the state. The answer to that question depended on what one thought the state was—not an easy point to reach agreement on in the 1650s. The result of this series of interlocking problems both local and imperial was a series of coups and countercoups in the Chesapeake and a vitriolic pamphlet war over the rights and wrongs of what had happened. Arguments over Maryland quickly turned into arguments about the nature and purpose of government and the measure of loyalty, placing the colony squarely within a more general discussion of colonies, states, and empires in the Anglophone world of the 1650s.[4]

* * *

The crisis of the 1650s in Maryland began with Virginia. Virginia's governor, Sir William Berkeley, was a royalist, and the colony had remained loyal to the king. By 1649, the Commonwealth's executive body, the Council of State, was ready to take corrective action. They were also being pressed to establish a government there more friendly to Parliament and to "allow free preaching of the gospel." The London merchants exerting this pressure were connected to the tobacco trade—and, in many cases, to William Claiborne. In addition, the long grudge against Maryland's existence held by erstwhile Virginia Company investors had not faded.[5]

Early in 1650, the Committee of the Admiralty, to which the Council of State referred many colonial matters, ordered Parliament to nominate commissioners to go to the Chesapeake, appoint a new governor and council, and bring Virginia's government into order. The official order drawn up by the Attorney General was to define the boundaries of the colony carefully "according to the ancient limits." Virginia's "ancient limits" might easily be understood to encompass Maryland as well, and indeed, one of the two men who signed the order was John Danvers, who was likely among those who pressed for a reconstitution of the Company back in the 1630s.[6]

The formal commission to "reduce" Virginia was issued late in 1651. Among the commissioners charged with enacting this change was William Claiborne—and the commission required the reduction not specifically of Virginia alone, but rather of "all the plantations within the bay of Chesapeake."[7] The series of political dislocations that followed reveals how deeply questions of power and authority within the Chesapeake were connected to the political divisions common to the English-speaking world as a whole in the 1640s and 1650s. The Commonwealth commissioners reduced Virginia, and then went on to reduce Maryland as well. But reduced to what, and to what end? The answer to this question was trickier than it seemed, for Maryland was "reduced" not once, but twice during the 1650s. In the first, in 1652, the commissioners removed some of Baltimore's officers. A more thorough purge was conducted two years later in 1654, when the commissioners and their supporters essentially repudiated proprietary authority, alleging popish conspiracy and abuse of power.

The charge of popish conspiracy was familiar, but the proprietor's rebuttal necessarily shifted somewhat with the times. By the 1650s he could not rest his authority on loyalty to the king or the prerogative powers of the crown. He maintained that he was a loyal subject with a legal charter, but altered circumstances shrank his options for demonstrating this—particularly given the increasing uncertainty as to what he, or any other English person, was meant to be loyal to. More than this, the proprietor's views of law and order in Maryland had scarcely changed, which made accommodation with the series of new regimes that followed the execution of Charles Stuart in 1649 even more difficult. He believed that law in the colony derived solely from him and his charter, and that opposition to either was not only nonsensical but also evidence of faction and subversion. This position pushed him into conflict with both his colonists and, eventually, the English state.

The process of recovery from the disaster of Ingle's raid created a series of logistical hurdles that soon turned into theoretical arguments about the nature of government in Maryland. In 1647–48, a procedural oversight caused a bitter controversy about the legal basis for a legitimate meeting of the provincial legislature. As the proprietary regime regained power, Governor Leonard Calvert briefly commissioned Edward Hill to act in his absence. In December of 1646, acting governor Hill summoned the Maryland assembly. When Leonard Calvert returned in early 1647, he did not issue a new summons for the assembly. The legislature passed some legislation with Calvert's consent. A year later, in early 1648, the freemen who met as the lower house objected to the laws passed by the assembly of early 1647, claiming that because Leonard Calvert had not issued a new summons under his own authority, the laws subsequently passed were void. Leonard Calvert had since died, but his successor in office, Thomas Green, refused to countenance this argument.[8]

The question boiled down to whether a legitimate assembly required a procedurally correct summons, or whether the approval of the governor was enough—was it following the laws that created legitimate authority, or merely the will of those in charge? Lord Baltimore's view of the matter was unambiguous. He did not believe that his brother had had the power to deputize Hill, thus rendering any laws passed by that assembly under Hill void.[9] But he considered anything acted by the same assembly once Leonard Calvert was back in charge acceptable. The assent of a legitimate representative of proprietary authority was what mattered. The question became entangled with the proprietor's demand that the assembly pass a list of laws that he sent, and the lower house's refusal on the grounds that they had found in these laws things that were "not convenient nor as we conceive it just to pass." They had instead drawn up some laws of their own as well as an address explaining their actions.[10]

Baltimore agreed to the proposed laws. But his outraged response to the assembly's objections to his laws and their nitpicking about the 1647 session—he wrote it in 1649 and the assembly received it the following year—is revealing. As far as the 1647 assembly was concerned, the only reason anyone could possibly have for questioning its legitimacy was a deliberate intent to breed "factions and divisions." Leonard Calvert had accepted it, and so it was legal. Indeed, even if a group of the freemen had shown up without any summons at all and called themselves an assembly, whatever laws they passed would be legal, if the governor of the province accepted them and Baltimore assented. (Such an action on the part of the freemen would, however, deserve "exemplary punishment.")

He ascribed the freemen's refusal to pass his list of laws to a "misunderstanding"—and yet it seemed to be rather more than that. The majority of the assembly had not done as he asked. Baltimore had concluded that this "unwillingness" was not the result of disagreement over legal matters but rather the work of malcontents whose "subtle suggestions" were part of a plan to raise "jealousies and discontents" between the proprietor and his colonists. Part of the laws he had directed the assembly to pass had included a recognition of his own rights and powers as proprietor. To reject this, he pointed out, was hardly in the colonists' interest, because no "well-affected person there not seduced by evil counsel" would hesitate to recognize "our rights there," given that it was on Baltimore's charter alone "(and upon it only), that their particular interests and rights in their lands and privileges in that province do solely and with most certainty depend." Baltimore suspected that blame for all this lay with some men who had acquired Indian lands directly from the Indians, not from the proprietor, and who wanted to raise "a great division and faction" which might be made into a "party . . . to revive their old pretended right." He did not specify who these men were, but no one fit this description better than the Jesuits. "Woeful experience," the proprietor concluded, demonstrated nothing "betrayed the people into true slavery" more often than "the deceitful suggestions of subtle machiavellians pretending religion . . . the direct road to bondage is usually found in specious pretensions of the preservation of liberty."[11] Had he not been by this point headless, Charles I could hardly have put it better himself.

Baltimore claimed that the freemen of the province ought to be eager to defend his charter rights, given that their liberties depended upon them. Like the proprietary policy of religious toleration, this statement was more contentious than it might first appear. After all, Baltimore had spent much of the 1630s doing legal and administrative battle with two separate parties, William Claiborne and the Jesuits, who had based their claims to what he saw as his property on arguments that turned on the idea that Baltimore's charter was not the sole or the fundamental source of law, rights, or authority in the colony of Maryland. In Lord Baltimore's opinion, there were no legitimate grounds for any hesitation to confirm his privileges. Not all his colonists were eager to support this view of the matter, however. The dispute over the legitimacy of the 1647 assembly suggests that many were uncomfortable with the idea that the numinous authority of the proprietor, rather than familiar English legal procedures, was the basis for lawmaking. What Baltimore took as a given, some Marylanders saw as a mistake. Baltimore's description of their objections reveals that some "stumbled at" phrases such as "absolute lord and proprietary" and "royal jurisdiction." It seemed that some in Maryland thought that the first implied "a slavery in the people there to us" and that the second "exceeded" the powers granted by the charter.[12] In addition to this, Baltimore's argument placed them in a strange situation as English subjects. According to him, their liberties and title to their land rested on the charter alone. What would happen if that charter were changed or revoked?

Alteration or even revocation was precisely the prospect Lord Baltimore faced in the 1650s. But the context in which scrutiny or revision might occur was much larger than the Chesapeake. The protracted battle over law, order, and legitimate authority in Maryland came at the beginning of a decades-long move to streamline and regularize the administration of English overseas possessions. The threat of revocation also came amid a deep crisis in government. In 1653, the Army dissolved the Long Parliament. Soon after, Oliver Cromwell took power as Lord Protector. The last institutional connection with the prewar regime had been broken—on what did the Protector's authority rest? This question was at the core of the controversial literature printed about Maryland in the 1650s. Both the dismantling and the defense of the proprietary regime required justification, and those doing the justifying had to place their claims within some familiar and convincing framework—and yet given the recent destruction and rebuilding of the English state, it was hard to determine what the best framework would be. Both the proprietor's opponents and his defenders drew on familiar tropes of dangerous papists, malicious sectaries, and threats to order—but in changed circumstances their arguments did not always work as well, or as consistently, as they might have wished.

In 1653, after the first reduction of both Maryland and Virginia but before the more dramatic purge of 1654, a defense of Baltimore's regime was printed in London under his name. The tract reveals Baltimore's concern with that ancient issue, loyalty—and also his awareness that loyalty was no longer enough. He had to demonstrate the congruence of his proprietorship with the evolving English state, an argument that required something more than personal loyalty to the new regime. In addition, he had to negotiate the tricky subject of religion. The relationship between political loyalty and confessional identity was no less fraught in the 1650s than it had been in the 1630s, but the 1650s offered a less hospitable climate for the argument that Baltimore needed to make, that his religion could and should be uncoupled from his relationship to the state. More than this, he had to offer an account of his opponents that successfully explained their opposition to his patent and criticism of his government.

The Maryland proprietor was aware that his proprietorship resembled a "hereditary monarchy," which some considered to be "inconsistent with this commonwealth." Baltimore argued that the seeming inconsistency was resolved by the distinction between kingdom and colony. A monarchy that had "any power over this commonwealth" would "not be consistent" with it, but "any monarchical government in foreign parts which is subordinate to, and dependent on, this commonwealth may be consistent with it."[13] What English settlers might think of being subjects of a commonwealth in England and of a subordinate monarchy in Maryland, the proprietor did not address. He regarded Maryland not as a part of England or Britain, but as "foreign parts." Baltimore, it seemed, would retain his rights and privileges as an English subject should he go to Maryland. If he did not, his patent would be meaningless, since he owned it by a gift from the king, under English law. But his argument indicated that the colonists, in his view, did not retain this protection. They did not own what they owned under English law—they owned it under Maryland law, as dispensed by Baltimore. And yet, English, Irish, and other British inhabitants of Maryland considered themselves subjects of the English crown—there is no evidence to suggest that in general they believed crossing the Atlantic changed that. At the same time, Baltimore argued that much of Maryland's system of government was familiar and English. Baltimore himself had great and unusual privileges, it was true, but these were necessary to offset the risks involved in sponsoring a colony. Besides, "such necessitous factious people as new plantations consist of" if not kept in check would "make laws to dispose of him, and all his estate there, without his consent."[14]

Alongside this legal and practical argument Baltimore placed a loyalty one. He had made a similar case for his own loyalty to the commonwealth not long before, when a plan was floated to combine the governments of Maryland and Virginia. In that case, Baltimore had stressed his "fidelity and affection to this commonwealth" and argued that the structure of the proprietorship itself contributed to its loyalty. Maryland had a "dependence on him and he upon this commonwealth, as he had before on the late king," and his residence in England meant that the colony was tied more closely to the administrative center than it would be if it were placed in the hands of those "whose interest and residence" were "wholly there."[15] Now, in 1653, he said much the same thing. His governor, William Stone, was "zealously affected" to Parliament, had submitted to the Commonwealth "in all humility," and "diverse of the Parliament's friends there were, by the Lord Baltimore's special direction . . . well treated there."[16]

But assurances of loyalty and demonstrations of the proprietary government's neat fit with England's ran up against the old problem of religion and loyalty. Baltimore's defense of his privileges moved seamlessly into the argument that even though he was "a recusant," his government in America was an asset to the Commonwealth. If English people such as himself did not take possession of America, the land would be in the hands of "Indian kings or foreigners." Besides, "the Lord Baltimore knows of no laws here against recusants which reach into America."[17] Baltimore's choice of words was astute. He was not a Catholic; he was a "recusant." The term was associated with Catholics, but it referred in general to a person who absented him- or herself from the state church—a term which might have been applied to many a Protestant Commonwealth loyalist in the past. With this statement Baltimore also revealed once more his model of the relationship between religious affiliation and political allegiance. He strenuously asserted his loyalty to the English state. But whatever it was in the state that he was loyal to was distinct from statutes operative in England—the state was distinct from its laws, which might operate differently in different places, and a proper connection to that state as a subject did not require one to be a Protestant.

More than that, English law did not cross the Atlantic with English people. Baltimore's charter connected his regime to the state, and the charter alone provided the legal framework for government in the colony.

The other thing that the proprietor had to account for was opposition to his regime, and to his patent in general. This was more difficult in the 1650s than it had been in the 1630s, because the powerful connection between "factious persons" and disloyalty and disorder from below was difficult to articulate without reference to Puritans, and the audience Baltimore now played to was far less interested than Charles I had been in this particular framework for explaining conflict. Baltimore referenced "factious fellows" and "ill-affected person[s]" in his explanation for a petition against his government that the committee of the navy had received "in the name of the inhabitants of Maryland."[18] He implied that Claiborne and the remnants of the Virginia Company were acting out of private greed rather than the public good in their efforts to restore Virginia's ancient boundaries, since the "inhabitants of Virginia . . . abhor the memory" of the Company "in regard of the great oppression and slavery they lived in under it."[19]

Baltimore was defending a valuable colonial charter from a series of serious threats to its continuance. At the same time, the variety of problems he had to address and the difficulty of generating a powerful defense of his patent that would answer the objections of his critics forced the Maryland proprietor to engage with issues at the center of the long crisis the English state underwent in the 1640s and 1650s. The process by which this crisis was resolved required the articulation of what the nascent English state and its empire were, how they functioned, what held the whole together, and how to judge loyalty to it. Working out what connected authority in England to English overseas possessions was a part of that process, as was the controversy over what to do with Maryland—Maryland's confessional oddities reflected the many connections in the English world between debates about authority and legitimacy and debates about religion. As the pamphlet war of the mid-1650s over the colony's government revealed, arguments over Maryland and its proprietor devolved with alarming speed into arguments about the nature and purpose of government, how authority worked, and what made a state legitimate.

Baltimore and those who supported him did not accept the 1652 "reduction" of Maryland's government without a murmur. The proprietor took steps to bolster his authority in the colony, requiring among other things that all judicial writs run in his name (accompanied by a statement that this "cannot in any ways derogate from our obedience to [the] commonwealth").[20] This double assertion that the proprietor's power was entirely undiminished and also completely consistent with obedience to the commonwealth aligned perfectly with Baltimore's printed tract of 1653. But the combination of still-powerful—perhaps too powerful—proprietary authority in Maryland and regime change in England proved too much for Claiborne and the Protestant nonconformists who had recently settled in Anne Arundel County to resist. They staged a more thorough coup in the summer of 1654. Baltimore's authority remained a threat to Claiborne's claims, and the Anne Arundel group had long been hesitant to submit to the proprietor's authority.[21]

Since the execution of Charles I in early 1649, England had been governed as a commonwealth by the remains—or, as contemporaries put it, the Rump—of the Long Parliament that had been in session since 1640. Turning a legislative body into an executive one was no easy task. Moreover, the Rump had long been at odds with the Army. The Rumpers' evident reluctance to enact constitutional and social change—particularly reform of the franchise—and their failure to endorse the radical Protestantism shared by Army leadership and the rank and file led to public agitation against Parliament and accusations of corruption and self-interest. Dearth of source material leaves aspects of the Rump's dissolution difficult to determine, but it is fair to say that by 1653 Cromwell and many of his allies and supporters felt that this Parliament no longer could be trusted to act in the best interests of the Army, the revolution, or the Commonwealth of England as they understood it. In dissolving the last points of continuity with the prewar English state—the next Parliament to be called would be summoned by Cromwell himself—Cromwell held the Rump up to a standard that would have struck most MPs and magistrates of the prewar world as both oddly familiar and profoundly dangerous: the interests of liberty, the nation, and true religion—as determined by Oliver Cromwell and the Army.[22]

That is, it was not antiquity, continuity with precedent, or constitutional propriety that made a government legitimate, but rather divine backing and conformity with a certain style of Protestant godliness. Baltimore's government, presumed to be Catholic in allegiance and intent rather than simply in personnel, was clearly not legitimate judged by these standards. This situation offered the opportunity, to those who wanted it, to permanently remove Baltimore from power. The fear of ungodly government may well have been sincere for some of the Anne Arundel / Providence group; for Claiborne and the Virginia interest it was at the very least extremely convenient. To this was added the efforts, beginning in the 1650s, to tighten the previously ad hoc administrative apparatus for the colonies—the same looseness of organization and diversity of structure that had allowed Baltimore's colony to exist in the first place. The result was a near-perfect storm for Maryland as all of the issues of law, religion, and authority that had plagued the colony from the beginning came together.

The so-called Battle of the Severn between Governor Stone's militia and the forces of their opponents early in 1655 decided events in favor of the new regime. Soon after, a series of pamphlets was published in London attacking and defending the proprietary government. These pamphlets reveal both continuity with the political world of the prewar years and substantial change. The familiar tropes of anti-popery and anti-Puritanism continued to shape the controversy. At the same time, the events of the 1640s and 1650s forced the participants to reconceive—with varying degrees of success—some of their assumptions about loyalty, religion, and the nature of the state. The controversy was of interest to those connected directly to Maryland, but this was not the limit of the audience. During the 1650s, more pamphlets were published about Maryland in London than in any other decade of the seventeenth century, including the 1680s.

Those attacking the proprietary regime used tropes about Catholics and power that would have been familiar to a Jacobean or even late-Elizabethan audience. Leonard Strong, self-described "agent for the people of Providence [Anne Arundel County] in Maryland" and a member of the colony's council after the second and more thorough purge of 1654, spoke in frightening terms of "arbitrary and popish government" and argued that the oath of loyalty that inhabitants had to take to become landowners or residents was in effect a requirement to "uphold Antichrist." His reference to the Maryland council receiving secret orders from Baltimore about a plan to "raise forces against the lawful power of the commonwealth of England" evoked longstanding associations between Catholics and conspiracy as did accusations of abuse of power and bloodshed, including the blood "of the Saints in Maryland."[23] Ship's captain Roger Heaman, whose ship the *Golden Lyon* was involved in the conflict, echoed Strong's charges, noting how "subtly the interest of the Lord Baltimore was carried on."[24] Both Heaman and the anonymous author or authors of the anti-Baltimore *Virginia and Maryland* leaned on the association between Catholic worship and idolatry. As the latter put it, when Governor Stone and his party retreated, "all the place [was] strewed with Papist beads where they fled."[25] Baltimore's regime as represented in these pamphlets was the textbook example of conniving, disloyal, idolatrous Catholics who attempted to undermine and supplant lawful Protestant authority.

The conventional inverse of these anti-Catholic tropes appeared in several pamphlets written in support of the proprietary regime. John Hammond described the Anne Arundel group as "inhuman, ingrateful and blood-sucking sectaries" whose "hypocrisies" deserved exposure and whose motives were of the most venal kind. His portrait of them was a near perfect replication of the scheming, grasping, hypocritical stage Puritan of late Elizabethan and Jacobean theater.[26] But these sectaries were also the dangerously subversive, disorder-mongering Puritans that Charles I had so feared. For Hammond, the crew on Roger Heaman's ship stood in for those Heaman supported: "disordered . . . mutinous . . . and quarrelsome."[27] John Langford, a second defender of the proprietary regime, stressed the dubious social origins of the Anne Arundel crowd and tried to undercut their attempts to tar all supporters of the proprietor with popery. Discussing the controversial oath of fidelity to Baltimore, he noted that Protestants "of much better quality" had taken it without a murmur.[28]

Writers on both sides of the dispute made a confessionally inflected argument about the disloyalty of their opponents. This was the easy part. The idea that popery undermined the rule of law had a long history, as did the complementary trope about subversive Puritans, disloyal to both church and king. But the events of the 1650s—and the fact that they were writing about an American colony—pushed polemicists like Strong and Heaman in unexpected directions. Native Americans made an appearance in Strong's text as potential agents of popish subversion, anticipating the more elaborate Indian-Catholic conspiracy theories of the 1670s and 1680s.[29] In a move more specific to the 1650s, Strong claimed Baltimore's oppressive powers were too great for a subject and "unsuitable to the present liberty" from "arbitrary and popish government" that the English currently enjoyed.[30]

But the nature of that government—what prevented it from being arbitrary—was more difficult to determine. Another anti-Baltimore pamphlet, *Virginia and Maryland: or the Lord Baltimore's printed case, uncased,* wrestled with that very problem. The association between Protestantism and lawfulness, or at least the opposition between Catholicism and lawfulness, was hardly new for readers of the 1650s. But what determined lawfulness or its inverse was a tricky question. It had been so decades before as James I, Charles I, and their allies and opponents sparred over the relationship between the prerogative and the common law, and it was certainly so now in the 1650s. *Virginia and Maryland* was written by persons connected with William Claiborne's longstanding campaign against Maryland's government, and rehashed some fairly hoary grievances. It was not merely that, however.

The writer or writers argued, in essence, that the proprietary regime was illegal. They challenged the charter on the grounds that its terms were contrary to English law despite its having been a royal gift. In granting the charter to Baltimore, Charles had believed that he was within his prerogative to give the powers contained therein to the proprietor. America was a royal dominion, not subject to the common or statute law of England. Prerogative powers covered it, and thus Baltimore's powers as described in the charter were legitimate. Baltimore certainly had followed this line ever since. Royal prerogative had suffered since 1632, however. One of the most fundamental points at issue during the English Civil War was the relationship between law and prerogative, and many among the victors had held that the king could not order anything contrary to the laws of England, and if he did so, the order was void by its very nature—this, indeed, was what allowed the possibility of waging war on the king in the first place. If the actions of the king threatened the well-being of the English people as protected by the customary and statute law of England, then the law was to be defended before the person of the monarch.[31] This position, that royal actions that violated the law were automatically invalid, was the position the writers of *Virginia and Maryland* implicitly took up against Baltimore's claims.

During the 1640s and 1650s in England a variety of people claimed that it was possible, sometimes even necessary, to dispense with the common law for the greater good, whether it was the royal prerogative that allowed the king to do this, or whether, as some parliamentarians and revolutionaries insisted, it was godliness or deeper concerns about liberty that permitted subjects to do this. The status of the common law as fundamental to all thinking about politics in England broke down in the 1640s in part as a result. As the English political historian Glenn Burgess has noted, "by 1642 'legal' meant for many not 'warranted by the common law' but 'justifiable by some guiding principle that overrode particular laws in the interests of public welfare.'"[32] In the Maryland context, what emerged was the argument that the king could not override the law and do illegal or unjust things, and if he did do things that were illegal, they were void. *Virginia and Maryland* even seems to imply that things that were merely unjust, if not technically illegal, were void. What this tract amounts to is a kind of extreme common law argument, but one made in the mid-1650s, when there had already been several technically illegal or at least unprecedented constitutional upheavals. This of course begged the question of how "illegal" was to be defined, and perhaps implied a more radical sense of inward spiritual promptings, or an innate and universal sense of justice, than the authors intended—they had, in other words, been drawn into the same legality vacuum that Burgess describes as present in England in the 1640s. The writer or writers of the pamphlet, though, seemed to do their best to ignore the problems revolution posed to their common law claims, either because it did not suit the claims they wanted to make, or because they thought the argument still stood.

The pamphlet argued that that Baltimore's "usurpation of royal privileges" in his colony was "incompatible to the English nation." The proprietor's insistence that the "Durham palatinate" clause in the charter permitted him to comport himself in this way was bogus, since "those privileges of Durham" had been "taken away as dishonorable, and incongruent to the English nation" by Henry VIII. Charles, in other words, had not been legally capable of giving such privileges to Baltimore in 1632, and they were consequently invalid now. Besides, even the patent itself stipulated that it was not to be interpreted in such a way as to "prejudice" or diminish "the commonwealth of England."[33] Baltimore would have argued that his royal style and the rest did not conflict with the laws of England because they had been granted, legally, by the king. *Virginia and Maryland* claimed instead that even royal grants were checked by the law. The use of "nation" here implies a standard above even mere law—there was an "English nation" that existed prior to the decisions of kings, and subsequent charters and privileges must be measured against it.[34]

The controversy over local government in Maryland was bound up in a series of problems concerning legitimacy. What made a government legitimate? How could one tell? More broadly, where should arguments about such things begin—what were the terms on which this conversation should be conducted? All the participants in this controversy confronted these questions. Occasionally they appeared to deliberately avoid confronting them. The authors of *Virginia and Maryland* moved very quickly from the problem of the Maryland charter's incompatibility with the English nation, however defined, to a comfortably familiar indictment of the proprietary regime on the grounds of corruption, royalism, and popery.[35]

But even here they ran aground. The author or authors mentioned Lord Baltimore's controversy with the Jesuits over the validity of ecclesiastical law, but seemed unsure what to make of it. Baltimore, "a professed recusant," had made his colony "a receptacle for papists, priests, and Jesuits . . . but hath since discontented them many times and many ways, though intelligence . . . from the pope and Rome be ordinary for his own interests." The writer probably had little idea of the details of the dispute and was unable to explain conflict within the presumably monolithic edifice of international popery. The author also mentioned the Act Concerning Religion of 1649 with the statement that the proprietor "now admits all sorts of religions," but did not elaborate. The commonplaces of anti-popery essentially broke down at this point. The reference implied that tolerating sectaries proved once more the danger the proprietor posed to true religion, but this was not a typical anti-papist position. Usually, popery crushed true religion by explicitly forbidding it and using violence to back up the prohibition, or, alternately, by seducing Protestants away from their faith by lies and false promises, as the authors of *Virginia and Maryland* elsewhere asserted.[36] Catholicism was equated with atheism and indifference, and fringe sectaries were sometimes accused of being Jesuits in disguise or suchlike, but popish toleration for radical Protestants was not customarily a part of the deal. It would be, of course, by the late 1680s, when James II attempted to provide liberty of conscience for both Catholics and Protestant dissenters, but in the mid-1650s the only people to link popery and "sectaries" had been men of far more conservative political credentials than the godly men associated with the commissioners' regime in Maryland in the 1650s, and even they—and many of them were anti-popish enough in their own way—had never claimed that it was a policy of Catholicism to tolerate radical Protestants.

The authors of this tract stumbled repeatedly as they attempted to offer a coherent and politically advantageous indictment of the proprietary regime in Maryland. It was simply not clear how to do this. The various available strategies did not fit easily together. The authors of *Virginia and Maryland* made a jump from equating Catholicism and abuse of power to what was basically an extreme form of the prewar common law argument that alleged that the basic laws and traditions of England limited the powers of the crown, not the other way around, and if the king did something contrary to those laws, that act was in itself void. The book also claimed that the laws against Catholic nonconformity or recusancy in England applied to colonies, including Maryland.[37] What the authors were trying to do was to argue that Catholicism was fundamentally incompatible with the basic constitution of the land; the statutes in England elucidated this; and thus they were valid in Maryland, whose charter did not permit anything at odds with the English constitution. Thus again, what Baltimore was doing was illegal, no matter what powers the king had had written into the charter. Making this claim was a way of fitting the anti-Catholicism argument in with the legal argument against the charter. This argument resembled older common-law arguments about things at odds with the English constitution; the implied standard, however, for figuring out what those things were was not the common law strictly read, but a vaguer sense of things incompatible with law, justice, and Englishness—including popery.

Roger Heaman grappled with a related problem. How—if the matter was one of papist conspiracy—was he to explain the role of the undeniably Protestant governor of Maryland, William Stone, who despite his religion appeared to be motivated by genuine loyalty to the proprietor? Heaman's solution was to turn Stone's experience into a conversion narrative. Heaman implied that as governor, Stone was a lukewarm Protestant at best, and it was only after his defeat at the Severn that he began to see his situation clearly—he "conceived that he was cursed." Stone, according to Heaman, was distraught that he had been "in company with those he knew were the very direct and absolute enemies of the people of God, and did much relent his ever undertaking their designs." Stone "declared further, that it was just with God to blast his company and him, and for his part, [he] did wholly disclaim the Lord Baltimore's cause and interest, and engaged, he would choose rather to die than . . . to join with the Catholics."[38] Stone, in other words, had been written by Heaman into a Puritan conversion narrative. The erstwhile governor had seen the extent of his sins, realize that God might justly "blast" him, and declared he preferred death to allegiance to Catholics. He had moved from being a nominal Protestant, deceived by papists, toward—at least according to Heaman—a better spiritual state. Like *Virginia and Maryland,* Heaman's account of William Stone's interior state aligned political divisions and confessional ones, with true Protestants loyal to the English state. More than this, whether Heaman intended it or not, his story about Stone got at an additional problem, that of goodness in government. Must rulers be good, or even godly, to be legitimate? Heaman implied that the answer to both these questions was yes.

Defenders of the proprietary regime argued differently. They evaded the question of goodness or godliness and offered a legal defense of the proprietary regime. But their arguments did not imply a principled withdrawal from the matter of religion. Rather, they argued a very different theory of the English state, that the state had a core of authority that was prior to confessional allegiance and to the common law, and that core of authority legitimately passed from Charles I to the Commonwealth to Cromwell. The patent had been issued legally by Charles I, and because the transfer of power from monarchy to republic to protectorate had been legitimate, then the patent and all it contained was so too, including the proprietor's right to allow Catholicism in Maryland.

Baltimore's backers started off at a disadvantage. As the proprietor had done in response to Ingle's charges in the 1640s, he and his supporters prefaced their positive arguments in favor of the proprietary regime with denials that the religious situation in Maryland was what writers like Heaman and Strong said it was. John Langford insisted that Stone was a "zealous and well-affected Protestant," as were the "chief officers under my Lord [Baltimore]" and added the obligatory explanation that no one in Maryland was "sworn to uphold Antichrist."[39] John Hammond stressed the "liberty of conscience" available in Maryland and downplayed the presence of the "few papists" who lived there.[40] The matter of the proprietor's doubtful loyalty to the new regime in England was dispatched in Langford's case with the observation that Charles Stuart had given another man, the poet William Davenant, a commission for the governorship of Maryland precisely because Baltimore "did visibly adhere to the rebels in England."[41]

Langford also defended the controversial oath of fidelity that colonists swore to Lord Baltimore, which as he said did not "bind any man to maintain any other jurisdiction or dominion of my lord's, other than what is granted by his patent."[42] His defense of this oath was part and parcel of his defense of the proprietary regime in general, which was that neither Baltimore nor his subordinates had done anything "other than what is warranted by his lordship's patent."[43] Neither here nor elsewhere did Baltimore or anyone writing on his behalf answer the specific charges leveled against the patent—that the "county palatine" clause was illegitimate, or that it was not legal for an English subject to assume a "royal we" over other subjects. Each time, the defense was simply another assertion that that was what the patent said, and thus the whole package was ipso facto legitimate. Essentially Langford was arguing that to pick at various aspects of the patent was to undermine the whole, and thus to undermine the authority that had issued it.

Although the causes of this pamphlet war and the terms on which it was conducted were rooted in the politics of the 1620s and 1630s, the political world had changed by 1655. Charges of popish disloyalty or the anarchical qualities of sectaries might work in a broad sense to argue that one's opponents did not have the common good in mind or that they were in general hostile to order and good government. But specifics were trickier. In 1655, the regime to which all the participants were ostensibly loyal was the Protectorate. But this was a revolutionary regime that had replaced a commonwealth, which had replaced a monarchy—the legal, or moral, or theoretical justifications for its authority were murky. What all of the writers in this controversy tried to do was to make a case that their opponents were disloyal to this regime. In doing so, they fell into familiar patterns. Intermingled with the anti-popery and anti-Puritanism were legal arguments that reached back decades before the civil wars. The trouble was that none of these strategies did precisely what these writers wanted, and they end up arguing quite complex, even internally inconsistent positions.

Langford, for example, was using an argument that had originally been based on a personal loyalty to the monarch. There were three distinct stages to his claim. First, the original charter had been legitimate. Second, the transfer of power from Charles I to the Commonwealth and Protectorate had been legitimate. Third, given all this, the charter was still in force, and to critique some of its provisions was to undermine it in its entirety, and, implicitly, to undermine the power of the present government. Langford offered a view of government based on legitimate holding of authority rather than on laws. If the authority that granted Baltimore's charter was legitimate, criticizing specific parts of it was both pointless and potentially seditious. This approach proved problematic for two reasons. One, it was best suited to government under a monarch—particularly a monarch like Charles I. If the government in question was one that claimed to be based on a specific set of laws, or principles, it was less clear why Baltimore's charter must not be measured against those and amended if necessary. And indeed, this was precisely the criticism leveled at the charter and the proprietary regime by Langford's opponents—that it was inconsistent with good government in general, or at the very least legitimate government now established.

Despite such vitriolic controversy, the dispute over government in Maryland in the 1650s ended with a whimper rather than a bang. The colony remained formally in the commissioners' hands until 1657, when Baltimore prevailed upon Cromwell to return it. A local settlement was reached early the following year.[44] The political uncertainty that resulted from Cromwell's death in 1658 provoked a revolt in Maryland in early 1660 headed by none other than the newly installed proprietary governor, Josias Fendall. Fendall and his supporters appear to have known of the situation in England and made an extraordinarily unlucky guess as to the direction events were taking.[45]

They did not repudiate Baltimore's authority entirely, but appear instead to have attempted a version of the commissioners' regime of 1652–54, in which the proprietor was still powerful, but his authority was reduced by the need to make Maryland's law and government congruent with England's. This rebellion was suppressed without incident later in 1660 when proprietary appointees, including the proprietor's kinsman Philip Calvert, now commissioned governor, proclaimed Fendall's tenure at an end. Fendall and his associates had, in fact, done Baltimore a useful service. The proprietor's speedy and decisive opposition to the Commonwealth-minded Fendall placed him ipso facto on the side of the newly restored monarch Charles II, which position would substantially assist whatever efforts the proprietor might be making to consign to oblivion his past assertions of loyalty to the Commonwealth and Protectorate.[46] The move seemed to work; Charles II ordered the governor of Virginia to assist Lord Baltimore against the "faction" Fendall had raised.[47]

The end of the turbulence of the 1650s in Maryland was of a piece with what happened in England. Armed conflict ended, order was seemingly restored, but in such a way as to bury rather than resolve the disagreements that had caused it. The Restoration in England also saw the beginning of a new attention on the crown's part to events in the colonial world. This shift involved continuity with the prewar years but also some dramatic change. Charles II and James II shared their father's desire for proper acknowledgment of the power of the crown and his willingness to countenance Catholicism—in the case of James it was not toleration but conversion. They were vulnerable to the same cultural narratives about the dangers of colluding with foreign papists and the threat overweening authority from above might pose to English laws and liberties. But things had changed since the 1630s. The colonial world was growing larger, more populous, and more profitable. The push to centralize and regularize colonial administration in the late seventeenth century was part and parcel of a similar process within the English state itself. The expansion of the English colonial world also changed daily life and local politics in the Chesapeake. The complex interaction between the growth of empire, the politics of colonial administration, and local governance in America and the unresolved confessional and political disputes that had caused the civil wars would create the dramatic conflicts Maryland experienced in the last decades of the seventeenth century. In the earlier part of the century, the ad hoc administration of colonial projects and the divisive politics of the 1620s and 1630s both created a space for Maryland's existence and undercut it at every turn. After the Restoration, even the things that remained the same—the politics of religion, problems of law, the challenges of accounting for conflict—would be transformed.

PART II
Colony and Empire

5

CONFLICTS *of* INTEREST

Old met new in the English empire during the 1660s, 1670s, and 1680s. The political culture and confessional fractures of the early Stuart period persisted—the events of mid-century had laid bare but not solved the conflicts that had led to revolution. Charles II was restored to the throne without conditions in 1660, creating a double-layered problem. The Restoration left longstanding issues unresolved—and the fear of a return to the 1640s made questions of law, prerogative, and religion so much the more difficult to address.[1] At the same time, the world of 1660 or 1670 was not that of 1630 or 1640. The English Atlantic empire was growing in population, in territorial extent, and in financial importance. The decades after the Restoration saw an entwined growth of state and empire; how the crown governed its colonies and the nature of the relationship between them were understood to reflect fundamental characteristics of the English polity itself.

The administrative debate over tobacco production in the 1660s offers a window into this process of transformation. Chesapeake tobacco production expanded significantly in the decades after the Restoration. The price of the commodity was falling, however, which meant that while tax receipts on shipments might rise, profits for growers shrank.[2] The result was an extended transatlantic policy conflict over what, if anything, ought to be done. Planters, Maryland assemblymen, and royal councilors were wrestling with a problem of expanding empire, but their assumption that there must be a single solution that would benefit everyone if all parties were honest would have been familiar to anyone who remembered the 1610s and 1620s.[3] Ultimately, no lasting solution was found. But the sense that economic troubles were necessarily rooted in human selfishness—or as contemporaries put it, the pursuit of "private interest" over the common good, with some parties far more likely than others to be guilty of such self-interested behavior—is key to understanding the tumultuous decades of the late seventeenth century.

After 1660, the term "interest" appears with increasing frequency in controversies ranging from the debate over the tobacco trade to the question of whether Lord Baltimore could be relied on to "espouse the Protestant interest." In the decades before 1690, this new term still contained a very old idea, that sustained conflict was necessarily the result of faction, malice, or ill will on the part of a few.[4] But the type of conflict in which accusations of "private interest" tended to emerge is important. Contemporaries used this word when navigating complex large-scale problems that proved persistently unamenable to solution because of the diverging needs of those affected. The expanding empire, with its increasingly elaborate administrative apparatus and vast conflicts emerging between Native peoples in America and European newcomers, proved productive of precisely this kind of problem; this was the case in the empire at large and in Maryland itself, with its fundamental disagreements about the nature of government and legitimate authority in the colony, increasingly troubled tobacco economy, and an almost-impossible-to-maintain diplomatic balance between English colonies and Indian nations. Blame tended to fasten on familiar characters; anti-popery, anti-Puritanism, and claims about "interest" went hand in hand in these decades. The result was ever more elaborate accusations of malice, conspiracy, and subversion. The tobacco controversy was not about religion. But, even here, in circumstances under which one might not expect to see modes of argument so closely tied to assumptions about order in a cosmic sense, participants made dark insinuations as to one another's motives and offered increasingly shrill explanations of the conduct of those who persisted in disagreeing with them.

* * *

Attempts to raise the price of Virginia tobacco had been made since the post-1620s fall in prices, but these had had little effect on the long-term downward drift in prices.[5] Before 1660, no such efforts had been made in Maryland, but with the return of familiar patterns of government and the continuing decline in prices, planters and administrators began to make attempts to improve the trade that required the cooperation of both colonies.

In May 1662, Virginian planters and merchants petitioned the king to accept a series of proposals for limiting tobacco production in Virginia and elsewhere. First, they asked that no tobacco be planted in Virginia or Maryland after June 1663, and that no ships be allowed to depart from either

Chesapeake colony before May 1, 1664. The goal was not only to reduce tobacco planting, but to encourage the production of other commodities, such as silk, hemp, pitch, and so on. The cessation of planting was to be renewed yearly until the price reached a satisfactory level. On May 26, the Privy Council rejected the petition, and stated "that thenceforth they would receive no petitions of that nature." Some of the petitioners, however, pressed for a reconsideration, and on June 13, the council agreed to review the matter.[6] On June 29, an order was issued that commissioners be appointed in both Maryland and Virginia to consider the best way of improving the tobacco trade.[7] No further progress on the cessation occurred, however, until August 26, when William Berkeley and a handful of other prominent inhabitants of Virginia and Maryland petitioned the king once more to enforce a limitation of tobacco planting, and to forbid ships from leaving the Chesapeake until after May 1.[8] The request was reiterated in September.[9]

Berkeley wrote to the Maryland council in April 1663 to seek their cooperation in reducing the volume of tobacco produced in order to increase the price. He pointedly implied that cooperation was in their interest, referring to the Privy Council's order of June 29 and adding that he wished to offer an account of the two colonies' meeting to the crown. Governor Charles Calvert's "acceptance or refusal" of the proposal would be of interest to the king, and an instance of the latter might reflect poorly on him.[10]

Governor Charles Calvert pronounced himself "ready to join in anything which may conduce to improving our only commodity," and at the subsequent meeting in Virginia on May 12 commissioners from both colonies concluded that the only way to "advance" the tobacco trade was to plant less tobacco. They agreed that no tobacco would be "planted or sowed in either colony" after June 20, 1664. This stint would last one year, but it might be renewed; the governors and councils of both colonies were to take an oath to enforce it.[11]

Charles Calvert was not among the Maryland commissioners, and when he and his father Cecil received word of the agreement, they suspected the Virginians were trying to cheat them, since the slight difference in latitude between the two colonies might allow the Virginians to begin planting earlier in the year. Charles himself did not seem utterly convinced as to the capacity of the commissioners; he added that "the calling our assembly here first was a great oversight in [the Maryland commissioners], and they could give me no good answer to't, only that it was much pressed by the other party the result of our assembly."[12] Probably the Virginians were anxious that the Maryland assembly approve the agreement because they suspected that Baltimore would not agree to the stint, and having an act of assembly, assented to by Charles, would provide some leverage in getting the stint into action. In the end, the Maryland assembly that met in September 1663 did not approve the bill, and over the course of the session both houses drew up lists of reasons why such an act should not be passed.[13] The records for that session are incomplete, however, and we have little information about the debate over the stint, or the reasons that the two houses produced against it.

The Virginians tried again the following year. A petition to the Privy Council resulted in a meeting between the council, delegates from Virginia, and Lord Baltimore in October 1664, after which the council ordered the Virginians to speak to Baltimore privately "to see whether [they] could jointly fix upon any fit proposition . . . for the lessening the quantity" of tobacco. The Virginians reported back a month later that they had attempted to do so, but Baltimore would not agree to "any thing we could propound." Baltimore's own proposals were unpromising, and in the end they had decided to "[present] our proposals apart," and leave them to the council's consideration.[14]

Their proposals reiterated the familiar problem that Chesapeake tobacco had "glutted all markets" and as a result did "little more than pay his majesty's customs." If prices were not raised via a stint imposed on both Maryland and Virginia and a regulation of when ships entered and left the harbor, the average Chesapeake planter would likely become "desperate . . . endangering both the peace (if not the ruin) of his majesty's country." They stressed that the stint was "so much desired by his majesty's governor [Berkeley] and . . . generally approved by his majesty's country" and that whatever Baltimore might object, they had "with tender respect . . . considered the interest of his Lordship's province" and found that it accorded with theirs.[15] The distinction between the interest of "his majesty's country" and that of "his lordship's province" was probably not an accident. The true interest of Baltimore's province was the same as Virginia's—but Lord Baltimore's own was perhaps a different question. Later complaints from Virginia about Baltimore's objections to the stint would make far less veiled charges of private interest and imperfect loyalty to the crown.

Baltimore remained skeptical. As he explained to the Privy Council later in November, he "wonder[ed] to meet with [the stint idea] so soon again," when it had been "reviled by his majesty's royal council board." He thought it would be impracticable to enforce and would not work, and he considered it an unfair experiment with the livelihood of so many farmers, potentially enough so to drive them to "despair and mutiny," especially given that the law would "restrain the planter . . . in their liberty, which they conceive is their birthright as Englishmen of planting what quantity they please." Besides, if any planters "live in a poor manner," the fault lay not in the economy but in "their own sloth, ill husbandry," and expenditure on "brandywine and other liquors."

But the danger was deeper than this. Baltimore thought that "knowing men . . . may perhaps have a design of their own interest in it" and that those in favor of a stint were doing so out of personal animus towards him and Maryland. He had reason to suspect "that the petition from Virginia for this stint was a design, either to cause some ill reflections on him or Maryland" or at the very least to place his colony at a disadvantage to Virginia. Baltimore's fears of "designs" against him were not entirely unreasonable—in 1661, William Berkeley had complained to colonial administrators that the ancient "dismembering" of Virginia, including the creation of Maryland, had been an "impediment" to the king's colony and would in time "be found more disadvantageous to the Crown" than was now apparent. Two years later he termed Baltimore's colony a "destructive government." Baltimore turned the language of royal interest back against whomever might use it against him. The stint would "be very prejudicial to his majesty . . . by notably lessening the customs and excise upon that commodity, which he [hoped] will be alone sufficient to put a stop to the proposal." Maryland, he noted further on, produced about £20,000 a year for the crown through customs and excise on tobacco.[16] Baltimore did not mention that his own duty of two shillings per hogshead on all tobacco exported from Maryland would also be affected.

In the end, Maryland's proprietor succeeded in preventing the stint. On November 25, 1664, the Privy Council made a report of the proceedings to the king. They concluded that the proposed stint "will be prejudicial both to the planters and his majesty's customs." Rather than limit tobacco production, they recommended encouragement of other commodities by lifting the customs duties on hemp, pitch, and tar from Maryland or Virginia for the next five years.[17] Interested parties turned then to more local solutions. The Maryland assembly found itself wrangling with the question of potentially competing economic interests in April 1666, when the two houses debated not a stint, but a complete cessation of tobacco planting for the following year. The argument over tobacco policy devolved with alarming speed into an argument over authority, characteristically infused with charges of malice and faction.

The lower house of the assembly opposed the cessation—or at least they demonstrated reluctance, requesting that the proprietor be informed that a cessation was under consideration so that he might "consider how the same may quadrate with his lordship's interest here." A cessation "may prove very prejudicial to the proprietor," and they hesitated to "determine anything which may reflect upon his lordship's rights, interest or prerogative without special direction from himself." The members of the assembly likely knew of Baltimore's opposition to limiting tobacco cultivation, and on this point they and he agreed. Stressing the need to sound the proprietor on the matter was, in this case, to their advantage. In addition, there might well have been a sincere sense that proposals for economic regulation on that scale, which would indeed have an effect on the proprietor's interests, really should be submitted to him beforehand.[18]

Within just a few days, the upper house—the governor and council—had grown frustrated by the assemblymen's persistent refusals to do as the upper house had asked and pass the bill authorizing the cessation. Discounting as spurious objections that the cessation might "depopulate the province," they began to "suspect that businesses are either not carried on in a due way in your house but managed by the artifice of a few." Whatever concern the lower house had voiced about Baltimore's privileges, "you have neither care of his interest here nor respect for him nor his governor nor his government even now when it is managed by his son and heir apparent."[19] The lower house's refusal to pass legislation the upper house considered necessary and appropriate had caused the governor and council to charge the burgesses with what amounted to sedition. Evidently, members of the upper house did not think it within the privileges of the lower to utterly refuse legislation the upper house had repeatedly urged on them, especially when the more prestigious house had explained why it was necessary. Probably, too, some of the governor's and council's insistence came from their knowledge of Baltimore's rejection of the previous plans for a stint. If they got the consent of the lower house, and Governor Calvert assented to the bill for a cessation, it would be legal at least until Baltimore disallowed it.

The issue was in part one of economic interest. The governor and council of Maryland and men of equivalent wealth and prestige in Virginia wanted a cessation. They had the resources to go a year without new income and they could afford to make the gamble that a small or no crop for that year might be followed by a boom the next. Less wealthy planters, such as those who made up much of the lower house of the Maryland assembly, as well as those the burgesses represented, probably could not.[20] It might help them in the long term, but the short term would be hard. The local economy depended on credit given out on each year's crop, and one year in which debts went unpaid might easily unravel many people's finances.

But those involved did not express the conflict in terms of reconciling the needs of people of varying wealth. They made arguments in terms of the public good, whether it was the lower house's reference to depopulating the province, or the upper house's subsequent assertion that if the cessation were not passed, tobacco would be worth so little that the province would be unable to buy arms and ammunition for defense against the Indians, and thus, as they put it "as you tender the preservation of yourselves, your wives and families . . . prepare yourselves . . . to settle this business of a cessation."[21] The language used by the upper house of the assembly reveals their sense that they were the body whose job it was to determine the interest of both province and proprietor. The lower house was there to debate and consent, and if they refused to debate or did not consent to a self-evidently reasonable proposal, this was evidence not of disagreement in good faith but of stubbornness, faction, and self-interest. The subject matter was new, but the terms on which the upper house understood the problem were virtually identical to Cecil Calvert's framing of his disputes with the assembly in the late 1640s and early 1650s. If the members of the lower house had had the "due respect to the governor you pretend," they would have deferred to their superiors' wishes without dragging their feet.[22]

Ultimately, the lower house acquiesced. The reasons for their sudden reversal cannot be fully uncovered. Perhaps a minority of prominent planters who favored the cessation plan extracted either deference or agreement from the rest. Legislative management may also have played a role. Of the commissioners soon sent to treat with Virginia about the matter all but councilors Philip Calvert and Henry Coursey had been members of the lower house, although one of the commissioners, Notley, the speaker of the lower house in 1666, was later reported as writing to Baltimore to express his opposition to the cessation.[23] But however consensus was achieved, achieved it was. Provided an agreement was reached with Virginia and Carolina to do the same, no tobacco was to be planted between February 1, 1666/7 and February 1, 1667/8.[24] The assemblies of Virginia and Carolina approved similar measures, and by the end of the autumn it seemed that the cessation would go into effect as planned. Lord Baltimore had received news of the Maryland assembly's act, however, and in November he disallowed it, undoing several months of intercolonial diplomacy.[25]

The proprietor's disallowance of the law caused no violent outcry in Maryland or Carolina, but the Virginians were livid. Berkeley and his council complained to the Privy Council about both the Maryland assembly and the proprietor, although they focused their sharpest criticism on the latter. They claimed that both were stubborn, self-interested, ignorant or careless of the common good, and potentially even disloyal. In 1663, Maryland's "obstina[te]" assembly had "utterly disowned and quashed" the plan for a stint, "to our and their own extreme disadvantage." The Maryland authorities had pretended to entertain the plan only "as a means to preserve them from being thought contumaciously obedient to your royal commands." When an agreement was finally reached in 1666, the Virginians were pleased not only at the prospect of avoiding "utter ruin" and "extreme poverty," but also because "we had fully and effectually obeyed your royal commands." But "contemplation of future happiness and prosperities" was cut short by the "absolute and princely" behavior of Lord Baltimore, whose disallowal of Maryland's part in the cessation "overtook us like a storm and forced us like distressed mariners . . . to throw our dear-bought commodities into the sea, when we were in sight of the harbor." All hope of future prosperity was thus "drowned," and the "mariners" were "divided and enforced to steer by another's compass whose needle is too often touched with particular interest, this unlimited and (as it appears to us) independent power and authority of the Lord Baltimore." The Maryland proprietor's authority "doth like an impetuous wind blow from us all these seasonable showers of your majesty's royal care and favors, and leaves us and his own province withering and decaying in distress and poverty." Baltimore had placed his own private interests above those of the polity as a whole, and distress and poverty was the result. He damaged not only the interest of his own colony, but the Chesapeake as a whole; his arbitrary action had occasioned enough "grief and anger" in Virginia that pains had to be taken to prevent "disturbances" there. The Virginians were fudging the issue of obedience a little. The order of June 29, 1662, had directed the two colonies to appoint commissioners and put in place what measures they saw fit; it was a long step from here to the assertion that because Baltimore had disallowed the Maryland assembly's cessation act four years later he was contumaciously disobedient. Nevertheless, the king and Privy Council had ordered the two colonies to come up with a solution, and the Maryland proprietor's sudden undoing of all their efforts did give the Virginia authorities room to argue that Baltimore's extensive powers were interfering with the best interests of Virginia and weakening the king's authority in the Chesapeake. Berkeley and the other councilors asked the king to "protect . . . your majesty's loyal and most ancientest colony from the violent and ruinous attempt of our neighbors armed (as they pretend) with absolute authority" and impose some solution.[26]

Lord Baltimore did his best to turn the Virginians' accusations on their head. He explained that he had disallowed the 1667 cessation act because he assumed it fell under the 1664 order that there was to be no stint. This was perhaps a slight stretch of the intent of the 1664 order, which did not forbid stints or cessations in perpetuity. The king and Privy Council in 1667 had not rebuked any of the tobacco colonies for negotiating such a plan, and the Virginians' complaint to the king in June 1667 seems to indicate they believed the question of future cessations was still open. But Baltimore's explanation stressed his loyalty—he had done what he had out of obedience. More than this, he professed himself concerned with the public good, noting that the cessation would reduce customs and ruin poor planters, whose distress would "very probably endanger the peace of the province and provoke the people to sedition." Thus it was not Baltimore, as the Virginians had alleged, who was acting only out of concern for his own interest. Indeed, it was the motives of his opponents that were suspect. In a criticism that was probably not far from the mark, Baltimore argued that the support for a cessation came only from a relatively small group of rich planters and merchants who were ignoring the interest of the poorer sort. He was not at all surprised that "the council and major part of the assemblies of both colonies (which consist of the ablest planters) should agree to such cessations, or that the merchants here should desire the same, it being in truth the way to make them rich in one year."[27]

Plans to engineer an improvement of the tobacco trade in the 1660s ended not with a workable solution but rather a series of increasingly harsh recriminations. On one level, the problem was simply an economic one. The expansion of the market was slowing, and tobacco prices were low. Contemporaries believed that controlling or limiting the market was the only solution. Solving the woes of the tobacco trade by stints or cessations, however, would have had drastically different effects on the various parties concerned in it. The men involved knew this. The poorest planters in the Chesapeake would likely, as Baltimore said, have suffered extremely in the short term. Richer planters who had the money to go a year without a crop would have done better. These men were by and large those behind efforts at limiting production. Most probably believed that despite the short-term difficulties their plan would pose to less wealthy planters, the long-term benefits would be to the advantage of all. Baltimore, a significant portion of whose income derived from a duty on the amount of tobacco exported, not the value of the shipped commodity, had little reason to agree to it. The same was true for the crown, whose revenues were in a fairly dire state by the late 1660s.[28] Customs duties provided a significant and growing amount of income.[29] Finally, there was the fear of social instability or even rebellion if too many poor freemen in the Chesapeake were left destitute. As the upper house of the Maryland assembly put it, increased economic stress might lead the poorer sorts to commit "outrages . . . for want of necessaries."[30] This point was argued on both sides of the question, and was probably as much a result of fear of a return to the chaos of the 1650s as of accurate calculations about the advantages and disadvantages of planting little or no tobacco.

The conflict was economic, but the fault lines it revealed were political. Most of the pressure for the stints and cessations came from wealthy Virginia planters rather than their counterparts in Maryland, and much of their invective was focused on Lord Baltimore. Prominent Maryland planters probably saw the potential benefits to themselves, but by 1667 at least, they would have known of Baltimore's opposition to tobacco limitation. Whatever support they might otherwise have voiced for a cessation had to be weighed against the patronage and authority Baltimore provided, and which they stood a chance of losing, or not getting in the future, should they do anything he considered rebellious or disobedient. They were willing in the end, of course, having been, at least according to Berkeley, convinced by the latter's arguments in favor, but only up to a point—the reluctance Berkeley describes as occasioning a confirmatory meeting in December 1667 could not have come from the assembly alone, which did not meet between April 1666 and April 1669. The main push for tobacco limitation came from Virginia, and the dispute ultimately devolved into an argument about the extent of the Maryland proprietor's authority and his apparent reluctance to submit to the authority of the crown. Berkeley and the others wanted to convince the king and Privy Council that they were in the right about the cessation, and to claim that Baltimore had more independence than was fitting for a subject while stressing their own obedience and loyalty. This was a fairly obvious line to take in the 1660s. Baltimore's Catholicism, though, and that of his most prominent underlings in Maryland, was not mentioned once. Berkeley and the others mentioned "arbitrary power" alone, not "popery and arbitrary power." Militant anti-Catholicism was not the best way to gain Charles II's approval, and no doubt they knew this.

The battle over tobacco limitation in the 1660s drew the developing economic tensions of a New World society into the political hothouse of Stuart England. Through the 1630s, '40s, and '50s, much of the controversy around Baltimore's colony had been focused around its unusual religious makeup, the political claims of its proprietor, and what those two things implied about both local government in Maryland and the English polity in general. The decades after 1660 saw continuity with the earlier Stuart period in the sense that English-speaking people spoke of questions of loyalty and order in confessional terms. The questions of law and royal power that had sparked the civil wars remained largely unresolved. But in the Chesapeake, early modern English colonials employed familiar political frameworks in a new environment and with the goal of dealing with local and imperial concerns that were becoming ever more difficult to navigate.

6

WAR *and* PEACE *in the* CHESAPEAKE

The controversy over the tobacco trade in the 1660s extended across the Atlantic and southward from Maryland into Virginia and Carolina. The web of Chesapeake politics also reached north and west into the interior of the continent and back many centuries before the arrival of the English.[1] In the earliest decades of the seventeenth century, English numbers were small, and their patterns of land use and ecological impact did not place them into immediate conflict with the Piscataways, Susquehannocks, and others who lived around the Chesapeake. By the 1660s, however, several independent strands—longstanding conflicts in the American interior; an upsurge in European and African migration and an increase in circulation of people, commodities, and disease; the expansion of both English and French possessions throughout eastern North America—twisted together to produce several decades of precisely the kind of complex problems that tended, for the English, to lead to charges of grand and terrifying conspiracy. Colonists' attempts to account for the threats they saw about them at every turn helped to create a specifically American anti-popery narrative, one in which the dangerous outsiders with whom papists conspired included Jesuit missionaries, Frenchmen, and—as the English often so vaguely put it—"the Indians."

* * *

Conflicts between Native Americans and European migrants over land and livestock were as persistent in Maryland as they were elsewhere. Before 1650, the small numbers of the English and the focus of many early settlers on the fur trade rather than farming obscured differences between natives and newcomers over land use and ownership. After midcentury, a combination of developments produced increasing conflict. The fur trade declined, and the number of English immigrants grew, making the presence of Indians from the English perspective a source of frustration rather than profit. Alliances among Indian traders, English factors, and elite colonial merchants early in the century had created an interethnic network of influential people whose interest lay in limiting land-intensive farming; as competition and warfare caused the trade to dwindle later in the century, the English portion of that interest evaporated.[2] The same process that created conflict over land edged out those among the English whose primary economic interest lay in maintaining good alliances. Some causes of conflict reached far beyond the Chesapeake—the expansion of the Atlantic trade after midcentury increased the likelihood that European diseases would cross the ocean; native communities reduced by disease were less able to resist land-hungry English planters, who did not hesitate to make the most of their newfound advantage.[3]

Native communities in the Chesapeake used a range of strategies to adjust to new circumstances.[4] But even those who had longstanding relationships with the English found that this offered no security against encroachment or abuse. In 1666, for example, Piscataway representatives voiced concern that despite an alliance that reached back to the 1630s, the English were not dealing fairly with them. They desired that "as they treat the English friendly so let not Indians be beaten without cause." There should be no "quarrels for killing hogs no more than for cows eating Indian corn." English livestock were often left loose to forage, which they often did in unfenced Indian cornfields; when Indians took or killed English pigs or cows that caused damage, the English demanded compensation. The spread of English farms, animals, and boundaries, the Piscataways explained, "drive us from place to place . . . we can fly no farther."[5]

Conflicts over land and livestock were not peculiar to Maryland or the Chesapeake.[6] But the course these conflicts took in Maryland and the motives and interests of those involved were rooted in the political landscape of the mid-Atlantic. The English in Maryland were aware that much of this landscape was obscure to them. In 1676, for example, the assembly considered what to do about the children of two planters, George Watts and John Dickenson, who were "in the possession of the Indians at Murder Keel." The assembly was reluctant to "demand" the children because this might "suggest a jealousy and suspicion to the emperor of Nanticoke that we are minded to pick a quarrel with him and create further mischief than we may possibly be aware of."[7] The Nanticokes were among the most powerful peoples of the Eastern Shore. They had tenuous ties to the Iroquois, who were frequently at war with the Maryland-allied Susquehannocks—"picking a quarrel" with the Nanticokes was not on the colonists' agenda, even if they were not always sure what would or would not help them avoid it.[8]

But there was a profound ambivalence to the English desire to keep the peace. They were well aware that much of their information about the local political landscape—as well as a significant amount of military support—necessarily came from Native American sources. At the same time, they often deeply distrusted those very sources, fearing betrayal at every turn. In 1676, for example, at a time when the threat of war was particularly acute, the Maryland assembly provided the Piscataways, Mattawomans, Pamunkeys, and others with matchcoats, corn, powder, and shot in return for military help, but they also took hostages to ensure loyalty. Not long afterward, the upper house of the assembly needed the linguistic assistance of a Mattawoman leader to interrogate some Native American prisoners and determine whether they were friendly and what their business was in the colony.[9]

Neither the physical nor the political landscape could be neatly demarcated by English surveying lines. Relationships among the English, Piscataways, Nanticokes and others did not operate under English direction, and were shaped by conflicts that reached far beyond the official jurisdictions of Lord Baltimore or Governor Berkeley. At the center of the events of the 1660s and 1670s were the Susquehannocks and the Five Nations of the Iroquois, whose enmities, mode of warfare, and diplomatic decisions had a profound effect on events in the Chesapeake.[10] The English did not know it, but the tangle of warfare and feuding that they were drawn into by the later seventeenth century had roots that reached back to at least the sixteenth century, when the Iroquois created the Great League of Peace and Power; this framework for mediation resolved decades of internal conflict by creating a mechanism to maintain harmony within and turn violence outward. The Five Nations engaged in "mourning wars" that replaced lost individuals with captives taken in warfare; their internal league required that captives come from outside, which put pressure on neighboring people who bore the brunt of their raids. Among these neighbors were other Iroquoian people who shared the mourning war custom, which could result in a vicious cycle of war and captive taking.

Such pressure caused the Iroquoian-speaking Susquehannocks to move southward to the Chesapeake by about 1600, which drew local people there into the longstanding Susquehannock–Five Nations feud. It also placed the

Susquehannocks in a position to trade for furs with the English—and may have also inadvertently cut the Iroquois off from direct access to European traders in the Chesapeake and on the Delaware.[11] They established a trading relationship with the Dutch in New Netherland, a key factor in their western military successes of the 1630s and 1640s.[12] The forces that shaped the creation of trading ventures, economic rivalries and Atlantic colonies were part of a political narrative that reached deep into the interior and was largely invisible to European newcomers.

The year 1650 proved a turning point in this story for several reasons. The Susquehannocks negotiated an alliance with Maryland in 1652. This was useful for the English and the Susquehannocks, but it created a host of problems for some smaller Chesapeake nations, whose own alliances with Maryland thus translated into enmity with the Iroquois. This change in the Chesapeake coincided with a turn in Iroquois policy. Previously the Five Nations had gone west and north for captives, but their success there was such that after midcentury they began to look southward.[13] The twin offerings of Europeans—trade goods and, inadvertently, disease—also influenced the geography of Iroquois warfare. During the earliest decades of the European presence, the geographic position of the Iroquois kept them relatively isolated from contagious disease, which gave them an advantage over some of their neighbors. But their isolation from European diseases ended by the 1630s and 1640s, when successive epidemics of smallpox killed over half the population. Mourning wars to replace lost numbers overlapped with conflicts over access to trade—and these wars, conducted with European weapons, were far more deadly than in the past.[14]

Their midcentury conflicts proved ruinous for the Five Nations.[15] The situation only worsened after 1660. The Iroquois' important trading relationship with the Dutch deteriorated during the early part of the decade and dwindled to nothing when the English conquered New Netherland in 1664. At this point, the Susquehannocks posed the greatest threat to the Five Nations.[16] Intermittent raids for captives and trade goods wrought more and more damage, and other Indian nations to the north and east of the Chesapeake were drawn into the conflict, as were both the Dutch in New Amstell (part of modern-day Delaware) and the English in Maryland. This war between the Iroquois and the Susquehannocks, as well as other Iroquois campaigns farther north in New York, would determine much of Maryland's Indian diplomacy over the next few decades.

Initially the English colonists in Maryland experienced the conflict second or third hand, as Iroquois war parties raided the villages of their neighbor Indians. The Susquehannocks had negotiated an alliance with Maryland in 1652; by the early 1660s they and their allies sought assistance from the English against the Five Nations. In December 1660, the Indians of the Portobacco area asked governor Philip Calvert for assistance. As allies of the English and the Susquehannocks they were in danger from the "Cinigoes [Senecas, i.e., Iroquois], who are a potent nation" and had "lately killed five of their men and threatened their fort [palisaded village] for being friends to [the English] and the Susquehannocks who are at war with the said . . . Cinigos, wherefore they desired that for pay they might have four English men to help them make their fort." The governor said he would consider the proposal, but no answer is recorded.[17]

The conflict soon required a more decisive response, though the English still lacked a complete understanding of what was happening. In April 1661, four months after the Portobacco Indians made their request for help, the Maryland assembly passed an act "empowering the governor and council to raise forces and maintain a war [outside] the province and to aid the Susquehannock Indians." This act was necessary because the province was in "imminent danger" from a "war begun it [seems] by some foreign Indians . . . [and] in humane probability our neighbor Indians the Susquehannocks are a bulwark and security of the northern parts of this province." The governor and council were licensed to levy fifty men and provisions to support them, which men and supplies would be sent to the Susquehannock fort.[18] As the explanation of the war that appeared to have been started by unspecified "foreign Indians" suggests, the English were aware that their Native American allies might be of use to them, in this case as a buffer, but they had no more specific information.

This Susquehannock-Iroquois conflict in which Maryland was becoming embroiled was not always distinguished or distinguishable from the periodic small-scale violence between Indians and English characteristic of these decades. Conflict over access to and use of land led to increased friction. English settlers were quick to suspect Indians who came near their widely scattered plantations, and if there seemed to be a threat they attacked even Indians from groups allied to the English. The relatives of Indians who had been killed took reprisals against the English, and just as Europeans did not always distinguish among Indians, the latter might raid the home or farm of English colonists unrelated to the original instigators. Indians also occasionally robbed traders or raided other parties, which led to further reprisals and counter-reprisals. Moreover, unlike European magistrates, Indian headmen or elders had little coercive power over others. While a "king" or an "emperor" of a particular nation might sign a treaty with the Maryland government, such leaders could not prevent other members of their community from raiding settlements or killing Europeans.

In August 1665, for example, a Mattawoman man named Maquamps, also known as Bennett, was charged with a gruesome murder in Charles County. The Mattawomans were friendly with the Maryland government, but this man and three others nevertheless assaulted a woman with a tomahawk, killed her son, and gave a third woman a "dangerous wound in the head." One of the servants who witnessed the attack, a young woman named Elizabeth Brumley, knew enough of the Indians' language to ask Maquamps/Bennett "why did he so? who answered in Indian, because he would."[19] Similarly, one Delaware Bay headman told the council that he was willing to negotiate peace despite his own loss of men because "he did believe all those outrages were committed by the English without order from the governor and council" just as the "revenges" under discussion "were taken by his Indians without his or any of his great men's knowledge."[20]

For many English colonists, the result was fear of a generalized and worsening "Indian threat" that did not make fine distinctions among Native Americans. In May of 1661, for example, when the Maryland council ordered anyone who had "suffered any damage by the Indians" or "engaged with them in a hostile manner" to appear at the former councilor Nathaniel Utie's plantation Spesutia on the fifteenth, the accounts of murder and plunder that were reported or sent in were probably not all directly related to the Iroquois-Susquehannock conflict that was the focus of the Maryland authorities' attention.[21]

Even from the vantage point of those in authority in Maryland, distinctions between allies and potential enemies were not always clear. Until the mid-1660s, the English believed that the best choice was to assist the Susquehannocks against the Iroquois, but even so they often suspected that the Susquehannocks were unreliable or disloyal. Soon after the information-gathering session at Utie's plantation, Captain John Odber was sent to the Susquehannocks' fort to gather information about "the process of the war between them and the Cingao Indians" and to "press them discreetly to a vigorous prosecution of it" if he found them "slack." Officials also instructed Odber to see if some of the perpetrators of the murders reported at Utie's plantation might not be among the Susquehannocks. If they were, he could order them "shot to death" or sent to Maryland for prosecution.[22] The Maryland-Susquehannock alliance was reaffirmed in 1666, and through the early 1660s the colony's authorities firmly considered themselves at war with the Iroquois.[23] But the Maryland authorities did not want their allies too close, and in August 1663 ordered Major Samuel Goldsmith of Calvert County to tell the Susquehannocks to come south to "treat with" the commissioners of Calvert county, and to remind them in forceful terms that they had agreed not to enter Maryland or approach an English settlement without an elaborate series of warnings to the English.[24] The Maryland authorities wanted to keep the Susquehannocks' friendship, but a military alliance did not always imply trust.

A major diplomatic realignment occurred between the mid-1660s and the mid-1670s, one that would have profound effects in the Chesapeake: the English, formerly allies of the Susquehannocks, sought peace with the Iroquois. Relations between the English and the Susquehannocks soured, leading to an incident at the Susquehannocks' fort in 1675 in which the English killed several Susquehannock leaders in cold blood. The massacre at the fort is well known in its relation to Bacon's Rebellion in Virginia.[25] This episode of violence also revealed differences among authorities in Maryland about how best to pursue relations with Native Americans and how English people should be punished—or not—for crimes committed against Indians. Suspicion of higher-ups' seemingly too cozy relations with Indians sparked suspicion in both Maryland and Virginia in the later seventeenth century. The massacre at the fort and the debate surrounding it played into deepening fears of conspiracy in the 1670s. Why were such frightening events happening—and who was to blame?[26]

Key to the events of these years was the Susquehannocks' decision to move. Their war with the Iroquois had continued through the 1660s and into the early 1670s. The Susquehannock population was falling for the same reasons as that of the Five Nations, warfare and disease. Sometime in 1673 or 1674 they abandoned their village, and by early 1675 at least some Susquehannocks had settled along the Patuxent River in Maryland. Iroquois military pressure was partly responsible for the move into Maryland; one scholar has argued that the Maryland authorities pressured the Susquehannocks into moving in order to reach a peace with the Iroquois: the Dutch had temporarily re-taken New Netherland in 1673–74, and the English feared that they would incite the Iroquois against them, so any potential roadblocks to peace with the Five Nations—including the Susquehannocks—had to be removed.[27] Either way, the Susquehannocks were no longer in a position to act as a buffer between the English and the Five Nations, and the Maryland government was well aware that "peace [with the Iroquois] may bring a war with the Susquehannocks."[28]

But as members of the Maryland assembly saw it, the threat of war with their erstwhile allies was more than simply the unfortunate consequence of a geographical and diplomatic realignment. They suspected connivance on the Susquehannocks' part. When some Susquehannock leaders came to the upper house during the February 1674/5 assembly, after their move into Maryland, to find out "what part of the province should be allotted for them to live on," the subsequent discussion revealed fears in the lower house of conspiracy among the Indians. They suspected the Susquehannocks "may corrupt our Indians, and mold them . . . to their own future designs." The Susquehannocks had not come to Maryland to ask where they might live, but rather "purposely to discover the strength of our province." The conspiracy was not limited to Maryland's former allies—"the Susquehannocks and Senecas have private correspondence together notwithstanding the seeming war between them." Even if the Susquehannocks and the Iroquois were really at war, it would be dangerous to have the former in the province because it will "exasperate the Senecas for us to entertain them."[29]

The assembly pressured the Susquehannocks to move to "a place above the falls of the Potomac," but by the summer of 1675 they were living in a deserted Piscataway town on the Maryland side of the river.[30] It was here that their story intersected with an already tense situation in Virginia. In July 1675, a Stafford County, Virginia, man was killed by some Doeg Indians, who fled across the Potomac into Maryland. The local militia, led by Col. George Mason and Capt. George Brent, pursued them, and killed not only Doegs but also several Susquehannocks. The Virginia militia's intrusion into Maryland brought a letter of complaint from Charles Calvert to William Berkeley, indicating irritation both with the trespass and the trouble Brent's and Mason's mistake would likely cause. Soon, though, faced with retaliatory attacks by the Susquehannocks on both sides of the river, the two colonies decided to join forces and march on the Susquehannocks' fort.[31]

The Virginians requested assistance from Maryland in seeking out the "true causes of several murders and spoils that have been done by the Indians," and the Maryland council ordered that a regiment of five troops of fifty men each be raised to assist the Virginians against the Susquehannocks, headed by councilor Thomas Truman. They also ordered that the Susquehannocks be forced to move where they had been pressured to go earlier, above the falls of the Potomac.[32]

The Maryland militia under Truman reached the Susquehannocks' fort in late September. Truman invited Harignera, who had negotiated with the council earlier that year, to come out and speak with him. Harignera had since died, however, and five other headmen emerged instead. Truman accused them of the murders along the frontier, to which the Susquehannock leaders replied that the Iroquois were responsible, and they had since left the area. The Virginia militia arrived the following day. They too charged the five headmen with the Stafford County deaths, and again the Susquehannocks replied that the Senecas had been responsible for those killings. One of the Susquehannocks brought out a medal on a piece of ribbon, stamped with the faces of Baltimore and his wife, explaining that it had been given to him by a former governor of Maryland as a token of peace. Truman ignored it. He had his men carry off the five headmen, and before they had gone far ordered them killed. The Virginia and Maryland militias besieged the fort for the next seven weeks, until the Susquehannocks escaped into the woods.[33]

The Susquehannocks retaliated against the English early in 1676, and as they sought allies against and ultimately reconciliation with the English, this war—from the perspective of the Virginians—became part of the conflict between Nathaniel Bacon and William Berkeley that plunged Virginia into disorder.[34] But Virginian problems did not remain in Virginia. As the events leading up to the murders at the Susquehannocks' fort revealed, the Potomac was a very porous political boundary. English differences of jurisdiction were not always apparent or meaningful to Indians; the governments of Maryland and Virginia often acted with a mixture of cooperation and antagonism. Bacon's Rebellion might easily have spread outside Virginia's borders. As the Maryland council explained in a letter to Charles

Calvert, who had succeeded to the proprietorship after the death of his father Cecil in 1675, there was cause to fear that Nathaniel Bacon would "embroil your province in a war" via an attack on the Piscataways.[35]

The threat of disorder from across the river was not merely the result of proximity. Virginia suffered the same economic and demographic woes as Maryland during the late seventeenth century. Opportunities for social advancement diminished, the price of tobacco remained low, and servants or tenants were more likely to remain so for life.[36] Hard times and a widening gap between rich and poor meant that taxation was a touchy subject on both sides of the Potomac. Maryland Governor Thomas Notley was more than aware that the ordinary people of Maryland were not so different from those of Virginia—as in Virginia, taxes and fear of Indians "hath given occasion for malignant spirits to mutter . . . for the common people will never be brought to understand the just reason of a public charge . . . never body was more replete with malignancy and frenzy than our people were about August last, and they wanted but a monstrous head to their monstrous body." Fortunately they had not found one.[37]

The threat of disorder did not derive merely from warfare or economic troubles. In both Maryland and Virginia, the troubles of the 1670s led inhabitants to express their frustration in terms of divided interest. Those in positions of authority appeared unable to address ordinary inhabitants' fears. Or perhaps they were not unable but unwilling—it might be that they had private goals of their own that conflicted with the public good. Many who joined Bacon believed that the governor of Virginia was unwilling to take effective measures against the Indians because he did not want to jeopardize his large private profits from the Indian trade.[38] This opinion was voiced in Maryland as well, where accusations of how Berkeley "relished Indian presents" were linked to his unwillingness to defend the province. The issues at stake were as porous as the boundary between the two colonies. The Maryland council had worried that Bacon would incite an attack on the Piscataways; although Bacon did not allege Catholic conspiracy, he might have found support for such an act in Maryland, as some English people there believed that the Piscataways were plotting against the English, possibly with the help of Catholics.[39] Those who accused Berkeley of placing presents above public defense saw an obvious connection between Berkeley's misgovernance, economic hard times, Indian raids on Maryland, the proprietor's Catholicism, the looming threat of the French, and the plans of papists "determined to over turn England with fire, sword and distractions."[40] A sense of general crisis required a general conspiracy to explain it, and the terms on which general conspiracies tended to operate meant that Maryland was in as much danger as Virginia.

The appearance of private interest or conspiracy was augmented by the difference between local politics as viewed by members of the council and politics from the perspective of assembly members or ordinary inhabitants. The events of the 1670s repeatedly revealed differences over what courtesies of diplomacy—if any—English colonists owed to Indians. Those on the council were usually (but not always) better informed of events beyond the horizon and more cautious in their dealings with Native Americans than were many men who sat in the lower house or the English population of Maryland at large. Plenty of people who bore the effects and the expenses of the war more directly than Thomas Notley or Charles Calvert witnessed or heard of conversations between their betters and Indians and saw not slow and careful diplomacy but rather delay, self-interest, and even conspiracy.

This difference in attitude was evident in the controversy in the Maryland assembly in the summer of 1676 over how or even whether to discipline Truman for his conduct at the Susquehannocks' fort. The governor and council were far more eager than the men in the lower house to punish him. Of particular concern to the council was Truman's possible submission to Virginia militia commanders when he murdered the five Susquehannock leaders, a point about which the majority of the lower house were far less concerned. The crux of the issue was that the council knew that the murder committed by Truman would cause diplomatic problems for them with the Susquehannocks, and they wanted to avoid further warfare if they could. Thus, when the lower house proposed merely to fine Truman, the upper thought this too "slender and slight" a punishment. They believed that by a fine alone, "the government will not sufficiently be cleared," and the world would not be certain that the major's actions were "detested and disowned by us." Moreover, "it will not give any satisfaction to the heathens, with whom the public faith has been broke, and until such actions are in a more public manner disowned . . . it is not to be expected that any credit will be given to any treaties we shall have with them." Despite their disinclination to have the Susquehannocks any closer to Maryland than the falls of the Potomac, utter repudiation of the alliance was not what Baltimore or the council intended. The lower house, though, remained reluctant to give

Truman a harsh sentence merely for killing Indians, and in the end they got their way.[41]

This was not the first time such a conflict had occurred. In 1674, the assembly considered the estate of the Billingsley orphans, whose father had purchased seven hundred acres from Mattapany and Patuxent Indians. John Billingsley appears to have had a patent for the land, but the Indians were still living there and the council and burgesses had to decide whether to force them to leave in the interest of Billingsley's children. The council recommended that the land be purchased by the country and given to the Indians, but the lower house disagreed, partly because the owners were orphans but mostly because "to force any to sell their land upon the humor of the Indians may prove of dangerous consequence to the province in general as being too much condescension . . . and showeth too much of fear to disoblige them."[42] Far less was at stake in this small land dispute than would be a few years later during and after Bacon's Rebellion, but differences over whether it mattered if English people "disobliged" Indians—or what it meant that the proprietor and his council seemed to "oblige" them—would play a significant role in the province in coming years.

* * *

Between 1660 and 1675, inhabitants of the Chesapeake, both English and Native American, found themselves in an increasingly fraught situation. The growth and increasing interconnection of the English empire brought more Old World diseases to the region, as well as more Old World people. Conflicts over land, trade and resources common to the American world from Canada to the Carolinas and deep into the American interior became interlocked with political struggles local to the Chesapeake, and these in turn shaped the internal politics of Indian towns and English colonies. English colonists and migrants in the latter half of the seventeenth century faced reduced opportunities in a political landscape that seemed ever more dangerous—and their social and political superiors feared for the preservation of order if discontent gained a "monstrous head," as it did in the person of Nathaniel Bacon. No one could be privy to every detail of this vast political landscape; there was no ready explanation for this welter of difficulties, and neither was there an obvious solution that all parties could accept. In Virginia matters came to a crisis in the 1670s—Marylanders would have to wait a few years more.

7
The PROPRIETARY REGIME *and the* MACHINERY *of* EMPIRE

Thomas Notley described the threat to order in the 1670s as bubbling up from below in the form of the common people's terrifying "frenzy" at the threat of war with Indians and the prospect of higher taxes to pay for it. The pressures placed on the proprietary regime in Maryland in the decades after 1660 were not limited to unruly tobacco farmers, however. The proprietor and his officials were increasingly caught between local and regional sources of conflict that they could not always control and the expanding administrative machinery of the late seventeenth-century English empire. The continental was interwoven with the Atlantic.

The irritating thing from the perspective of Lord Baltimore was that both criticism from below about his use of his powers and increasing curiosity from above as to whether the operation of his colony squared with the plans of the Stuart monarchy had a worrying tendency to converge on a single point: the proprietor had too much power. Baltimore's basic assumptions about the nature of the royal power from which his charter derived were not out of step with the political views of Charles II or James II, just as they had been congenial to Charles I. But the nature of the relationship between crown and overseas possessions had evolved, rendering Baltimore's regime a more doubtful fit with such views than had been the case in the 1630s.

* * *

Much of the murmuring against the provincial government in Maryland would have been familiar to residents of Virginia. Like their neighbors to the south, Marylanders complained of taxes and the petty exactions of local officials. Many of the poll taxes passed by the assemblies of the 1660s and 1670s were for defense, and conflict arose several times over whether expenses for war could be levied on the inhabitants without an act of assembly, and what the respective financial obligations of the proprietor and the freemen were. These issues remained unresolved into the 1680s.[1] To taxes were added fees for all official services. Such exactions were not limited to Maryland, and there is little evidence that inhabitants of Baltimore's colony were mulcted much more heavily than residents of other colonies. Nevertheless, official fees, some legal and some not, generated plenty of complaint. In 1666, for example, the assembly addressed the "cruel exactions of several clerks of the respective [county] courts within this province" and limited what they could charge for, and how much.[2] In February of 1674/5, efforts were made to "curb the exorbitant exactions of the several deputy surveyors."[3] In 1676, the assembly passed an act to stop the "great extortion and oppression" committed by various officials "under color of office."[4]

Occasionally complaints about taxes and fees shaded into resentment of Baltimore's officials and the monopoly of office held by the proprietor's cozy circle of friends and relations. In early 1684, the lawyer and assemblyman Robert Carvile complained about the provincial secretary's fees and "discoursed of and concerning his lordship's council, that Major Sewall and Mr. John Darnall were nothing but boys, and what was Col. [Henry] Darnall or Col. Digges[?]" Told that they were "his betters," Carvile "answered that my lord put none in office but knaves and fools," and "if it was not for him, that there was not a man in the country that durst speak his own right." He called Baltimore a "fart . . . there is little difference between him and a fart . . . what are the Calverts? My family is as ancient as the Calverts." Depositions also implicated another Carvile, Thomas, who allegedly said Baltimore "was not fit to govern the people of this province, and that the tower of London was a more fit place for him . . . [he was] an old papist rogue." Thomas Carvile, who believed he had been ill-treated by the Maryland authorities, likened Baltimore to Cromwell, who "sent his rogues before and stayed behind himself." Thomas Carvile's wife, who had gone to Lady Baltimore to plead on her husband's behalf, added the observation that the proprietor's lady was a "spiteful toad."[5] The Carviles presented more sound and fury than thoughtful political discourse, but some of what they said in the midst of complaints about personal grievances real or imaginary—that the proprietor was Catholic, and that his family arrogated more power to itself than they properly deserved and did not use it wisely—would be repeated later by more skillful critics.

Of greater consequence than the grievances of the Carvile family were Charles Calvert's attempts in the 1670s to decrease the number of representatives that sat in the lower house of the assembly. His plan to shrink the lower house devolved into a long argument about the nature of the proprietor's prerogative that would have been familiar to colonists of the late 1640s. Baltimore and his critics agreed that it was his power as proprietor that allowed the assembly to be called at all, but they differed as to whether and how that power might be limited and regularized. Embedded in that argument was a conflict over the meaning of "English liberties" in the New World and the power not only of the proprietor but of the king himself.

In 1676 Charles Calvert, now third Lord Baltimore, decided that of the four deputies elected from each county for that year's assembly, only two would sit. Members of the assembly quickly dispatched a petition indicating their dissatisfaction. They freely acknowledged "that it is your lordship's prerogative to call what number of delegates or deputies to a general assembly out of the respective counties as your lordship shall think fit." At the same time, the proprietor ought not to change his mind at the last minute. "Some of the inhabitants of this your lordship's province" were concerned that "they have not their free vote." The assembled burgesses thus requested that "for the future, to prevent all discontent touching the same," Baltimore would call every representative that he had ordered elected. Charles Calvert was not at all eager to do what the petitioners wished. He claimed that agreeing to the request would "make void" his father's "declaration . . . relating to the settlement of assemblies." Cecil Calvert had repeatedly insisted that he and only he decided what constituted a legal assembly and who might sit in it. Charles did not dismiss the petition, however. He declared himself willing to grant the request, but with the requirement that in the future, every elected representative, including those who had been elected but not summoned in 1676, must "take the oath of fidelity to us" before the session began.[6]

Although Baltimore seemed to have granted that he had not acted fairly in not calling all the burgesses he had ordered elected, his response to the petition implied that those who had objected were perhaps not quite so loyal to him that a reaffirmation of that loyalty would be unnecessary. The reason Baltimore usually gave for postponing assemblies and limiting the number of delegates was the great expense the meetings placed on the province, which, given the protest in Virginia against the expense of assemblies, was not incredible. The presence of an economic explanation, however, did not prevent some from putting a more sinister interpretation on his actions.[7] Even a sincere attempt to limit public expenditure looked dubious when carried out in such a high-handed way.

The delegates matter rankled for years. It came up during the assemblies of 1682 and 1683, and was not laid to rest even then. The problem was not simply the limitation of elected representatives, but rather that the proprietor resisted every attempt to regularize the process or agree to a procedure that could not be changed at will. Baltimore, for his part, leaned on the matter of expense, and explained that his reservation of his prerogatives in this instance had not only the advantage of being cheaper—refusing to define election procedures via legislation was for the inhabitants' own good. As the debate unfolded, both Baltimore and the members of the lower house circled around the accusation—never made, but at times implied—that the proprietor did not have the province's best interests at heart.

In his opening address to the autumn 1682 assembly, Baltimore reiterated his argument for decreasing expense by limiting each county's delegates to two. He reminded the assembled councilors and burgesses that "in this I have proceeded according to the undoubted rights, privileges and powers of my charter . . . I very confidently assure myself that I shall not be thought by any member here present to have other design in this than the public good and welfare of the freemen of Maryland."[8] Despite the proprietor's somewhat circular self-confidence, the lower house continued to press for a reconsideration of the issue. They drew up a law that would have allowed the counties to return two, three, or four delegates as they chose, and petitioned the proprietor to accept it. The upper house replied that Baltimore might "by his undoubted right" resolve the matter by issuing an order "under his great seal." He could also direct the assembly to pass an act that would close the issue. The implication of this response was that all decisions about the composition of the assembly and the number of delegates per county were ultimately Baltimore's to make. The freemen might petition, but they had no legal ground for making claims of their own. Soon after, Baltimore gave a formal answer to the lower house's request about the delegates bill. Not answering them directly, he had decided, would cause him to "run some hazard (as . . . you seem to hint) of having my good intentions toward the freemen of Maryland called into question by you." Thus he had resolved to reply, but the answer he gave was a negative one. Their "request is of that nature that it will as well be inconvenient for the freemen to accept as it may be dangerous for me to grant." His "privileges and powers," including the power of calling assemblies, derived "from the king," and "I cannot deem it honorable nor safe to lodge it in the freemen, for it would be as reasonable for me to give away my power of calling and dissolving of assemblies as to give that of choosing the number of delegates." He was "resolved never to part with powers my charter gives me," but rather hold them and use them for the benefit of the inhabitants.[9] As his father had argued in the 1650s as he and his clients had defended the proprietary regime from its revolutionary critics, if the powers contained in the royal charter were legal, than all of them were legal—to chip away at them, or to slice a few off as not strictly necessary, would be to endanger the whole.

The members of the lower house were not satisfied and sent up another elections bill a few days later, which the upper house dismissed as a "needless bill, his lordship having already settled" the matter.[10] The lower house continued to push the delegates bill throughout the rest of the session, often stalling on other legislation in hopes of getting the upper house to take some action on it, but it was not considered or passed.[11] The issue was not simply the reduction in the number of burgesses from four to two, but the knowledge that Baltimore could change the rules for elections at his pleasure. As the lower house explained the following year, when they again pressed for an act of assembly to determine election procedure, "the best and surest foundation whereon the peace of the province depends" was "the making of good and wholesome laws." Such laws "cannot be made without the consent of the freemen of this province" through their deputies, "and since hitherto the form of assembling" the freemen's representatives "hath been altogether diverse and uncertain, this house considers that no better way can be used in this particular for settling the minds of the freemen and reducing a matter of this moment to a certainty for the future" then by passing an act outlining the process." They stressed that "all due honor and regard ought to be had to his lordship's ordinances and proclamations," but since these were not binding on his successors and could be "altered and abrogated at his and their wills and pleasures," the additional certainty of an act of assembly was needed.[12] As in 1682, the bill met with small success.[13]

The crux of the issue was that members of the lower house wanted the composition of the legislature to rest on a firmer legal basis than the proprietor's pleasure. If Baltimore could limit or increase each county's delegates as he chose and determine the procedure for elections at will, the composition of the assembly was not really in the hands of the freemen. This, of course, was what Baltimore wanted. Perhaps even more than his father Cecil, Charles Calvert was prickly about his privileges and irritated, even suspicious, when appropriate deference was not rendered.

He tended, for example, to view assembly sessions as a benevolent concession on his part rather than a right of the inhabitants—the session of October–November 1683, for example, was "the meeting I gave you."[14] To negotiate with the lower house was demeaning. "Tis not fit nor reasonable," he declared in 1683 when the lower house attempted to trade his agreement to one act for theirs to another, "that I should be thus imposed on when I only seek the general not my private advantage[;] when you catch me at the latter, gentlemen, I will give you leave to make bargains."[15] He was irritated when presented with bills he disliked, and when he had indicated the sort of thing he would not agree to, he expected the burgesses to draft legislation accordingly.[16] In this view, the ideal lower house of the assembly was small, compliant, and deferential. They were there to assent, not to assert. The lower house was the mechanism by which Baltimore's government was government by consent of the freemen, as expressed in the charter. They were an instrument to the proper functioning of the charter—to fulfill the legal requirements and provide the appropriate social flourishes to the proprietor's authority. It was not in Baltimore's interest to grant the lower house any powers or privileges that lay beyond his control or that he could not alter or revoke.

The conflict was analogous to that in England over passing an act requiring a parliament every three years. Members of Parliament wanted some guarantee that they would be called, while both Charles I and Charles II viewed such a guarantee as an infringement on their rights. The dispute over the number of delegates in the Maryland assembly was essentially another version of the argument over whether power derived from the king and flowed downward—and thus that Parliament existed because the king said it could—or whether there were liberties and privileges inherent in English subjects that included assembly in parliaments and were not under the king's control. If the king failed to call Parliament for too long, the absence of a meeting was a legitimate grievance. Thus, argued those in favor of the English Triennial Act, Parliament must be called regularly, and it was necessary to pass a law, with the consent of the king, to ensure it. This argument, of course, assumed that the king could not dispense with laws and merely ignore the act.[17]

The arguments at work in Maryland were similar. Like Charles I and his sons, Charles Calvert had a top-down view of power, which led him to believe that to let the assembly determine its election procedures was a violation of his rights. Many colonists, in contrast, thought that the freemen had chosen how many deputies they sent in the past and they ought to continue doing so. If Baltimore claimed that he feared the expense to them of so many deputies, let them be the judge of it themselves in each county. Having election procedures tweaked at proprietary whim was a grievance, and so again a legislative act was necessary, with Baltimore's assent, of course, to determine and fix the correct procedure. The issue at stake was not that members of the lower house thought they had an absolute abstract right to a legislative assembly under their sole control, but rather that many thought the rules that governed its composition should be based on law, or local custom—there had always been more than two delegates per county—and not the personal whim of the proprietor.

The issue ran parallel to the tension between Charles I and his Parliaments over money, the law, or religious change. In England in the 1620s and 1630s, it would have been hard to find many willing to claim that the prerogative power of the crown was not a natural and necessary part of the state. Likewise, few in Maryland would have said outright that Baltimore did not have the final word on how the assembly was constituted, or that its existence did not ultimately depend upon his authority. Rather, they wanted the proprietor's "prerogatives" to be well-defined, and have more limits and structure than the proprietor himself preferred. They did not trust Charles Calvert to use his power exactly as he should, and pressed for the security of a law agreed upon by him, and them. Like Charles I when members of Parliament appeared to question his motives or press for explanation or explicit assurance that he would follow the law, Baltimore saw the assembly's request as an attack on him, and their failure to trust him as evidence of sedition.

The delegates issue as well as other limitations placed on the franchise by the proprietary regime were responsible for a striking moment of political protest in the summer of 1676. A group of men from Calvert County—William Davies, William Gent, Giles Hasleham, and John Pate—wrote a tract entitled "The liberties of the freemen of this province." A few days later, they assembled at the plantation of Thomas Barbary, on the Patuxent River, "with force and terror of arms . . . to the number of sixty persons." They wanted from the governor and council "certain immunities and freedoms," which according to the governor and council were not within their power or the proprietor's to give them. The council ordered the sixty or so people to "lay down and yield up their arms & to retire to their own houses," and promised "to propound their requests to the next assembly." If they dispersed they would be pardoned, with the exception of Davies, who would be tried at the next provincial court. These offers were "slighted and contemned by the said Davies, Gent, Hasleham and Pate and their accomplices, and . . . they did from thence march away with drums beating and colors flying." After this confrontation on September 3 they dispersed, although the governor and council suspected that they "lie lurking till they can find a fitter opportunity to work out their malicious and wicked designs." When they failed to turn themselves in, Davies, Gent, Hasleham, and Pate were proclaimed outlaws.[18]

No more was heard from the men who had assembled at Barbary's plantation, but through the fall and winter of 1676 there was a "great clamor . . . against the greatness of the taxes" and grumblings about the exclusion of poor freemen from the franchise. Voting had been restricted by proclamation in 1670 to those with "a visible seated plantation" of fifty acres or more, or £40 sterling in personal wealth. Governor Notley issued a proclamation in late 1676 chiding the clamorers for "ingratitude," reminding them of the anarchy similar insubordination had so recently caused in Virginia, and reminding them that "as Lord Proprietary" Baltimore could "call assemblies by his patent whensoever and in what manner to him shall seem most fit and convenient." Besides, a restriction of the franchise based on land or personal estate was "most agreeable to the law and custom of England."[19]

Although he intended his words to quell dissent rather than encourage controversy, Notley's statement highlights the connection between the specific matter of the delegates to the lower house of the assembly and a much larger problem: the operation of the law in Baltimore's colony. As Notley noted, a property-based franchise was indeed consistent with English law—but it was not a settled issue how far Maryland's law was required to match that of the mother country. After all, Maryland's Act Concerning Religion was in direct conflict with English statute law on church attendance. Theoretical legal questions such as these were accompanied by more practical ones. Because of the use of temporary statutes and the proprietor's power to disallow laws after they had been passed, it was often difficult to tell what laws were in force in the colony at all. Maryland's laws were not well systemized or codified, and this haziness proved a source of frustration for the inhabitants. The 1660s and 1670s saw several attempts to solve this problem via the legislature, most of which quickly unraveled into arguments over the basic political architecture of Baltimore's colony.

Attempts in the Maryland assembly to clarify the province's law became tangled in a number of interlocking constitutional problems. The first was to what extent Maryland law should be identical to English law, or as a member of the 1662 assembly phrased it, "whether all laws of England how inconsistent soever with a plantation shall be admitted here."[20] Was a wholescale importation of English law required, and if it was not, would it be useful? Copying English statutes verbatim might sound attractively simple—but not every law in England was necessary or appropriate for an American colony. In 1674, the burgesses and the upper house agreed that it was necessary to draw up a list of all English laws "as are necessary for his lordship's justices and justices of the provincial court to proceed upon in all criminal cases" in the colony, and that an act should be passed requiring judges to use them. This effort simply to determine what laws were in force raised the question of how much of English law was valid in Maryland. The lower house at one point thought that the act under consideration was unnecessary because "the laws of England ought to be esteemed and adjudged of full force and power within this province." The upper house countered that the assemblymen ought to "consider of the dangerous consequences which will of necessity happen by this house's condescending that all laws in England should be in force in this province for the trial of criminals," given that there were so many English statutes and they "often times are repealed without our knowledge." It would be "unsafe" to proceed against criminals "by such uncertain laws." In the end, the act was not passed.[21]

The combination of proprietary privilege and transatlantic distance created a second, related problem. Many of Maryland's laws were temporary and expired after a few years or at the next session of the assembly if they were not renewed. Periodic legislative housekeeping of this type was a normal part of the assembly's business. But in addition to this, the assembly faced the prospect that even if a law were temporary, the proprietor might disallow it—and given the time it took papers to cross and recross the Atlantic, he might do so after several months had elapsed. The assembly that met in 1676 articulated several of these issues at once in the course of a discussion over what to do about the colony's confusing legal situation. The question of a change in proprietary policy was probed as far as securing advance consent for laws so as to save the effort of drawing up legislation that might be rejected: the lower house asked whether Lord Baltimore, who was then resident in the colony, could be requested to "declare whether he will consent to laws in general" before he was given "the particular laws desired to be passed." The upper house did not think this a good idea.[22] But the two houses did join in a general review of the province's laws, a significant portion of which involved "ascertaining what laws" were actually "in force within this province." Inhabitants of the province were confused, "not knowing what laws are in force . . . and by the multiplicity of laws to one and the same thing which many times interfere with one another," which had a way of fouling up due legal process. "Experience" had also revealed that "many of the laws" on the books" both "perpetual [and] temporal [temporary] are become useless or repealed in other private acts not sufficiently taken notice of."[23]

The assemblies of the 1670s confronted at many turns the challenges created by a shifting and uncertain legal code. But the most sustained debate about the problem of law in Maryland had taken place a few years earlier, in 1669, when a sermon given at the beginning of the session raised the thorny question of what sort of a body the Maryland assembly was. Might it be compared to the House of Commons in England, or was the best analogy a different kind of legislative or corporate organization?[24] How ought it to legislate?—how were its members to judge which laws to propose, or to pass, or what might be styled a legitimate grievance? Arguments over these questions and provincial grievances more generally raised once more the tricky problem of how to judge legal and illegal in Maryland. The session records suggest that some members of the lower house and the freeholders they represented thought that the proprietary regime was doing things that violated their liberties; the Maryland council regarded such claims as dangerous and seditious: if the council, or the proprietor, acted as allowed by the charter, by definition this could not be a violation of anyone's liberties.

The sermon that proved so contentious was given before the lower house by a minister named Charles Nicholett. Nicholett told the assemblymen that "they were now chosen . . . by God and man" and that there had never been such "great expectations" from an assembly "as from this." He "wished they had read the proceedings of the Commons in England to see what brave things they had done," and asked the assemblymen to "consider the poor people, for the Lord will hear their cause" and remember "how heavy the tax was upon them the last year." Nicholett's comparison between the Maryland assembly and the House of Commons went further when he urged them to "make such laws . . . agreeable to their own conscience"—if they did not, "this was no liberty, but a seeming liberty and [they] had better be without it." Nicholett was censured by the upper house for these "seditious speeches" and forced to apologize.[25] The comparison between the Maryland Assembly and the English Commons had hit a proprietary—or at least a conciliar—nerve.

Nicholett claimed that if the assembly did not legislate according to conscience, their liberty was an illusion. The Maryland council saw things differently—in their view, it was precisely this sort of loose talk of liberties, liberties that were really no such thing, that was the source of potential danger. Later in the session, the upper house found reason to accuse the lower of delaying business and leaving the province lawless and vulnerable. They were stirring up trouble among the inhabitants, the councilors alleged, giving the people a false sense of their liberties and teaching them to style the proprietor's rights as grievances. The "people [are] discontented, and jealous that their just liberties are denied them, when in truth, we only vindicate that just power in my lord [Baltimore] which the king hath given him by his charter and which is no way communicable to the people." Contrary to what Nicholett had said in his sermon, their "privileges" did not "run parallel to the commons in the Parliament of England." The Maryland assembly met only "by virtue of my lord's charter, so that if they any way infringe that, they destroy themselves." Proprietary political theory had not budged much since the 1640s or 1650s. The charter was the only source of power in the province, and to attempt to change it threatened anarchy.

The members of the upper house argued that the English institution most like the Maryland legislature was not the House of Commons but rather "the common council of the city of London, which if they act contrary or to the overthrow of the charter of the city, run into sedition."[26] The members of the upper house might not have realized it, but the comparison between the assembly and London's common council highlighted an important point about the nature of political power in the colonial world.

When they made this comparison and said that the assembly had no rights that did not derive from the patent, the council probably did not mean to imply that residents of London had no privileges but those derived from the government of the city. The problem in explaining what liberties the inhabitants or the assembly in Maryland did have was that nearly all the inhabitants came from a society where there were layers of competing liberties and privileges. These included Magna Carta, the common law, statute law, royal prerogative, borough charters, and so on. Baltimore's charter was derived from a single one of these layers, the royal prerogative. Even in England, it was not always clear how royal prerogative interacted with all the others. In claiming that that single layer, the royal prerogative and the charter derived from it, was the only one valid in Maryland, the upper house was arguing something outside both experience in England and practice in Maryland. The persistent criticisms of the charter suggest that many Marylanders assumed that there was more than one single source of liberties and privileges in the colony; inhabitants usually referenced "English liberties" or the "liberties of freemen" as did both the Davies-Pate group in 1676 and the authors of the near-contemporary anti-Baltimore screed "A Complaint from Heaven."[27] Like the lower house in 1669, the Cliffs rebels and the writers of "A Complaint from Heaven" argued that charter or no charter, what Baltimore was doing in Maryland—or, what was being done in his name—constituted a violation of the inhabitants' liberties. The proprietor's, governor's, and council's actions were not merely unfair, or unpleasant, but illegal. Various members of the lower house and some others were willing to argue that just because Baltimore did something by virtue of the powers delegated him in his charter, that did not ipso facto make it legal. In 1669 no one in the upper house of the assembly proved responsive to any such claim of violated liberties. The entire council continued to maintain that all authority in Maryland derived from the charter, and that no further discussion or negotiation was possible. Moreover, any questioning of the charter or description of Baltimore's privileges as illegal or even problematic was, the council claimed, seditious.

But what had the lower house of the assembly done to provoke this lecture about proprietary authority? The council's hackles had been raised by a list of grievances drawn up by the lower house. Most of these were familiar complaints. The proprietor's disassenting power was placed front and center on the list. The lower house had earlier requested that a procedure be put into place whereby the proprietary veto would require the assembly's consent, but the upper house refused.[28] Dissatisfaction with the proprietor's disassenting power in this case focused around his disallowing an Act for Quieting Possessions, which had regulated the transfer and sale of land and was intended to stop the endless lawsuits that resulted from informal sales or transfers and unofficial or missing titles. Failures of "formality in the conveyance" made up to the time of the act were not grounds for lawsuits, although in the future formal written documents would be required.[29] Other grievances included illegal taxation and seizure of goods, the creation of offices whose holders collected illegal fees, and, finally, "vexatious informers."[30]

The upper house responded that even things that might seem illegal or unfair were not to be styled grievances if they were permitted by the charter. In the case of the complaint about newly created officers charging exorbitant fees, they pointed out that they knew of no such persons, and even if there were they would not be legitimate grounds for complaint, since "it is but what his lordship hath power to do by his patent, and whatsoever he lawfully doth by power of his patent must not be styled a grievance unless you mean to quarrel with the king who granted it."[31] Arguing that proprietary rights were public grievances was a serious, even seditious charge, and the upper house was very sensitive on this point. They demanded that the lower house "raze the mutinous and seditious votes contained in the paper entitled 'The Public Grievances'" from the records; if they did not do this, the upper house would "treat with them no further," and the threat Governor Charles Calvert had made earlier to "make an end of this assembly" would be carried out. The so-called grievances were "an arraignment of the lord proprietor, the governor and council," which could not be tolerated. Members of the lower house rejected the charge of mutiny or sedition. The demand that the grievances be erased was a "breach of the privileges of this house," since the grievances were "real and public" and did "not any wise tend to the arraignment" of the colony's appointed leaders.[32] It was the debate over the grievances themselves and their legitimacy that caused the upper house to lecture the lower so vehemently and in such detail about the power of the charter.

Efforts to close the breach thus opened followed forms as familiar as those that had created it in the first place. Over the next several days the members of the upper house offered to "put no sinister interpretation" on the grievances and join with the lower house in a "petition of grace and favor (not of right)" to the proprietor about the officials' fees and a few other limited matters—but not the list as a whole.[33] Implied was the suggestion that it would be very easy to put a "sinister" interpretation on such grievances and they were doing the assemblymen a great favor in offering to solicit Baltimore's voluntary agreement to amend a situation that he had every right to leave alone. The lower house took a familiar English parliamentary line and offered to blame the problem on a failure of communication. They protested that they had no wish to "style his lordship's rights grievances" and that if there was a problem, it was because the proprietor had simply not been made aware that his just rights as they were "now exercised [were] indeed" grievances.[34] In the end, the lower house agreed to erase the offending passage from its records, and the upper house removed the words "mutinous and seditious" from its own.[35]

Legislative peace was restored, but the competing views of power and politics in Maryland that the dispute had revealed had not been reconciled. The problem of the proprietor's disassenting power recurred in 1683, and Charles Calvert, now proprietor rather than governor, explained that he had agreed in 1681 to signal assent or disassent to laws within eighteen months, but more than that promise he could not give, as it would not be "convenient . . . to oblige my heirs and successors" to such limits or the "mischiefs" they might cause.[36] Specific issues like the disassenting power did not vanish, and neither did the assumptions behind the controversies—or the ways in which participants interpreted the behavior of their opponents.

The assumptions at work in this dispute emerged with particular clarity in an argument over the colony's charter in 1678. The threat of war with Native Americans, which was growing acute by the late 1670s, led the governor to ask both houses to "make a recognition of the Lord Proprietary's power so that the soldiers might be better governed and ruled." The lower house said that they would have to look over the charter first "so this house might see his lordship's power and so know what they did acknowledge." They asked the upper house for a copy of the charter, which was sent to them with the request that they read over the clause "where the king's articles of war are marked." Later, the lower house requested that the copy of the charter they had been given be "signed [by the governor and council] as a true copy of the lord proprietary's charter."[37] This delicacy over the accuracy of the copy caused things to take an unexpected turn. The governor and council refused the request, voicing their surprise that the lower house "should impose such an impossibility on the members of this house, who never did see the original patent in Latin, and therefore could judge of no translation, much less of a copy of it." But even asking for the copy was dangerous. After all, the lower house had as much right to question the accuracy of the copy as it did "to question the authority by which they were called and now sit, having no other warrant but custom grounded upon this translation, which hath always been taken for good." The lower house insisted that it was "very necessary both for his lordship and the good people of this province that an authentic copy of the true translation of his lordship's charter be recorded in the secretary's office of this province," alongside a copy of all the laws "as being the foundation of the same."[38] The dispute went no further, but the difference between the two houses over the accuracy of the copy is telling. The representatives in the lower house wanted to make sure that the copy the assembly had of the charter was accurate, and contained everything the original charter contained. Proper proceedings depended on the accuracy and legitimacy of legal documents. The upper house's response revealed that it was not so much the wording of the charter but the fact that it was there that was important. The translation they had had "always been taken for good," and the lower house could not question its accuracy, or they questioned the legality of their own presence. Authority derived from the fact that the king had given a charter in Latin to Baltimore, by virtue of which the assembly was called. Whether the English translation of the charter was accurate in every detail was simply not the point.

Divisions in Maryland over the function and legal status of the legislature and how law in the colony was to be made had been evident from the beginning. They deepened in the decades after 1660, just as a changing political landscape seemed to create threats of invasion or revolt at every turn. In 1669, the upper house noted that that delays on the part of the lower house left the province vulnerable to Indian raids and disaffection among the ordinary people—a variety of new circumstances rendered the province more vulnerable and its stability seemingly more fragile. Charles Calvert and the members of his council were quick to react to threats of sedition or mutiny: as they saw it, their power—the maintenance of which was in the interest of everyone—depended on their doing so.

But the Calverts and their relatives and supporters also faced criticism from above. Questions about the sources of the colonists' liberties, and how or whether the power of a holder of a royal charter might be limited, remained unsolved in Maryland because these same questions remained unresolved in England, as did the issue of whether a Catholic like Lord Baltimore was a legitimate recipient of royal authority in the first place. In England the priority of law or royal prerogative was contested; the relationship between confessional and political identity was a subject of fierce controversy; and by the 1670s the political nation was once again debating whether papists or Protestant sectaries offered the greatest threat to the stability of the realm. Meanwhile, the growth of the colonial world meant that a more uniform and systematic mode of administration was needed, one that would ensure uniformity in law, tax collection and—perhaps—religion. As a result, the Maryland proprietor's religion, his policy of religious toleration, his vast and hazy powers as head of Maryland's government, and the many people who had reason to resent both the vastness and the haziness of those powers, drew Lord Baltimore once again into a worsening political storm.

The 1670s in England was a decade of increasing political polarization and tension, which culminated in the combined crisis of the Popish Plot and the furor over the possible exclusion of Charles II's younger brother and heir James, Duke of York, from the throne. The 1670s also saw the beginning of a significant change in colonial policy, as the Navigation Acts were more strictly enforced and attempts were made to systematize and regularize colonial administration. The crown intruded more directly on local elites' management of their colonies and asked more searching questions about how such operations were being run.[39] Colonial charters in general came into question—in the 1680s Lord Howard of Effingham, the royal governor of Virginia, gleefully anticipated the end of the Maryland patent as part of a general retraction of charters that would, as professional administrator William Blathwayt had explained it to him, "make the king great and extend his . . . empire in those parts."[40] The Popish Plot and Exclusion crisis raised the ancient issue of confessional identity and loyalty—could papists be trusted with power? If Protestantism was a gauge of political reliability, did it matter what sort of Protestant one was? The Scots rebellion of 1679 and Rye House Plot in the early 1680s suggested that it did.[41] If one intended to reel in wayward colonies, requiring not only obedience to the law, but conformity to the Church of England seemed a good place to start. The politics of confessional difference and questions of allegiance and obedience were impossible to separate in the 1670s and 1680s, and the need to govern a growing and increasingly important Atlantic empire made such problems impossible to ignore.

In Massachusetts, for example, the colony's royal customs surveyor, Edward Randolph, was driven into a near-constant state of impotent fury as a result of his attempts to enforce the Navigation Acts. While the Massachusetts General Court agreed to enforce these laws, they made it clear that they did so because they chose to, not because they had been ordered. Randolph complained loudly and bitterly to his superiors on the Privy Council, and among his complaints were constant reiterations of the disloyalty and flouting of royal authority characteristic of the dissenting Protestants, heirs to the upheavals of the 1640s, who made up the government.[42] The problem of how to govern such a strange and various empire and its contumacious colonists was pushed even further to the forefront by politics outside the control of any English person—King Philip in New England, the Five Nations of the Iroquois, and the Susquehannocks in the Chesapeake pursued their own diplomatic and political interests, often causing division and fear among the English and undermining the perceived effectiveness of local authorities. In the 1670s, the politics of the English Atlantic and the politics of the American interior meshed to create a crisis that reshaped the empire.

In New England, the prospect of disloyal dissenters undermining the authority of the crown placed the Massachusetts charter in jeopardy. Similar forces were at work in Maryland, although here Protestant dissenters and Catholics combined to create the menace. An anti-popish and anti-Baltimore paper entitled "Complaint from Heaven with a Hue and a Crye," probably written in late 1676, had been transmitted to Whitehall and there had been found significant enough to keep, perhaps because it was a tidy, if unlikely, synthesis of anti-Catholicism and criticism of local government in the Chesapeake. The "Complaint" described proprietary tampering with the assembly, misgovernment in Virginia, and the looming threat of the French and the Iroquois, all neatly synthesized into a damning indictment of the proprietary regime via the capacity of popery to turn the world upside down, invert loyalties, and undermine English law, monarchy, and religion.[43] In May 1676, slightly before the "Complaint" was written, a Church of England minister named John Yeo articulated the problem in slightly less apocalyptic terms when he wrote to the Archbishop of Canterbury with his own litany of grievances. Maryland lacked "an established ministry," and the few Anglican ministers there were unqualified. Nevertheless, these men were performing Christian rites and "sow[ing] seeds of division amongst the people so that here is a great necessity of able and learned men to confute the gainsayer." Yeo also equated Jesuits and Protestant dissenters, and indicated the danger to order the presence of each implied. The "popish priests and Jesuits" were cared for by their own, "the Quaker takes care and provides for those that are speakers in their conventicles, but no care is taken or provision made" for Anglicans, with the result that "many daily fall away either to Popery, Quakerism or Phanaticism." Yeo knew that Charles Calvert planned to leave Maryland for England in June, and had heard that part of the reason for his trip was "to receive a farther confirmation of the province from his Majesty." Perhaps the Bishop might "prevail with him" and establish "a Protestant ministry" just like "in Virginia, Barbados and all other his majesty's plantations"? If these steps were taken, there was hope that "the generality of the people may be brought by degrees to a uniformity."[44]

Yeo's complaints were taken seriously enough that Baltimore was called before the Lords of Trade to explain the religious situation in Maryland; questions of religious uniformity in Maryland had become entangled with a broader attempt at increased crown control, religious and otherwise, in the colonies. When Archbishop Gilbert Sheldon received Yeo's letter, he forwarded it to the Bishop of London, Henry Compton, under whose jurisdiction the colonies fell. Sheldon approved of Yeo's design, and asked Compton to bring it up when Maryland affairs were next discussed by the Privy Council. There would likely "be a convenient opp[ortunity] to obtain some settled revenue for the ministry of that place as well as the other plantations."[45] Maryland, in other words, was not the only colony whose interior workings required scrutiny. Compton presented the Lords of Trade with a list of "abuses crept into the churches of the plantations" in July 1677, followed by Yeo's letter a few days later. By then Baltimore, who had attended the first meeting but was unprepared then to respond, had drafted an explanation. He presented a memo explaining the religious situation in Maryland. There were few Anglicans there, and it would be "difficult" to compel the others to pay for an Anglican ministry. The Act Concerning Religion of 1649 promised that inhabitants of the colony would suffer no "penalties or payments" on account of their religious beliefs—and the use of public money to finance the Church of England would seem to fall into this category. Besides, Maryland was not unique. Similar policies of religious toleration were in place in Rhode Island, New Jersey, and Carolina. Nevertheless, the Lords of Trade decided that a settled Anglican ministry would be a good thing for the colony, "to which . . . Lord Baltimore seemed to consent, and then withdrew." The committee was not entirely satisfied: they wanted more detailed data on non-Anglicans in Maryland "and in general an account of the number of the planters in Maryland and of what persuasion they are in matters of religion."[46]

Royal information gathering was not limited to questions of religion. Even before the Lords of Trade decided to quiz the proprietor about the religious disposition of his colonists, they had sent him an earlier set of more general "Queries about Maryland." The questions centered on the mechanics of government and law, population, relations with Native Americans, and trade and revenue. Baltimore was able to provide more information on some of these points than on others. He could direct them to a map of the colony, printed and available in London, and did not hesitate to explain that the "greatest obstruction" to trade was the Navigation Acts. But he did not have the documents available to list the number of vessels entering and leaving, the population (including the number of servants), the laws then in force, or "the number of acres patented or settled," because the records were all in Maryland. Besides, inquiries into population, marriages, religion, and burials "endanger insurrections," since many of the inhabitants had left England because "they could not live with ease there." Even if he had access to the law books or the land records, they would "make up a very long and tedious volume" to transcribe or to read. As far as money was concerned, Baltimore did "not conceive that their lordships intend there to make an inquiry into or to expect from me a particular of my own rents, and of what is my particular property and revenue," and so gave account of public revenues only. Taxes were levied by the assembly, as occasion required, "and these occasions being always various and uncertain, it is impossible for me to give any certain account of them or of their various applications."[47]

Baltimore's answers probably did not tell the Lords of Trade all they wished to know, but there is no record of their having pressed the proprietor any further. Despite the complaints of the bishops, the Church of England was not established in the colony in the 1670s or any public revenue set aside for the support of its ministers. Why was there no further pressure to do so? The most obvious reason was that Maryland remained a proprietary colony. There was no royal governor there, and all commands or even requests for information had to go through Baltimore or the men he had appointed to govern the colony. Baltimore had little information at hand about Maryland and no real incentive to dig any up. Unlike a royal governor who failed to make a requested report, getting rid of the proprietor would not be simply a matter of commissioning a replacement. Moreover, as he told the Lords of Trade, the colony was at least in part the private property of his family. Even if proprietary rents and taxes functioned as public matters as far as the inhabitants were concerned, it was unclear how far the Lords of Trade were justified in looking into the proprietor's private financial transactions. Administration of Maryland had to go through Baltimore, and the proprietor had an interest in opacity.

The Navigation Acts offered another reason Baltimore might dodge royal inquiries into his province. Evasion of these laws occurred in Maryland as it did elsewhere, and the Lords of Trade knew this. In 1662, Cecil Calvert was called before the committee for foreign plantations to answer questions about illegal tobacco trade in Maryland with the Dutch, which he promised to look into.[48] The proprietary government made some effort to prohibit smuggling, but enforcement relied more on local appointees than crown officials, a policy that was not uniformly successful.[49] Some traders were arrested from time to time for evasion of the acts, but this was probably closer to the exception than the rule.[50] Maryland and Virginia were known as areas where "neglects, or rather contempts" of the acts took place—and the crown was not the only loser. Lord Baltimore's own customs were frequently dodged. His two shillings per hogshead duty on tobacco was reportedly evaded by taking tobacco to the head of the bay, transporting it overland to the Delaware River, and shipping it from there.[51]

Baltimore, then, had reason to keep scrutiny off his province. The religious interests of the Privy Council were not his, he regarded too-detailed inquiries as an invasion of his privileges, and no doubt he preferred to have his own appointees rather than crown officials in charge of customs collection. Partly this was because compliance was difficult to enforce, and Baltimore himself did not see the navigation laws as working to the colony's, and thus his, benefit, and partly because the intrusion of royal authority seemed to threaten his own prerogatives. The murder of a royal tax collector, Christopher Rousby, by the proprietor's cousin in the 1680s demonstrated the tension that could arise between the authority of royal customs officials and that of the proprietor.[52]

The point on which criticisms from below and those from above converged was that Lord Baltimore was misusing his power—and perhaps he had more power than was in the interest of the crown, the Church of England, or the inhabitants of Maryland. The governor of Virginia, Lord Howard of Effingham, suggested as much after the Rousby murder, noting that "the king's interest here has suffered by Mr. Rousby's death."[53] Effingham had been out for the governorship of Maryland for several years, and was not above the occasional hint that Baltimore's exercise of his proprietary powers "lessen[ed] . . . as well the revenue as dignity" of "his majesty's government."[54] But Effingham was hardly the first to make this point, which had been articulated quite clearly in a memorandum about Maryland probably drawn up in 1677. This document listed a number of dubious activities in Baltimore's province, including the charges that Baltimore was coining his own money, that the oath of allegiance to the king was neglected in favor of an oath to the proprietor, that courts were conducted in Baltimore's name rather than the king's, and that Baltimore was using writs that mimicked the royal formula, reading "to our trusty and well-beloved in such a year of our dominion."[55] These were not wild accusations, even the charge of coining money. In October 1659, Cecil Calvert, then Lord Baltimore, had been summoned before the English Council of State on the charge of coining money for Maryland, and all the money itself, as well as the tools and molds used to make it, had been ordered seized.[56] Baltimore thought his charter allowed him to do this, but the Council of State disagreed.[57]

Similarly, complaints like those made in the "Complaint from Heaven" about mismanagement of or tampering with the Maryland assembly were not all a matter of wild conspiracy theories. Like James I or Charles I when they faced Parliament, the lords Baltimore used undertakers from time to time to manage the Maryland assembly. Evidence for such efforts on the part of Charles Calvert can be found in a letter he wrote to his father in 1672, in which he described how he had obtained places in the lower house for both Thomas Notley and one John Morecraft. The latter was, he explained, an excellent lawyer and a great defender of Baltimore's privileges. Moreover, "now that I have got Mr. Notley into the chair I have assured him, that with your Lordship's leave, I am resolved to keep him there as long as he and I live together." Religious loyalties also played a role, and Charles

Calvert seems to have expected a certain amount of what some contemporaries would have called popish conspiring. "It is most certain," he went on in his letter, "that some of the Catholics in the assembly did not behave themselves as expected, hereafter they will I hope endeavor to understand themselves better and their own interest."[58]

PART III

Crisis

8
RUMOR *and* POLITICS

Over the course of the seventeenth century, American colonists revised the script of English anti-popery. As early as the 1650s, anti-proprietary writers added a New World dimension when they connected Lord Baltimore's "nursery for Jesuits" with economic manipulation that caused foreign traders to provide weapons to Native Americans "to the total endangering of this colony."[1] By the 1670s and 1680s, the colonial variety of anti-popery—in which Catholics conspired with the French and the Native Americans as part of the grand plan to overturn law, right religion, and good government—was both familiar to English colonists and powerful enough to endanger colonial regimes.

This American version of the narrative accounted for local events with explanations that had transatlantic appeal, and its power was not limited to Maryland. Anti-Catholicism was a powerful destabilizing force in the later seventeenth century.[2] The long-familiar languages of confessional difference—both anti-popery and anti-Puritanism—were languages of political critique. They described the exterior world of government, law, and right relationships between states, subjects, and God. In a political culture that did not assume that multiple mutually exclusive or competing interests were a normal part of politics, they were ways of accounting for the frustrating, frightening or otherwise inexplicable behavior of other people—of which there seemed to be a great deal in the imperial world of the 1670s and 1680s.

Anti-popery could and did overlap with hot Protestant piety, but plenty of contemporaries knew better than to conflate the two. One could fulminate against the proprietor, the Jesuits, and "the Papists" but live more than amicably with the Catholics next door.[3] On the other side, colonists skeptical—or at the receiving end—of charges rooted in anti-popery reformulated the conventions of anti-Puritanism and subversion from below to fit the wider world of the later seventeenth-century English empire. Early Stuart anti-Puritanism had persisted well into the 1650s in Maryland.[4] Few after 1660 forgot the role of dissenting Protestants in overturning monarchy and executing the king, as post-Restoration Protestant dissenters were more than aware; links between Protestant nonconformity and threats to monarchy were not laid to rest with the Restoration.[5] This equation of Protestant dissent with political subversion worked for critics of some colonial regimes, such as those of New England, but it did not for others. The factious and tumultuous persons who threatened duly constituted authority from below in Maryland were sometimes Dissenters—Charles Calvert was not particularly fond of Quakers, for example.[6] But despite the presence of many Protestant nonconformists in Maryland, criticism of the proprietary regime did not come solely from that quarter in any consistent way—and besides, suggesting that his colony was swarming with subversive nonconformists was probably not in the proprietor's interest either.

Nathaniel Bacon inadvertently did Charles Calvert an enormous favor in 1676, because Bacon created a narrative of anti-monarchical subversion and disorder in the Chesapeake that did not require the presence or participation of Protestant dissenters. After 1676, the "factious" could now be classed as "Baconists," a term that Lord Baltimore applied to Josias Fendall and John Coode over and over again. Baconists were presumably Protestants—and indeed, the claim that trouble could come from conforming quarters reemphasized that Protestantism was not a transparent indicator of orderliness or loyalty—but their primary characteristic was that they followed their own selfish interests rather than the public good, overturning duly constituted authority and seeking plunder. Alongside these cries of "Baconism," the pejorative use of "popular" or "popularity" to describe subversion from below persisted. As late as 1706, the Virginia Council used language James I would have recognized when they referenced "popular arguments [that] may prevail with a mob and unthinking multitude when managed by turbulent and designing men."[7] But references to "Baconists" had the advantage of specificity. Such a narrative was not inconsistent with anti-Dissenter language, but it could also operate independently. In the end, this amalgam of anti-Puritanism and anti-Baconism proved not as powerful or as effective as anti-popery, probably because accusations of popish conspiracy resonated through the English polity as a whole in a way that charges of "rank Baconism" did not—the latter lacked both an obvious English equivalent and a threatening international dimension—but also because English people in the colonial world were far more likely to discuss and debate the dark machinations of the French and the Iroquois than they were to spread rumors of hordes of Baconists (or Dissenters) invading the province and killing them in their beds. The facts of American life stacked the ideological deck against Maryland's Catholic proprietors.

But words alone, however evocative or precise, do not make revolutions. The gap between mentality and action—between the presence of anti-papist narratives and concrete action against Catholics—was often filled by rumor and news. Rumor was a powerful force in colonial politics. Following the path from person to person of a rumor or an item of news offers a glimpse into the mindset of people who do not otherwise speak in the sources—and at least as importantly, it reveals the process by which longstanding assumptions about order and disorder, or religion and loyalty, turned into action.[8] We know that the language of popish or Puritanical conspiracy was not merely a cover for the "real," more material, motives lurking beneath.[9] Rumor reveals precisely *how* it was not. Rumor is not simply a thing: a statement that approximates reality. Rather, it is a collaborative process that individuals engage in when they lack crucial information in a situation that requires explanation. Bits of information are pieced together; narratives are fleshed out or stripped down through telling and retelling; the limits of the probable or possible are explored.[10]

Rumor is closely connected not only to news but also to myth and legend. Explanations of strange and frightening things travel farther when they connect to larger cultural scripts about the likely sources and consequences of good or bad behavior—but familiar elements can also be recombined in creative and terrifying ways.[11] Maryland colonists frustrated with the vagaries of the tobacco trade or the threat of war looked for malicious human agents at work. As they shared and elaborated on stories of Indian-Catholic conspiracy and the dark and selfish interests of the Catholic proprietor, they placed an array of otherwise inexplicable difficulties into a very familiar—and powerful—narrative.

* * *

Political information in Maryland followed many paths. First, there was news from England, the sources of which are often easy to trace. Some Marylanders received news books from England.[12] Christopher Rousby, a resident of Calvert County who ultimately became a royal tax official, was one such person. When he traveled across the Atlantic, Rousby also sent letters to two friends, Robert Ridgley and William Stevens, in which he gave detailed accounts of politics in London in the early 1680s.[13] Given the conventions of early modern letter writing and reading, these letters would likely have been read aloud to others or circulated among friends and acquaintances. Men of far higher rank than Rousby or Ridgley did the same—in May 1684, Lord Howard of Effingham, the royal governor of Virginia, noted in a letter to his wife that Lord Baltimore had "shewed [him] a letter . . . which specified the death of the Duke of Norfolk and some other Duke in the Tower."[14]

Even where the source is unknown, discussion and speculation about events across the Atlantic reveal Chesapeake colonists' interest in English news and their views on what they heard. When the Duke of Monmouth, an illegitimate Protestant son of Charles II, attempted to take the throne by force at his father's death in 1685, his rebellion was the subject of enough talk in Virginia that the governor there wrote the Lords of Trade that "so many took liberty of speech upon the rebellion of the Duke . . . that I was fearful it would have produced the same here."[15] In Maryland, the council received word in September 1686 that Giles Porter, while drinking with some neighbors, had "said he would drink the Duke of Monmouth's health for [James, the Duke of] York had been a bloody rogue and had poisoned his own brother King Charles and was the first invention of the burning of the city of London."[16] Monmouth's bid for power as the "Protestant Duke" in contrast to the Catholic James would not have surprised watchful consumers of news. James was known to have converted to Catholicism by the early 1670s, and fear of what he would do as king—not to mention what his elder brother, already cozy with Catholics, *was* doing as king—prompted a parliamentary campaign to exclude James from the throne. Some classic articulations of political anti-popery, such as Andrew Marvell's 1677 *Account of the growth of popery and arbitrary government in England,* were written in this context.[17]

Monmouth was defeated, and James succeeded his brother despite his religion. Most English people in 1685 preferred a legitimate Catholic monarch to an illegitimate Protestant one, and James's reign began with the appearance of stability and success. By 1688, however, many of his subjects had come to believe that he respected neither English law nor the Protestant religion, and an engineered invasion by the Dutch stadtholder, William of Orange, the husband of James's daughter Mary, removed him from the throne.[18] Reactions in the Chesapeake to the Glorious Revolution were mixed. Soon after news of the events of 1688 reached Maryland, a story circulated that one local Maryland official, a Catholic, "did hope before Easter Day to wash his hands in the Protestants' blood, and that if he had the Prince of Orange there he would thrust his sword up to the beam in him." Indians, too, had heard of recent doings in England, although those whose opinions we have emphasized trade more than confessional politics. A Virginian official reported one or more as saying "they did hear the English men in England had cut off their king's head and that there were abundance of Dutchmen coming . . . and that they should bring abundance of matchcoats and other things with them."[19]

The movement of local news is often easier to trace; its subject matter moved between problems and personalities peculiar to the Chesapeake and more common concerns about derogation of authority figures, confessional difference, and loyalty to the king. Christopher Rousby again offers an example both of the content of such talk and how stories moved from person to person within the colony. In early 1679, the Maryland council received word of "an aspersion cast upon Mr. Christopher Rousby by John Burdett of St. Mary's County, tending also to the dishonor of his lordship."[20] The council called in witness after witness as they tried to unravel the story. John Llewellyn, the clerk of the council, reported that around February 19 or 20, he, Burdett, and some others had been in the kitchen of the governor's house. Burdett had whispered "some private news (as he said)" to Llewellyn, asking the latter "not to divulge it, for that only himself and the person that told him knew anything of it." The news was that Baltimore "and Mr. Christopher Rousby had lately had some high words, that Mr. Rousby called his lordship a traitor to his face, and his lordship offering to speak again, Mr. Rousby told him he had best hold his tongue and say no more."

The source of Burdett's "private news" was a man named William Person who lived in the same house as Rousby. Or so Llewelyn said. When called before the council to explain, Burdett confirmed the story but said that it had not been Person who told him, but one Thomas Smith; a third man, Anthony Evans, had also been present when Smith told the story to Burdett.[21] Evans was summoned in turn and explained that Smith had told them that Rousby "had grossly abused his lordship, calling him 'runaway' . . . and that he ought to be sent home in chains." Baltimore "asked Mr. Rousby what was the reason he so abused him," and Rousby "rapped out a great oath and swore that what he said was true, that he had from under the king's hand

and seal for it." According to Evans reporting Smith's words, "her ladyship upon this discourse fell a crying." William Person denied hearing anything at all and was excused. Smith, the apparent source of the story, said he had in fact overheard another man, Arthur Hart, tell a third, Thomas Price, that "Mr. Rousby had called the Lord Proprietary runaway, which if a poor man had done, he would certainly have been laid neck and heels, but Mr. Rousby was not afraid to tell him so." Smith told Hart and Price that he could not believe such a story, whereupon Hart replied that it was indeed true and he himself had "heard it credibly reported at a christening or funeral."[22] Stories of authority undermined—or traitors receiving condign punishment—circulated all too easily.

In addition to local news centered on personal clashes like that between Rousby and Baltimore, there were also stories that centered on provincial government; the assembly and who might or might not be influencing it were a particular focus of discussion. During the 1661 session, for example, a statement was read from Lord Baltimore in which he discounted a rumor that a customs bill passed in 1646 "had been extorted by force or fears from the assembly" and assured the assembly that Marylanders would be taxed no more heavily than inhabitants of Virginia. "This," he wrote, "we hope will satisfy the people there that we neither have nor had any intention in the least to oppress them."[23] Similar talk circulated about specific provincial issues like the controversial oath of allegiance to the proprietor, discussion of which reached beyond the boundaries of the colony. Just days after the council attended to the Rousby rumor in early 1679, they learned that a ship's captain, Richard Covill, had "falsely and maliciously" said that the governor of Maryland, ordered by the proprietor, had "imposed an oath of fidelity on the people of this province by which they were to swear allegiance to his lordship against all princes whatsoever and more especially against his sacred majesty" the king, with threat of banishment for those who refused. This report prompted the governor and council to issue a declaration that to their knowledge "never any such oath was imposed or tendered to any person or persons whatsoever" in Maryland, and no one had ever been punished for refusing to take such an oath. The proprietor, governor, and council were all "true liegemen" to the king, and hoped that "full faith and credit" would be given to their words in England.[24] Incidents such as this echoed Richard Ingle's accusations in the 1640s, not in that they posed a serious threat to the proprietor, but in that the proprietary regime was obliged to address them—accusations of legislative tampering or disloyalty, especially when made against Catholics, could not simply be ignored.

But perhaps the most common and persistent sort of rumor was about the movements and intentions of Native Americans. English colonists often assumed that Indians acted at the behest or in the interest of the Catholics of New France, the Jesuits, and sometimes Catholics in general. A Dutch visitor to the colony around 1680, Jasper Danckaerts, framed his account of Catholics and Native Americans in terms of such connections. He described the freedom of religion that Catholics enjoyed in Maryland, "because the governor makes profession of that faith, and consequently there are priests and other ecclesiastics who travel and disperse themselves everywhere, and neglect nothing which serves for their profit and purpose." He reported an extensive Jesuit-Indian network linking Canada to Maryland.

> The priests of Canada take care of this region, and hold correspondence with those here, as is supposed, as well as with those who reside among the Indians. It is said there is not an Indian fort between Canada and Maryland, where there is not a Jesuit who teaches and advises the Indians, who begin to listen to them too much; so much so that some people in Virginia and Maryland as well as in New Netherland, have been apprehensive lest there might be an outbreak, hearing what has happened in Europe, as well as among their neighbors in Boston; but they hope that the result of the troubles there will determine many things elsewhere.[25]

The Maryland-Jesuit-Canada connection and the assertion that people in both Maryland and Virginia were afraid of an attack appeared in much greater detail elsewhere.[26]

Rumors do not merely describe events, however. They can also create them.[27] In a climate of deep fear and political and economic uncertainty, rumors can create covens of baby-killing Satanists, bands of marauding brigands instigated by aristocrats to destroy harvests, disguised policemen abducting the children of the poor—or, as in Maryland in the spring of 1689, regiments of Iroquois incited by the Catholics to massacre all the Protestants. The threat in each of these cases was imaginary, but the response was not.[28] Stories of order overturned and innocent persons abused needed no agitators to spread them. The rumor panic in Maryland in the spring of 1689 reveals how ordinary Marylanders turned assumptions and suspicions into action; it also shows stories evolving as they moved from oral form to manuscript text and back again.[29] The threat of an Iroquois invasion also profoundly frightened many people and may have disposed them to be more receptive to John Coode and the Associators' language of Catholic and Indian conspiracies the following summer.

On March 24, 1688/9, William Digges, a member of the Maryland council, received a panicked letter from fellow councilor and militia commander Henry Jowles, who told a story of dark conspiracy, divided interests, and imminent disaster. "We are all over the country [near the Patuxent River] in a great uproar and tumult," Jowles wrote, "and know not who to apply ourselves to" other than Digges, who they were sure would never, perhaps unlike some others, "betray the country to the common enemy." The enclosed depositions would prove that "we are sold and betrayed to the heathen by those whose interest it ought to have been to protect and defend us from them." The Indians had already been sighted and were "enfort[ing] themselves at the head of our river." Jowles and the others were making preparations for defense. They were also attempting to retrieve "the country arms and ammunition that were taken from us." Earlier that year, Catholic governor William Joseph had recalled the public arms for repair, an action that now looked extremely suspicious. Similar rumors of Catholics confiscating Protestants' guns had circulated in the 1640s, during Ingle's invasion. Digges would see from the enclosed depositions, Jowles continued, that some of "our great men" were implicated, and Jowles requested to know "your opinion on what is best to be done concerning them[;] our eyes are upon your honor as the only person left we can trust and if you please to espouse the Protestant interest the whole country you may be assured will faithfully stand by you." Digges's response, however, needed to be "sudden and expeditious[;] we do not desire any injury should be done them in their persons or estates but rather ready obedience to them in all things provided they show themselves ready to defend the country against the common enemy." If not, "we must do the best we can to secure ourselves against them and the Indians also." The papers that Jowles enclosed contained accounts of a story circulating that some Eastern Shore Indians when drunk had said they were "hired or employed by Col. Henry Darnall to fight against the English, but being asked when they were sober they would not say anything."[30]

Fear of invasion had placed Jowles in a tricky position. He had to act, or else people might form unauthorized military parties and engage in the type of indiscriminate vigilante action against Indians that could easily provoke the very violence that they feared. Military preparation required help from St. Mary's—but should the rumors turn out to be true, this was of course the last quarter form which aid would be forthcoming. Jowles clearly did not disbelieve what he had been told. He wrote to Digges because if the conspiracy were real, the Protestant Digges might not be in it. Should the rumors prove false, however, Jowles's letter placed him in a precarious position, since he had implied that he did not trust the Catholic majority of the Maryland council.

Perhaps to mitigate the doubtful impression his letter to Digges might leave on the council if it reached them, Jowles also wrote to Joseph and the rest of the council the same day to tell them about the "tumult and uproar" and the need for "speedy satisfaction." The letter was sent with the boat and men he had dispatched to collect the public weapons. Jowles's words to the council were chosen carefully. He explained that "there has been a rumor a great while . . . that the Catholics and Indians have plotted together to destroy and cut off all the Protestants in the province, and the Indians do already appear and begin to enfort themselves at the head of the river." He added that there was confirmation of this "from Virginia." The council should send a trustworthy person to bring "powder and bullets" and organize a defense, and they should do this quickly "for until you do that [the local inhabitants] do and will hold themselves betrayed by your honor to the common enemy." Jowles made here a point of stressing the imminent Indian threat, and gave no indication of his opinion of the plot's Catholic component. The threat in this account was posed by settlers further down on the social scale who believed the rumors and would think themselves "betrayed" by Joseph and the others. Jowles thus set up his plea for help as a request for aid in suppressing unruly poor and middling sorts, not Catholics. It had been necessary to suppress unruly poor and middling sorts in the past, as in 1676 and 1681,[31] and the council was used to the idea of imposing order on the rabble. If he explained the situation in this way Jowles did not look terribly anti-Catholic and might just get the weapons he needed to defend himself and others against what might, for all he knew, turn out to be a real threat of attack even if Catholics were not involved.[32]

Digges responded to Jowles's letter only briefly, telling him that he would take the information to the council and would give him "better satisfaction" soon and in person.[33] The council took the threat seriously. They reassured Jowles that "we will stand by you and by all the English and good people of Maryland" against the Indians. At the same time, they stressed the need for "true discretion" and the chaos that might arise from imprudent action. Jowles was to go up the river to seek further information. If the Indians were "in no hostile or unusual posture we are of opinion that it will be prudent to preserve the peace." But if they were not, Jowles could of course expect immediate assistance.[34]

The problem for the council was that while the Catholic conspiracy was unlikely, the threat of war with Indians might be real.[35] If it was not, they did not want panicked colonists to "rashly cut off or kill" innocent people and "thereby give occasion to the heathen to revenge the same upon the English."[36] Part of the power of anti-popish conspiracy theories, after all, was their seeming fit with irrefutably real things. If the threat were real, the council's order to Jowles to reconnoiter made sense. Even if the threat were not real, they would be seen to be taking action, and giving Jowles such an assignment added credibility to their assertion that he and they and all the English inhabitants of Maryland were on the same side.

The council knew the power of the Indian-Catholic plot narrative, which could not only frighten people but was also amenable to use by "ill-minded men of desperate fortunes" who might seize the moment to "pillage and plunder the people."[37] Their insistence on prudence and deliberation reveals the council members' awareness that events might easily spiral out of control, and they found it necessary to say, once more, that they were good, English, and loyal and would stand by other such people. They also took the added measure of sending Henry Darnall to Jowles's house "to inspect the premises" for military readiness to withstand "Indian enemies or others," an order that was not included in their letter to Jowles himself.[38] Perhaps they did not trust him as much as their letter to him implied—or at least did not trust him not to act rashly, willing as he was to entertain the possibility that the conspiracy might be real. Once Jowles had the weapons they had sent, any number of things could happen; if he was caught up in the panic, an armed militia leader acting outside the council's control was the last thing they needed.

As Jowles's letter to the council indicated, the threat was not confined to Maryland. The Virginians were involved as well. Authorities in Stafford County, across the Potomac River from Maryland, had investigated "some discourse talked by the Indians." These unnamed Indians had said "the great men of Maryland" had "hired the Seneca Indians to kill the Protestants." These "great men" included Henry Darnall, Edward Pye, and William Boreman, who was said to be "all one with the Senecas." Boreman, Darnall, and Pye had told the Indians that "they must make haste and kill the Protestants before the ships come in, for" after that "the Protestants would kill all the Papists and then all the Indians." This reference to the ships was likely related to the recent regime change in England, news of which had already reached the Chesapeake. Bur Harrison, one of the two Stafford County officials involved in taking the Indians' depositions, added that he had heard from other quarters that Pye said he "did hope before Easter Day to wash his hands in the Protestants' blood, and that if he had the Prince of Orange there he would thrust his sword up to the beam in him." The Piscataways, longtime allies of Maryland, were accused of "hir[ing] the Seneca Indians to kill all the Nanjatico Indians" so that "they might have the better opportunity to kill all the people of Virginia."

The Virginians' participation was not limited to discussion. The St. Mary's–based merchant John Addison, who was involved in the chain of letters by which the information from Virginia reached the Maryland council, wrote that the rumors must be quelled, by force if necessary, "or else it may be a cause of bringing over the Virginians, which I suppose wants but small inviting." Despite his concern that disorder in Maryland might provoke invasion from the south, Addison did not discount what his correspondents reported. He was "persuaded there is something abrewing amongst our Indians more than ordinary, for they have asked what makes the English men angry with them and that they intend to kill them as soon as they are all at the fort together."[39] Virginia officials also reported that "great numbers of Indians [were] flocking from Maryland," some repeating the story that Addison reported. The Virginia council wanted the Maryland government to prevent these Indians from crossing the river "to satisfy the present fears and disquiets" in Virginia.[40] The panic was potentially regional rather than local. News had crossed and recrossed the Potomac, and the story of Seneca invasion was not limited to the English.

Fear threatened to run out of control. The story grew bigger in the telling. Reports came to the council of "nine thousand French and Senecas . . . upon the cliffs in Ann Arundell County" and a "fort of foreign Indians" at the head of the Patuxent "being number as [the informant] could guess ten thousand," with nine thousand of them "landed on the coast of the mouth of the Patuxent."[41] Inhabitants soon threatened to take matters into their own hands. A group of Anne Arundel County men wrote to Digges and told him that they had heard all the reports and that "if we have not speedy advice and assistance from" those in charge "we must and will apply ourselves to those that will have greater regard to our present troubles."[42]

Who those more helpful individuals might be was revealed by Henry Darnall, who along with Digges had quieted a crowd that had assembled at Henry Jowles's house. There had been talk of "the people's sending for the Virginians to come to their assistance," which Darnall hoped he and Digges had "put a stop to." Not for the first time, some in Maryland clearly believed that the Protestant Virginians could be relied on to defend the public interest while their own leaders in Maryland could not. Maryland officials repeatedly insisted that the motives of any Virginians who did "come over" were not the preservation of the public good or the "Protestant interest" but rather their own personal, selfish interests: "the design of the Virginians to come over was purely for the love of the plunder."[43] The fear of mobilized Virginians was not unreasonable. Reports from south of the Potomac indicated that "the Virginians were actually in arms, horse and foot."[44] The Catholic-Indian conspiracy rumor threatened to replace the appointed chain of authority in Maryland with assertions from below that confessional identity trumped constituted authority as an indicator of one's reliability and public spiritedness. That the "public good" was the same as the "Protestant interest" was another worrying assertion. Maryland's Catholic leaders had battled this claim for decades, and not six months after this invasion scare they would battle it again.

The panic in March 1689 subsided within a few days. The council repeatedly issued assurances that the stories were false. At the same time, they were not convinced that there was not a threat from the Iroquois—or at least they did not want to appear unresponsive to such a threat—and patrols continued to range the woods. They also kept a "diligent eye upon the motions of the Virginians."[45] There was no grand attack by thousands of French and Iroquois, and armed Virginians did not come pouring across the Potomac. But the scare underlined the power of rumor to threaten the proprietary regime. News traveled quickly within the colony and beyond its borders. Even far less significant incidents, like the story about the confrontation between Christopher Rousby and Lord Baltimore, were repeated over and over. The proprietary regime could not control what was discussed in households or at christenings or funerals; merely the knowledge that a story was widely known could give it a reality and a significance that it might otherwise have lacked. Rumor not only offered people an opportunity to articulate fears or vent frustration—it also, as in the case with the Anne Arundel men who threatened to take matters into their own hands—could cause people both to take action and to justify why they were taking it. As Nicholas Spencer of Virginia put it, "disturbed minds" could be "violently carried into ruinous imaginations."[46]

9
NEWS, RUMOR, *and* REBELLION

Nicholas Spencer of Virginia complained in March of 1689 of common planters' "ruinous imaginations."[1] But the rumor panic of 1689 was not the first time that tall tales threatened the security of the proprietary regime. Maryland nearly had a Bacon's Rebellion of its own in the early 1680s. With some agitation from the former proprietary governor (and former rebel) Josias Fendall and a St. Mary's gentleman named John Coode, long-familiar local grievances coalesced via the American version of the anti-popery narrative into a dangerously coherent critique of proprietary government that seemed for weeks to tremble on the brink of armed revolt.

Fendall and Coode did more talking than plotting, however. In 1680 neither one proved willing to go through with the "rising" against Baltimore's government that their words suggested. Neither was the time quite right for rabid anti-popery as a political strategy. But the upwelling of confessionally colored political discontent between 1679 and 1681 revealed in stark terms how easily local tensions and fears could move into the familiar anti-Catholic narrative of conspiracy and cosmic disorder. Rumors about Catholics and Indians in Maryland were a discussion of the use and misuse of power, and allowed many people to voice criticism of the proprietary regime that might otherwise go unheard. The American version of the anti-popery narrative provided an explanation of events peculiar to Maryland, the Chesapeake, and the mid-Atlantic, and simultaneously placed these events in a framework that connected English colonists in the Chesapeake to their compatriots in the British Isles as well as the threat of war with the Five Nations and the "menacing shadow" Louis XIV had begun to cast in Europe.[2]

Yet the narrative had limits. Without indication from England that regime change in Maryland would be looked upon with favor, rumor could only go so far. As the royal governor of Jamaica noted a few years earlier in 1676 on hearing that some Marylanders had "revolted and declared for [Nathaniel] Bacon," he could not "trace the grounds of this report, so I suppose it only to be rumor, and probably raised by those who wish it."[3] Rumors might articulate wishes and fears and suggest what ought to be done, but given the administrative realities of the late seventeenth-century empire, without hope of support from across the Atlantic, rumor could do only so much.

* * *

The first part of the story lay both within and outside the colony's borders. The diplomatic reorientation of the middle 1670s in which the Susquehannocks went from allies to potential enemies and the English sought a treaty with the Five Nations, had not guaranteed peace. In the late 1670s, the Maryland council learned that the Susquehannocks had "submitted themselves to and put themselves under the protection of the Cinnigos or some other nations of Indians residing to the northward." In April 1677, the governor and council commissioned councilor Henry Coursey to go to New York and make a "firm peace" with the Susquehannocks, if they still existed as a separate nation, or with the Five Nations or "any other Indians now unknown to us." Indians allied to Maryland such as the Piscataways were to be included in the agreement.[4] The negotiations appeared to be a success.[5]

But the results of the treaty were not what the Maryland council had counted on. Coursey's was not the only treaty the Iroquois negotiated between 1676 and 1679. The Iroquois ended hostilities not only with the English, but with other Indian nations to the north and east. In addition, many Susquehannocks had been incorporated into Iroquois communities in the mid- and late 1670s. The Maryland council heard of this, as their reference to the Susquehannocks "submitting" to the Iroquois suggests, but they were not fully aware of its potential effects. Before this series of treaties, Iroquois war parties, although they did appear in the Chesapeake area, had tended to go north rather than south for plunder and captives. Afterward, with wars with peoples there now reduced or ended, Susquehannock adoptees among the Iroquois appear to have negotiated raids against enemies farther south in Maryland and Virginia in exchange for help with the Iroquois wars farther west.[6] The peace Coursey and the Iroquois negotiated may have been part of a process of diplomatic readjustment among both the Indians and the English that inadvertently led to the opposite of what the Maryland council intended—further wars in the Chesapeake. Coursey also misconstrued some elements of Iroquois law, assuming that the Iroquois would go through the English to resolve disputes with English-allied Indians; the Iroquois' understanding of what they agreed to did not require them to do this.[7]

This difference in understanding soon became evident with respect to the Piscataways, who were both old enemies of the Susquehannocks and allies of the English. The English had intended that they be included in whatever agreement Coursey reached with the Iroquois, but by June of 1678, there was a "common rumor" that the Iroquois "by instigation of the remaining part of the Susquehannocks now among them" intended to "come down and make war upon the Piscataway Indians." The interpreter Jacob Young was dispatched to the "old Susquehannock fort" to remind them of the agreement."[8] At a meeting between the council and the Piscataways in March 1679, an unnamed man who had "lately come from the Sinniquos" laid out a map of the Iroquois towns, with each town represented by a kernel of corn. The Susquehannocks were living half in one of these towns and half in another, and it was they who were responsible for attacks on English and Indians in Maryland, he said. The Susquehannocks would never make peace with either the English or the Piscataways, and they were drawing more and more of the Iroquois to their point of view. He and another man on the Piscataway delegation emphasized that the Susquehannocks' plans for revenge included the English in both Virginia and Maryland almost on equal terms with the Piscataways.[9] This was consistent with a rumor the council had heard the previous summer that the Iroquois intended to attack English settlements along the heads of the rivers in Virginia.[10]

The Iroquois and the Susquehannocks among them may have placed the Piscatways and the English on the same side of the conflict, but the English were not so sure. Local sources of tension—land, livestock, trade—rendered formal diplomatic alliance less straightforward than the various parties to it might have wished. At their meeting with the English in the spring of 1679, the Piscataway representatives stressed that the recent murder of "some English" in Maryland had been falsely blamed on them; the real culprits were Susquehannocks. The Piscataways were allies of the English and needed their support—arms and ammunition for defense. Lord Baltimore promised supplies.[11] But the matter of murders that the English blamed on the Piscataways and the Piscataways on the Iroquois was a tricky one. The English did suspect that the Piscataways had "privately done us several mischiefs and fathered the same upon the Sinnicos and other foreign Indians." Among these was the 1678 murder of the wife of a planter named David Cunningham, who lived at the head of the Patuxent River.[12]

The Cunningham murder was not an isolated incident. The Piscataways were not suspected of every act of violence, but there were plenty of such acts. In early 1677/8, for example, Governor Notley received word of a murder in Somerset County. A specific Indian man and his "accomplices" were suspected, and the English feared that this might be a sign of more violence to come.[13] In June 1678, the local official Augustine Hermann sent word to the council about the "great damage and injury" suffered by the settlers in Baltimore and Cecil Counties, in the northeastern part of the colony, by "the Delaware Indians driving away and killing their stocks, the said Indians pretending that most of the land in the upper part of the said counties doth properly belong to them." This was a painfully common conflict, in which foraging English livestock damaged Indian farms and fields and the farmers killed the animals. The English expected a familiar end to the story: Hermann and the interpreter Jacob Young were ordered to go and treat with the Delawares and find out "what satisfaction they require to quit . . . their claim" to the land."[14] In late August of 1678 another murder was committed by "some Indian on three English men on the east side of Susquehannock River, as they lay asleep on the riverside."[15] An alliance like that between Maryland and the Piscatways had to be negotiated through the noise of conflicts over land, trade, and livestock that did not always involve both parties but nevertheless undermined their trust in one another at every turn.

Maintaining the tricky balance between protecting the Piscataways and other native allies—whose own sense of their obligations to the English did not always match English expectations—their mutual obligations with Virginia, and the need to defend Maryland itself took up a great deal of the governor's and council's time. Meanwhile, the situation of the Piscataways, Mattawomans, and Chopticos grew desperate. By early 1680, they were continually under attack from Susquehannock and Iroquois war parties or both. The Maryland council's solution was to press all three groups to relocate to a single, defensible area; they promised to provide ammunition and assistance.[16] In February 1680/1, the Piscataways reminded the council of "the distressed condition they at present groaned under and which their friendship to the English" in the latter's war with the Susquehannocks "had reduced them to." They feared even to leave their fort to plant corn, all of which they blamed on their "friendship to the English." Thus they "crave[d] protection." It was ordered that military aid and food be supplied to the Piscataways, and the council strongly recommended that the Mattawomans, Chopticos, and Nanjemys "enfort themselves" with the Piscataways.[17] By April, however, the Mattawomans and Chopticos had not yet joined the Piscataways. Baltimore had met with their kings, who had "pitifully set forth to him the distressed condition they were in, being in continual expectation of their enemies' approach and being surprised and cut off by them." They repeated what the Piscataways had said, that they had not dared to plant corn for fear of attacks, and as a result depended on the English for both supplies and military assistance. Baltimore "assured them of a supply."[18]

Two Iroquois representatives met with the Maryland council in August of 1681 to discuss peace. The Iroquois intended to keep the peace with the English, but as for the Piscataways, "as they have brought the Piscataways' heads to be as small as a finger, they will now see if they can make an end of them."[19] The Five Nations and the English in Maryland clearly had different conceptions of what that treaty of 1678 had meant. The council asked Col. Randolph Brandt, who oversaw Maryland's military assistance to the Piscataways and sometimes encountered Iroquois, to reconfirm the colony's treaty with them if he spoke to any; Brandt himself wondered whether "those Indians I treated with were not real Sinniquos" and "had no relation to those Col. Coursey made peace with." A colleague of Brandt's observed that the "Sinniquos" were in fact a mixed group of Susquehannocks, Doegs, and others.[20] What Brandt and others observed was probably less a case of mistaken identity than the effect of the Iroquois' "mourning wars," in which they raided in order to take captives, who would be adopted to supplement a population depleted by warfare and disease. Depending on the timing and circumstance of the adoption, earlier identities were sometimes retained, and captives' previous alliances, grudges and, loyalties affected Iroquois policy.

But while the proprietor and council attempted to implement what they thought had been a treaty of peace—and, at times, figure out who they were in fact treating with—the alarming pattern of violence continued against both Iroquois enemies in the Chesapeake and their English allies. Sometimes it happened in the very heart of English settlement. In the early summer of 1681, a "horrid murder" of six English people, five men and a woman, was committed at Lookout Point at the "lower end" of St. Mary's, near the mouth of the Potomac.[21] In August it was reported that "the foreign Indians hath a fort above the eastern branch near the falls of Potomac," and four slaves belonging to George Brent had been captured by them and escaped. "The foreign Indians" had also been at Zachaia Fort recently (where Indians from several Maryland nations had taken shelter) and "cut up some of their [the enforted Indians'] corn."[22] Indians suspected to be Iroquois had attacked a farm in Anne Arundel County, destroying tobacco and livestock; another planter had been robbed of "of linen, blankets, and wearing clothes and rings to the value of £30 sterling." Eleven Piscataways were kidnapped. In Charles County, "inhabitants hereabouts . . . do say that if your lordship do not take some speedy cause to secure them" they feared for their property and their lives.[23] English inhabitants of Anne Arundel County were "in great distress, the Indians hollowing around their plantations, and attempting their dwelling houses."[24] And the frightening murders at Lookout Point were not resolved.

Some English inhabitants began to speak of vigilante action. The council warned Piscataways, Mattawoman, and Nanjemy Indians to stay away from "any English plantation" because those murders had "enraged" the English and since they did not know "how to distinguish their friends from their foes" they might assume that the Piscataways and others were "of the latter rank."[25] This was not a new problem; the previous summer planters had begun "raising men to see if we can find the Indians" and were promptly rebuked by the proprietor's council for such "rash unadvised actions."[26] The council spent a great deal of time talking to Indians. They were not accustomed to making their dealings public, so what many people saw was simply the proprietor conferring with "the Indians" and providing them with food, gunpowder, and ammunition—and yet the situation seemed to worsen rather than improve.

Overlaid on this tangle of violence and negotiation was a pattern of stories from abroad. At the house of Josias Fendall in Charles County in April of 1679 a number of people "fell into discourse" about the "late report of the troubles in England." Connected to this report was the assertion that there was "a frigate ready" to come to Maryland for Lord Baltimore.[27] Local official Christopher Roubsby's claim at about the same time that Baltimore would be taken home in chains, or that he was a traitor, suggests he and Fendall had heard the same story.[28] So had many others, and not only in Maryland. In Virginia, the captain of a ship from Bristol, William Nicklas, was accused of calling Baltimore a traitor and saying that he and others would not "clear [customs] with Lord Baltimore . . . because they would not pay any money . . . to any traitor." Nicklas was talking with another captain, Edward Blagg, who countered that he would be perfectly willing to clear with Baltimore, to which Nicklas responded by drinking "a health to the Duke of Monmouth as proprietary of the country, saying that my Lord Baltimore" had "forfeited his country" through treachery and there was no one better than Monmouth to take his place.[29] Ships trading in tobacco usually reached the Chesapeake late in the fall or early winter and left in the spring, before the weather got hot.[30] The Popish Plot in England was at its height in the winter of 1678–79, and Lord Baltimore and his cousin Henry Arundell had been among those that Titus Oates accused in October 1678 of accepting commissions from the Jesuits as officers in a Catholic army to overthrow England or ministers in the popish government to be established afterward; acceptance of such a commission would certainly count as treason.[31] There was time enough for this information to cross the Atlantic by March or April.

The Popish Plot of the late 1670s involved all the familiar elements: the Jesuits, foreign (in this case, French) subversion, the activities of covert Catholics in high places, even a potential link to the heir to the throne in accusations against the Duchess of York's secretary, Edward Coleman. The questions of a Catholic succession—what would the Duke of York do if he succeeded to the throne? Was it in England's interest to prevent this, and was it politically feasible, or right to do so?—mingled with fears of what James's ostensibly Protestant brother Charles II was already doing. As the poet and pamphleteer Andrew Marvell put it, "popery and arbitrary government" went hand in hand. Protestants feared not only a loss of liberty and the suppression of true religion, but even for their very lives. One MP from Kent reported that the people there were afraid that "a French armie would land" and "cut their throats . . . in their beds."[32]

English people in Maryland were at least as afraid of getting their throats cut by the Iroquois as by the French, but the Catholic French were rarely absent from the story. Even observers skeptical of the Catholic conspiracy narrative were concerned about the French. At the meeting between the English and the Piscataway representatives in 1679, one of the Piscataways, who had recently been among people farther north, told the proprietor and the council that there were Frenchmen among the Indians there. Lord Baltimore, who spoke French, asked him to bring one of these Frenchmen back the next time he went north so he could speak with him. The Piscataway man told him that this was impossible. The proprietor thought that there might be some French among the Susquehannock and Iroquois raiding parties; the Piscataways agreed that this might be true.[33] In 1681, Indians who had been prisoners among the Iroquois reported that there were "two Frenchmen" among them.[34] Reality lined up with narrative convention just enough to make some people's worst fears terrifyingly plausible.

Inhabitants of Maryland were not slow to put Indians, Frenchman, English Catholics, and "arbitrary government" together; neither were they reluctant to discuss and elaborate upon this exciting nexus. In early May 1681, John Mould reported to the council that while he and Henry Johnson had been out "seeking for deer or turkeys," Johnson had asked him "if I did hear of the Irish that was to come into this province." There were "forty families" on their way under the guise of ordinary colonists, but they came at the instigation of "my lord and that Irish fellow Talbot" and intended to "cut the Protestants' throats." Johnson hoped that the English parliament would "prevent their purposes" or that the Irish would "sink by the way" on their trip over.[35] The Irish had been a mainstay of English anti-popery narratives since Elizabeth's reign, as unruly papist savages likely to assist Spanish invasion forces and—after 1641—as agents of terrible atrocities against innocent English and Scottish Protestants. It was no great leap to combine or conflate them with the threat of "savage" Native Americans.[36] Neither was the link between Baltimore and Ireland a fabrication. The proprietor's title came from his family's Irish possessions, and the "Irish fellow Talbot" Johnson mentioned was Baltimore's cousin George, who served on the provincial council.[37]

Mould was not the only one to hear or repeat such a story. Not a month later Edmund McDermott reported to the council that Mordecai Hunton had told him about a boy who went "ranging for his master's horse." The boy met "a single Indian," who asked him "whether he met more Indians." The Indian was surprised when the boy said no, because "those English called the Romans and the Sinniquos are to join together and kill all the Protestants." Three Catholic priests were "certainly known" to be involved. When McDermott challenged Hunton that "the story was very idle" Hunton responded that "tis not so idle but I believe you know of it."[38] A few days later the governor of Virginia reported that the inhabitants of Maryland, having suffered a "breaking forth of the Indians" were making the "irrational . . .

conjecture" that it was the Iroquois "by the instigation of Jesuits in Canada and the procurance of the Lord Baltimore to cut off . . . the Protestants."[39] John Tyrling was soon after accused of "saying that his lordship . . . had furnished the Indians with powder and shot, and no wonder then the English had their throats cut when the proprietary gave them powder and shot for that purpose." Tyrling denied this, but did say he had been told that Baltimore "sent a packet of letters" to the Iroquois "for them to come and cut off the Protestants."[40] The Tyrling story soon became "general discourse among the people" causing at least one man to "fort in" his house.[41] Daniel Mathena of Charles County was questioned because it was rumored that an Indian had been at his house to bring "two packets of letters, one as big as both his fists and the other somewhat smaller, both in a grass silk basket." The letters were for the "Sinnoquo Indians and the French" in Canada.[42]

By the end of July 1681, Col. Philip Ludwell of Virginia reported not only a general fear of the Iroquois in both Virginia and Maryland but also that in Maryland people were "ready to break forth into acts of violence," and if their "grievances [were] not . . . redressed" by the meeting of the assembly in August, they would take matters into their own hands.[43] But were these rumors moving merely under their own power? Perhaps not. At the center of the talk of invasion and conspiracy were two men, Josias Fendall and John Coode. According to Lord Baltimore, Josias Fendall had "leapt the gallows very narrowly" in 1660, when he was involved in an ill-timed attempt to replace the newly restored proprietary regime. He also had connections to "most of the rascals in the north part of Virginia."[44] John Coode was a former minister turned gentleman by an advantageous marriage.[45] Less prominent than Fendall in the events of 1681, he came into his own as a political agitator eight years later, when he and the Protestant Associators overthrew the proprietary regime.

In 1681, Fendall did most of the talking, and much of what he said concerned the rumors of conspiracy and invasion current in the colony. He often spoke "concerning the Indians and particularly about the family that was cut off near Point Lookout." A man who worked for him reported that Fendall said "several times" that "he believed . . . the papists and Indians joined together." The proprietor and his government would support the Indians over the English, and "they together had a mind to destroy all the Protestants."[46] Thomas Mudd described a conversation about "news out of England and likewise of the news here" in which John Dent said Fendall had told him "the Sinniquos were coming down to assist the Catholics . . . he thought it would be troublesome times with the Catholics."[47]

But Fendall did more than repeat what he heard. He also implied that he might be in a position to do something about this problem—or at the very least that something should be done, or would soon be done. In early 1679, visitors at Fendall's house discussed the Popish Plot and the rumor of a ship's coming to fetch the proprietor. According to one member of the party, Fendall said that if all that were true, all the authorities in England had to do was "send two or three words to me" and he would "engage . . . to send him home myself" and "save [them] that charge."[48] A few months later, Fendall claimed to have "all the late proceedings in England at home" and stated that "my Lord was a traitor, and he could prove it." Soon he would "have more honor in the country than he ever had."[49] We have more of Fendall's words than Coode's, but the latter was certainly not silent. In response to a man who was concerned about some land, Coode exclaimed "what the devil need you trouble yourself with land, there is never a papist in Maryland will have one foot of land within these four month."[50] Both claimed to have numerous armed supporters they might call on. Fendall claimed thirty or forty men in 1679 and later said he had been offered forty in 1681 if he would "but undertake to alter things are they now are." The characteristically more colorful Coode claimed ten thousand.[51] But at no point did either do more than imply that something was to be done soon, and perhaps they might do it.

Others assumed that action was imminent and that it had a good chance of success. Fendall and John Coode were said to have gone to a friend in Virginia "to advise . . . what they should do in the business" about the "papists and Indians."[52] A man who had heard about the Lookout Point murders from Fendall said that Fendall would have no difficulty raising men even without a commission.[53] After his arrest in the summer of 1681, rumor had it that "Fendall was now going to call my lord to an account."[54] George Godfrey, a minor militia officer, attempted to raise troops to "rescue" Fendall.[55] Many people appeared to believe that Fendall was "ready to rise."[56] But he never did. One clue as to why not may lie in a conversation between John Dent and Fendall, in which Dent suggested that Fendall might postpone rising "until he had further news out of England." Fendall's response to Dent was that if he waited "it might be too late."[57] These were bold words, but Dent's point was difficult to discount. Fendall himself had said a few years before that he would send Baltimore home at the first opportunity—if he were ordered to do so. Perhaps he really did expect orders, or at the very least news, from England that would signify the time was right. His experience in 1660 had probably convinced him that a little patience in such matters could not hurt.

The proprietary regime was well aware of the power of Catholic-Indian conspiracy stories. They issued a proclamation reiterating laws against "false news, rumors and reports."[58] But their reaction to the threat that Fendall and Coode seemed to pose played right into the very stories the regime wished to quash. Colonel Ludwell of Virginia thought that the arrest of Fendall, Coode, and "several other Protestant gentlemen" had only increased Marylanders' fears of a Catholic plot. It was rumored that the men had been arrested so that they would not be able to sit in the assembly in August.[59] Lord Baltimore had required once more that each county send only two delegates and was unwilling to put into place a procedure for by-elections to fill vacancies between sessions. Col. Randolph Brandt informed him that even though "your lordship hath been pleased to signify the reasons" for his requirements, "the people . . . think it strange," and there was much talk about it. This was in addition to rumors that "your lordship doth favor the Romans."[60] But it was more than the timing of the arrest. According to the governor of Virginia, Lord Culpeper, the Protestant gentlemen had been "seiz[ed] . . . in the dead time of the night in their own houses in time of peace with force of arms without warrant shown and refused to be shown when demanded, contrary to the liberty of the subject."[61] In an effort to stifle dangerous rumors about a Catholic plot, Baltimore had done precisely what a dangerous Catholic ruler would naturally do.

Baltimore also made an ill-advised attempt to eject John Coode, elected for St. Mary's, from the lower house of the assembly when it met in August. The proprietor regarded Coode as guilty until proven innocent. He had been accused of "mutinous and seditious speeches and attempts tending to a breach of the peace" and ought not to sit "until . . . he hath purged himself." The lower house responded that "only felony treasons and refusing to give security for breach of the peace" could disable someone from sitting, and since Coode had merely been accused and released on bail, they could not see that he ought to be excluded. This and the question of delegates and by-elections set up the proprietor and the lower house of the assembly for yet another collision over privileges.[62]

Not for the first time, proprietor and assembly clashed over what sort of body the lower house was and the source of its privileges, which again raised the question of what liberties the English inhabitants of Maryland had and the limits of proprietary power—not to mention what motives might lie behind either agitation about liberties on the one hand or insistence on proprietary privilege on the other. As far as rules for elections and by-elections were concerned, the lower house considered the precedents provided by the English House of Commons "the only rule to walk by." Charles Calvert responded that this was utterly preposterous. The privileges they asked for—that the speaker be allowed to issue warrants for by-elections for vacant seats; they also wanted a sergeant-at-arms to keep order—had never been given to them. No other colonial assembly had such privileges, and in short they had grossly mistaken their business. Besides, the king of England had "sole power dispose of his conquests upon terms he pleases," and Baltimore's royal patent had given him the power of "enacting . . . laws." The patent was the framework for determining how elections should function, not the pattern provided by the House of Commons. The lower house confessed themselves "extremely grieved" that the proprietor would "make it a matter of wonder" that they looked to the "rules of England" for their "rights and privileges." After all, it was "our inherent right yea and birthright though born in this province." Just because they lived in Maryland did not mean that they had no rights or liberties other than those derived from the patent. The comparison of Maryland to a "conquest" was also worrying. If this was intended to mean "that we are subject to arbitrary laws and impositions" they could not believe that those words were Baltimore's own. Here they invoked a formula that English people had used for decades to suggest those in authority might possibly not be acting in the public interest: such disquieting words must be "the result of strange if not evil counsel." The proprietor objected strenuously to the phrase—he was "confident" it was the work of a faction in the assembly rather than the considered opinion of the whole.[63]

To Lord Baltimore and the council, Fendall and Coode were "rank Baconists" whose only goal was plunder, a view the council would reiterate in March 1689 when it seemed, yet again, that Maryland was in danger of a Catholic-assisted Indian invasion. As Baltimore wrote to the Earl of Anglesey in July 1681, before the assembly met, these "evil-disposed spirits" had been "stir[ring] up the inhabitants of Maryland" and northern Virginia "to mutiny." The proprietor believed that Fendall had counted on the "differences" between Charles II and Parliament—over the exclusion of James among other things—to cause "civil wars" that would dissolve government and allow him "and his crew" to "possess themselves here and in Virginia of what estates they pleased."[64] Religion was not the issue, and the claims about liberty were utterly specious.

When he and Coode were tried for the summer's "mutiny and sedition" in November of 1681, Fendall loudly asserted the opposite. He questioned each of the jurors about the juror's religion and took exception to those who were Catholics. When the court refused to give Fendall the evidence against him—one judge explained to Fendall that they knew he would have "taken . . . off" those who had given information against him "by your influence upon the people"—he objected that even "the persons impeached for the [Popish] Plot" were allowed to know the evidence against them.[65] Fendall's best chance lay in a narrative of scheming Catholics and heroic Protestants, and he knew it. That this might be a plausible defense was not entirely ludicrous. Even those who expressed dismay at the disorder Marylanders appeared to be about to fall into in 1681 could easily slide into confessional language in describing what was happening. Lord Culpeper, the governor of Virginia, referred to those criticizing Baltimore's government as "the Protestants." Philip Ludwell described those who were arrested in August as "Protestant gentlemen."[66] They were, of course—but Lord Baltimore would have objected that that was not the point.

News of the arrests of Fendall and Coode in the summer of 1681 quickly crossed the Atlantic and made a "great . . . noise at London."[67] Not everyone who heard about it believed in the conspiracy, but for the Privy Council it was further evidence that Baltimore's colony might bear some looking into. In October, before Fendall and Coode were tried, but late enough in the fall that news of the summer's confusion could have reached London, the council wrote to Baltimore about "information" they had received indicating that "there are very few of his majesty's Protestant subjects admitted to be of the council of the colony of Maryland, and that there is partiality and favor shewed on all occasions towards those of the Popish religion." They hoped that this was not so, but if it was, Baltimore was to correct the problem immediately. Power should lie in Protestant hands—as should the colony's public arms and ammunition.[68] Soon after this, ship's captain Richard Shepard gave them additional information about the events of the previous summer. Shepard stressed that despite what they might have heard there was "no quarrel between the Protestants and the Papists." The latter were outnumbered by the former thirty to one.[69] Perhaps there was no conspiracy after all.

But even if Protestants in Maryland were not being oppressed, there were aspects of Baltimore's style of rule that did not sit well with the Lords of Trade. He appeared to be obstructing the collection of royal customs in his province, for example. Early in 1682 the Lords of Trade resolved a long and acrimonious dispute that had pitted Baltimore against two royal customs officials, Nicholas Badcock and Christopher Rousby, who had accused the proprietary regime of interfering with royal customs collection. The committee concluded that "diverse undeniable testimonies" and "the confession of your [Baltimore's] own letters" indicated "you have obstructed our service and discouraged our officers in the execution of their duty." The proprietor was fined the £2,500 that the committee reckoned he had cost the crown in lost revenue.[70] Even if religion were not the root of the problem, royal power was not as well respected in Maryland as it might be.

The events of the summer of 1681 provoked another public airing of that ancient question: was anything rotten in Maryland—and if it were, who was to blame? Argument about this question was not confined to the chambers of the Lords of Trade. As were the 1650s, the late 1670s and early 1680s were a time of intense controversy, even crisis, in the Anglophone world over the relationship between confessional identity and political power. Could Catholics—a category that included the heir to the throne—be trusted with the latter? One anonymous pamphlet, *To the Parliament of England, the Case of the Poor English Protestants in Mary-Land,* was an address to Parliament that offered a resounding no. The tone of this tract was more generally anti-Catholic than specifically anti-Baltimore. Its author argued that the proprietor's only goal was "advancing popery," and to further this cause Lord Baltimore was willing to engage in horrific violence. The text was a typical early modern atrocity narrative. The raid on Kent Island in the late 1630s was described as a terrifying nighttime attack in which Protestants were driven from their homes and "hanged . . . at their own doors," including one man forced to watch his brother die. In another incident, "a poor woman who lay in child-bed" escaped her "flaming house" only to be caught and turned out naked with her infant into the "frosty cold weather" to freeze.[71] The colony's "great numbers" of priests and Jesuits did their best to convert Protestants; the great number of inhabitants who came as servants "not well grounded in the Protestant religion" made the population so much the more vulnerable to such persuasion. Since the "true Christian religion" was not taught, Maryland would "in a very short time be all papists." Its location near the geographical center of the English colonial world meant that Maryland might "in a small time infect all the rest." Government was "arbitrary" and "popish"—no Protestant could hope for justice. The proprietary regime punished efforts to show loyalty to the king, forbidding celebration of "Gunpowder Treason Day" and "threaten[ing]" a public-house keeper who dared to "drink the king of England's health."[72]

How had this horrific state of affairs come about? Protestants had relaxed their vigilance. They had foolishly believed Baltimore's false assurance that Protestant colonists would be "free from the popish yoke" and "enjoy the same privileges as the papists did."[73] So far, this argument was typical for anti-popish complaints about Maryland's government. The Native Americans, however, played no role in the popish conspiracy. They attacked "Baltimore's territories" in revenge after the Kent Island battle and "burn[ed] the priests," who they held responsible for the outrage.[74] After this, they were hardly mentioned. Despite the other (very) roughly accurate details of Maryland's history that the tract included, this omission suggests the pamphlet was not written by someone who had spent much time there—or at least by someone whose primary purpose was not to describe the problems of Maryland qua Maryland. This was a more general popish conspiracy story; the intent was probably to use Maryland to argue that in general Catholics should be removed from political power. It was, after all, addressed to "The Parliament of England," a body that by 1681 had spent a great deal of time attempting to do precisely that.

The argument of *The Case of the Poor English Protestants* was simple and familiar: Catholics were by their very nature subversive and destructive of everything that good and loyal English people valued. This particular pamphlet was not aimed solely at Maryland's proprietary regime, but this mode of argument was central to the attacks that had been made upon it. Defenders of Maryland, in contrast, focused on undermining the standing of people like Fendall and Coode as exemplary Protestant subjects, thus pulling apart the claim that loyalty and Protestantism went hand in hand. In 1682, a two-page letter from the proprietor's uncle Philip Calvert to Col. Henry Meese, a merchant, was published in London. The letter was dated

December 29, 1681, after the trials of Fendall and Coode. The letter was a concerted effort to turn Fendall's claims upside down. Here it was not the proprietor but rather Fendall himself who grasped for power he did not deserve. He had been barred from office after "perfidiously" breaking "his oath and trust" as governor in 1659–60, but "now he sets all his wits to work" trying to worm his way back into power. He tried to talk the people into "mutiny" and "tampere[ed] with some of the justices of the peace in St. Mary's county."[75] If there were lying and law-breaking in Maryland, it was Fendall who was responsible, not the proprietary regime. This favorable depiction of Baltimore's government was bolstered by the description of the arrests of Fendall and Coode, which in this account were models of legality and restraint. These took place "when it was light," and the man who arrested each of them, Henry Darnall, "entered [each house] alone, leaving his men without." Indeed, if anyone sought persons who did not have the public good at heart, one need look no further than Fendall's own supporters. Rather than "searching for the Indians, that had murdered some of our planters" and were daily expected to attack, Lieut. George Godfrey had "laid a plot to unhorse" his superior officer and "carry the troop to the rescue of Fendall."[76] Protestantism did not at all imply that one was committed to loyalty and order—and Catholicism did not imply the opposite.

The events of 1679–81 revealed the uneasy push and pull between ideology and administrative structure, local events and concerns that spanned the Atlantic. When combined with the danger of demonstrably real military threats, anti-popery was a powerful force. Even those unconvinced by the conspiracy theory could easily fall into confessional language in discussing political troubles in Lord Baltimore's colony. Ultimately, however, Fendall and Coode did not "rise" in 1681, and the panic abated. As Fendall's conversation with John Dent suggested, perhaps they were waiting for some more positive sign from England that regime change in Maryland would be welcome, and they did not receive one. By the summer of 1681, the urgency of the Popish Plot in England had faded. Indeed, by then the drift of politics there had shifted, as the reaction to the Exclusion Crisis linked Protestant dissent to threats of anti-monarchical subversion.[77] As the outcome of Monmouth's Rebellion in 1685 indicated, plenty of English people were willing to believe that a Catholic might wield power fairly, or at least that a legitimate Catholic ruler was better than an illegitimate Protestant one. Anti-popery had limits.

Charles Calvert made no effort to adjust to changing times in the 1680s.[78] With the memory of Bacon's Rebellion in Virginia still lingering, it was easy and effective to categorize Fendall and Coode as mere "Baconists" whose claims about Catholics and abuse of power might easily be discounted. Charles did not believe in the legitimacy of such critiques of his regime, and for the time being the Lords of Trade seemed to accept his reassurances that Protestants were not mistreated in his colony. And yet the ideological ground under Calvert's feet was shifting. By the early 1680s, the Lords of Trade had many reasons other than the confessional affinities of the proprietor to keep a closer eye on Baltimore's province. As the imperial administrative apparatus grew in the late 1600s, the crown and Lords of Trade were less tolerant of colonies that appeared to go their own way, whether those colonies were understood to be populated by Protestant dissenters as in Massachusetts, or both dissenters and Catholics as in Maryland. Lord Baltimore's construction of his powers as proprietor of Maryland derived from a theory of politics based on strong royal power, but ironically his sense of his own prerogatives often appeared to undermine his commitment to those of the crown. The administrative and ideological machinery of empire was not as friendly to proprietary power as it had been in decades past—when the timing was right, this in tandem with the power of anti-Catholicism could form a very dangerous combination.

10

GLORIOUS REVOLUTIONS

The Revolution of 1688 was a turning point in the long restructuring of the English—soon to be British—empire between 1675 and the first decades of the eighteenth century. In Maryland, as in New York and Massachusetts, it offered local elites the opportunity to overturn regimes many of them resented. Whether or not the outcome they envisioned was congruent with the plans of the new monarchs in England was a separate question; it would take at least a decade before the reengineered machine of empire ran smoothly. The language of anti-popery was crucial to the development of the British empire in the early eighteenth century, although the long term and the short term could be quite different—in both New York and Maryland, anti-Catholicism aided rebellion but it did not guarantee that those who wielded it would gain a permanent place in the new order.[1]

In Maryland, John Coode and the Protestant Associators overthrew the proprietary regime in the summer of 1689 using much the same language as Coode and Fendall had eight years earlier. Fendall had died by 1689; the Asssociators who toppled Maryland's proprietary regime were led by Coode and a number of other Protestant gentlemen, including Coode's two brothers-in-law, Nehemiah Blakiston and Kenelm Cheseldyn, as well as some who had figured dramatically in the anti-papist scare of the preceding March, including Henry Jowles and John Addison.[2] Henry Darnall, a prominent Catholic planter and officeholder and cousin of the proprietor, gave an account of the coup to the Lords of Trade later that year. According to Darnall, the revolt took the regime by surprise. Darnall received a message by night on 16 July "that John Coode was raising men up Potomac." He told the council, "who immediately dispatched a person to know the truth, but the said person was taken by Coode as a spy and by him kept, so the council had no notice until two days of anything," when they were told that Coode and his supporters were marching on St. Mary's. The council tried to regain control of the militia, but the rank and file were convinced that Coode, not the proprietary regime, was acting in the country's interest. While "we found most of the officers ready to come in to us," Darnall explained, the "men were possessed by the belief that Coode rose only to preserve the country from the Indians and papists and to proclaim the king and queen, and would do them no harm." As a result, Coode had several hundred more men than the defenders of the proprietary government.[3] By August 1, the state house and public records were secured and the garrison guarding the public arms at Mattapany surrendered.

The crucial part of the battle lay not in securing St. Mary's, however, but in convincing the new regime in London that the Associators were patriots and not, as Charles Calvert had described Coode years earlier, "rank Baconists."[4] It was a contest not of swords but of words—whose version of the proprietary regime was correct? Was Baltimore a scheming French-allied papist, or a just and legitimate governor troubled by malcontents? In the end, the Associators did not so much win the argument as Lord Baltimore lost it. The proprietary regime's defense of itself and its government had not changed over the years—but the monarchy and empire in which it operated had. There was far less space for the type of power Baltimore wielded than there had been in 1630 or even 1660.

There were still skeptics of anti-popery and critiques of militant Protestantism, of course—there always had been. The difference was that in the past, challenges to the proprietary regime had focused primarily on confessional difference as a way of articulating what was wrong with it, and a way of arguing that Baltimore's government was illegal, corrupt, and dangerous. But by the late 1680s, the need for a more systematic imperial administration had created a second challenge—the English state wanted more control over colonies like Maryland than the proprietor desired. Previously, Charles Calvert and his father could answer charges of Catholic conspiracy with the language of anti-Puritanism, loyalty, and respect for the prerogative powers of the crown. To impugn the patent was to impugn the king. When the state was not particularly interested in meddling with the internal affairs of colonies, this worked. But when proper colonial deference to the power of the crown came to involve calls for uniformity in religion and administration—not to mention more efficient tax collection—as it did in the last decades of the seventeenth century, the identification of the proprietor's vast powers with the king's prerogative was no longer an effective means of defending them. And in 1689, Charles Calvert's Catholicism, as well as some of the very real problems within his colony, made it difficult for him to counter the Associators' argument that the proprietary regime was in the interest of neither king nor colonists.

* * *

In the fall of 1688, Charles Calvert gave no sign of thinking that the justification for the way he governed his colony might have to change. He added to the provincial council the Catholic William Joseph, who, when he arrived, gave a speech to the assembly that articulated in the starkest possible terms the proprietary model of power in the colony. Power flowed from top to bottom, "from God, to the king, and from the king to his excellency the Lord Proprietary, and from his lordship to us." Monarchs, he repeated, "are the Lord's anointed," and subjects were "bound to fear and honor" them.[5]

Joseph stressed the indivisibility of interest among king, proprietor, and subjects by way of a specifically American problem. At the petition of merchants from both Maryland and Virginia, the king had ordered that tobacco could no longer be shipped to England packaged in bundles—it had to go in hogsheads. A few might "presume to question the advantage or disadvantage," of such a command, but this was "unbecoming subjects . . . as if the good and evil which thereby might . . . arise were not fully and duly considered of in England by the king's most honorable council." He also stressed the assembly's duty to Baltimore, particularly with respect to paying proprietary taxes. Here he "hope[d] there are not any . . . so wicked as (by Machiavellian principles) shall go about to divide the interests of my lord and his people which indeed are not two interests but one."[6] Joseph reiterated the longstanding proprietary claim that the only source of lawful authority in the colony was the proprietor, by virtue of his royal charter—and to criticize either was to undermine the king himself. King, proprietor, and subjects shared a single interest, and any person who might suggest that the actions of either James II or Lord Baltimore were not for the good of all was him or herself guilty of private interest and "Machiavellian" wickedness. There was no such thing as loyal opposition.

This was a powerful argument, calculated to be almost unanswerable. The essential problem with the English constitution as it stood after the Restoration was that the whole system depended on trust between king and Parliament, and the king's willingness to act within the law as his subjects understood it.[7] The political problems left unresolved at the Restoration remained so because most MPs and gentry were reluctant to think that there could be a true division of interest between the king and his subjects. They were unwilling to argue that what the king wanted, when fully informed and honestly advised, was not what was best for the polity as a whole. To argue that the interests of rulers and ruled might legitimately diverge was at once to argue that one did not or could not trust the king, and possibly also that monarchy itself was a flawed form of government—a dangerous idea given the memory of the 1640s and 1650s. To imply that critics of Lord Baltimore were doing precisely this was a strong statement indeed.

Equating criticism of Charles Calvert with republicanism was a difficult position to sustain, however. It implied that as far as the inhabitants of Maryland were concerned, Baltimore was to be immune to the charge of pursuing his private interests at the expense of the community. If to criticize Baltimore or question his motives was to subvert monarchy, this made Baltimore into an unusual type of subject. Privy Councilors or great landholders in Britain could have their motives assessed in this way, and, while it might be considered disrespectful, it was not seditious in the same way that the same charges would have been if leveled at the king. Joseph was claiming that Baltimore represented crown authority in such a way as to make him almost a sort of viceroy or sub-monarch. Such a stand would not have been congenial to James II himself for the same reason that the crown began proceedings to revoke proprietary and corporate charters and replace them with a more uniform colonial administration even before 1688.[8] Neither was it to the taste of William and Mary. In April 1689, the Lords of Trade discussed how to "better secure their majesties' interest" in proprietary colonies, Maryland included, as these colonies "do not hold themselves subject to [the king's] immediate government nor render any account to his majesty of their proceedings."[9] The following month they noted that Maryland in particular was not "under such a dependence on the crown as is necessary in the present conjunctures."[10] Joseph's assertion of the majesty of proprietary claims was potentially a dangerous move because it set the proprietor up for accusations of both abuse of power and insufficient deference to the crown.

Particular danger lay in the fact that such accusations contained an element of truth. Just as the proprietary regime spent a great deal of time talking to Native Americans (though not for the dark purposes the regime's enemies imagined) and just as the proprietor consistently refused to acknowledge assertions of familiar English liberties that did not derive from his charter (though not out of any malicious desire to subvert English law or enact tyranny), the charge that Lord Baltimore abused his power was not as wild as he might have wished. Neither he nor his father had done anything they believed to be illegal or wrong, but they had occasionally construed their authority in ways that those above them found alarming. The example of this most vivid in local memory—John Coode harped upon it constantly—was Baltimore's interference in customs collection in the early 1680s, for which the Lords of Trade fined him, and the subsequent murder by his cousin George Talbot of one of the royal collectors, Christopher Rousby. The murder was ultimately tried in Virginia in part for jurisdictional reasons but also because the Lords of Trade did not trust the proprietary regime to handle it properly.[11]

Most unfortunate of all—coming as it did on the heels of the rumor panic of March 1689—was the proprietary regime's failure to proclaim William and Mary. Lord Baltimore told the Lords of Trade that he had dispatched instructions to do so but the instructions never arrived.[12] According to provincial secretary of Virginia Nicholas Spencer, the inhabitants of Maryland were "ragingly earnest" for the proclamation of their new sovereigns and "will not believe but . . . that the [Maryland] government have concealed their commands." Back in March some had threatened to take matters into their own hands if not permitted to defend themselves against the Iroquois they imagined were about to descend upon them—and now they threatened to do so again and "proclaim their majesties without the order of the government." This, Spencer concluded, would "unhinge" Maryland's "whole constitution" and "dissolve the whole frame of it."[13]

In 1679 and 1681, Josias Fendall had said several times that given only a few words from England he would dispatch Baltimore's government in an instant. He did not get them, and his predicted rising never happened. But in 1689, John Coode and his associates apparently decided that the proprietary regime's failure to proclaim the new king and queen was word enough.[14] During July and August he and the self-described Protestant Associators staged their successful coup. Henry Darnall later noted the power of the Catholic-Indian conspiracy fear to motivate support; another glimpse into Marylanders' reasons for supporting the Associators came from the Catholic planter and official Peter Sayer, who said that Coode threatened inhabitants with "the loss of their estates" and provoked them to fear that "their throats should be cut by the papists."[15] The Protestant loyalist and militia commander Richard Smith noted that local people told him they would "march with him upon any other occasion, but not to fight for the papists against themselves."[16] The difference between 1689 and 1681 was transatlantic—a decade before, wild fears had remained wild fears. But the seeming failure of the proprietary regime to proclaim the new monarchs tipped the balance: as the Associators' historically resonant name implied, when there was truly a dire threat to the maintenance of loyalty to the legitimate Protestant sovereign, it was lawful to act.

It was not as simple as that, of course. The Associators had taken control of the colony, but as Jacob Leisler was to learn in far grislier a fashion in New York, that was not the end of the story. Indeed, stories and whether or not one had an opportunity to tell them were a crucial part of the revolutions of 1688 and 1689.[17] Coode and his supporters had overturned a government, rendering them vulnerable to charges of rebellion, even treason. They had to convince both their neighbors in Maryland and the authorities in London that they were not grasping malcontents but rather patriotic Protestants—that they acted in what Henry Jowles had earlier that year called the "Protestant interest" and not for their own selfish purposes. While the Associators did their best to make this case, members of the proprietary regime itself and those in Maryland who supported it argued the opposite. Baltimore's government was peaceful and lawful, his religion caused no problems, and Coode and the others had no legitimate reason to do what they had done. There was no "Protestant interest"—there was only the common interest of obedient subjects loyal to the crown, a category that included Lord Baltimore but not John Coode.

The contest reduced to an argument over the nature of the English constitution—what sort of a place, if any, should Catholics have within the English polity? Were loyal subjects bound together and to the (Protestant) monarch by a common religion, with Catholicism necessarily a source of subversion and disorder? (And if that were true, how broad was the definition of "Protestant"?) Or might loyal subjects differ in religion; if this was the case, what ensured their loyalty—and how were actions such as John Coode's to be explained? William and Mary were in the midst of answering these very questions.[18] Their decisions about the colonies would help to shape the meaning of the revolution throughout their dominions. After all, if Lord Baltimore remained in power, either popery was not so dangerous a presence as some might claim—or uniformity of religion in colonies did not matter. If it did not, that in itself was a statement about the nature of the relationship of American provinces to the crown as well as the role of confessional uniformity in securing political allegiance.

Coode, Blackiston, Jowles, and the others engaged in a series of polemical moves aimed at various audiences—their fellow Marylanders, the authorities of Virginia and New York, the new monarchs and council. The first of these was their name itself, the "Protestant Associators." They offered no direct explanation of their choice, but the name was likely intended to evoke the Bond of Association of 1584. This was a document created by the Elizabethan regime in the wake of the assassination of William I of Orange by a Catholic Frenchman and in the midst of what the regime understood to be a longstanding threat to Elizabeth's life and throne by Mary, Queen of Scots. Those who signed it and swore to uphold its terms bound themselves to pursue "to the uttermost extermination" anyone who attempted to harm the queen "and to resist the succession of any individual on whose behalf such acts might be attempted."[19] It was an astute piece of propaganda on the part of the regime: signatories, which included a range of men from Privy Councilors to freeholders, engaged in a dramatic public attestation of loyalty to the queen in the face of dangerous international Catholic conspiracy.[20]

The Bond did not drop from memory after Elizabeth. In 1696, several years after the Maryland Associators' coup, William's government in England responded to an assassination plot with a revived Bond. Copies of the 1584 original were reprinted with pointed references to Catholic conspiracy, and swearing to the 1696 bond soon became a requirement for office.[21] This second Bond reached into the empire; signatories registering their loyalty to William and horror at the reputed plot included a long list of free men in Maryland, who were anxious to signal their repugnance for "so flagicious a design."[22] In 1689, reference to the 1584 bond evoked a Franco-Spanish Catholic threat to a Dutch prince (William I's assassin, Balthasar Gerard, was French, but admired Philip II of Spain, considered William a traitor to his prince and to the true religion and—perhaps not unimportantly—knew of the significant reward the Spanish king had offered for William's death) as well as memories of the long drama of suspected popish subversion that had surrounded Mary Stuart. The 1584 Bond was an elaborate public statement of loyalty, in which the Protestant political nation arranged itself in opposition to a Catholic threat; such a drama was precisely what the 1689 Associators reenacted in Maryland.[23]

The Associators' basic claims were outlined in a statement entitled *The Declaration of the Reasons and Motives for the Present Appearing in Arms,* which was issued on July 25 and soon printed in London. The title was a fairly obvious crib of William's *Declaration of his Highness William Henry, by the Grace of God Prince of Orange, Of the Reasons Inducing him to appear in Armes in the kingdom of England,* and for good reason.[24] In their own tract, the Associators presented their coup as an act, like William's, of Protestant patriotism. As typical papists, Lord Baltimore and his advisors and adherents had not only abused the Protestant English people in their charge, but also "shrouded" this "injustice and tyranny" from "the eye of observation and the hand of redress."[25] As loyal Protestant subjects, the Associators were stripping away the shroud and revealing to the new monarchs the true state of affairs in their kingdom.

The catalog of Catholic abuses that they presented was the typical world-turned-upside-down narrative of anti-popery. Rather than offering justice to his inferiors and obedience to those above him, Baltimore had usurped crown authority and interfered with Marylanders' allegiance to their monarch—the Associators emphasized in particular the demand during the fall 1688 assembly meeting that the representatives take an oath of allegiance to Lord Baltimore that did not reference the king.[26] The things that ought to have held colonists together—properly governed families, the law, loyalty to the crown, religion—were undermined or overturned. Protestant churches were converted to Catholic ones, and Protestant orphans were placed in Catholic households. The laws protecting the proprietor's own interests were "severely imposed," while Catholics could commit "outrages and murders on Protestants" and run scot free. They reiterated once again the cases of Nicholas Badcock and Christopher Rousby. The former had faced harassment by the proprietor in his attempts to report violations of the law, and the latter was "barbarously murdered upon the execution of his office by . . . an Irish papist" with close ties to the proprietor. The regime did its best to "disunite us among ourselves" and divide Maryland from Virginia, "whose friendship, vicinity, great loyalty, and sameness of religion" ought to have made that colony Maryland's strongest friend. Here was not government in the interest of the people, the Protestant religion, or the crown, but rather a dark network of "private designs."[27]

In short, a "great inundation of slavery and popery" threatened to "overwhelm their majesties' Protestant subjects." But this had been the case for some time. The event—or rather lack of event—that had prompted the Associators to take military action was the failure of the proprietary regime to proclaim William and Mary. The Associators had hoped that the new regime in England would bring an end to the "unlimited and arbitrary power" of Lord Baltimore, but he seemed determined to prevent this. His regime had actively supported James II. Catholics both lay and clerical had "vilified" William and Mary, and used "all the means . . . that art or malice can suggest, to divert the obedience and loyalty of the inhabitants from their most sacred majesties." Support for Catholic monarchs in Europe had American consequences. Baltimore's government appeared not only to support French designs against England in Europe, but also in America, so that the Associators had "great reason to think ourselves in imminent danger" from the combined forces of the French, the Jesuits, and the "Northern Indians." Here they recalled the events of 1681, when the French Jesuits had led the Iroquois "into the heart of the province," which the proprietary government tried to use to force the assembly to give them "unlimited and tyrannical" control over the militia.[28] The Associators wanted the world turned right way up again in the form of a "just and legal administration" free from "the yoke of arbitrary government, tyranny and popery."[29]

This was a powerful statement, all the more so in that it contained elements of fact, most obviously the failure to reach Maryland of proprietary orders to proclaim the new monarchs. But convincing the Associators' various audiences that this explanation of events was true was not easy. Their claims that they spoke for all Protestant Marylanders and that any problems in the colony should be laid at the door of popish tyranny were repeatedly undermined. When they summoned an assembly, many counties proved reluctant to send representatives because to do so would be an endorsement of the coup—and not to do so communicated very succinctly that the Associators' version of events should not be taken at face value, a fact the frustrated Henry Jowles was clearly aware of when he threatened to "fetch [representatives] down with the long sword" if the inhabitants "would not choose [them] freely."[30] The assembly's claims to be the "representative body" of Maryland's "most dutiful and loyal subjects" were far from universally recognized.[31] Two Protestant men arrested as "delinquents" for refusing to support the coup or the assembly wrote to the Bishop of London to offer a complete inversion of Coode's description of events. They explained that the alleged papist-Indian conspiracy was a fraud intended to serve "the designs of some prejudiced persons" who wanted not freedom from tyranny but rather power that they did not deserve. Protestant subjects were being "abused and imprisoned" in Maryland, but they were being abused by Coode and his adherents "under pretense of displacing the popish officers."[32]

Those who opposed the Associators' actions were anxious to make their opposition publicly known both in Maryland and to their king and queen. In the autumn of 1689, many counties drew up congratulatory accession addresses to William and Mary.[33] Some of these expressed wholehearted approval of the Associators and reiterated their claims to speak for all loyal Protestants. One from Kent County described how "we with the consent of all the rest of your majesty's most loyal subjects" in Maryland "in a Parliamentary way assembled have displaced all Roman Catholics whatsoever from bearing any office civil or military," and asked for the crown's approval.[34] The St. Mary's County address, of which Coode was a signatory, mentioned the "pit of destruction" that James II's continued reign would have deepened for "our religion, lives and liberties," and noted that the inhabitants remained loyal to the king and queen "in despite of all the oppositions and contradictions of the priests, papists and their adherents with which we are surrounded."[35] Another from Calvert County, signed by Jowles and others, described the recent assembly as "the late convention of the whole province."[36] The pro-Associator addresses if read alone would have offered a picture of loyal Protestant unity in the face of popish oppression.

Other addresses, however—some from the very same counties—were far less sanguine about the coup. The self-described "ancient Protestant inhabitants of Kent County" recalled the "halcyon days" under the proprietary regime, and argued that their "rights and freedoms" were "so interwoven with his lordship's prerogative" as to be a single political interest, indistinguishable from that of other English subjects. Coode and the Associators, in this view were guilty of "falsehood and unfaithfulness," had "stir[red] up unjust jealousies and dismal apprehensions," and "disposed the people to mutiny and tumult." Their coup was illegal and tyrannous, their assembly composed of "factious persons of no commendable life or conversation," and they had abused good and obedient subjects "of unquestionable loyalty and affection to the Church of England."[37] Coode and the Associators had erected the inversion of what they claimed. Well-preserved rights and liberties were ended and replaced with tyranny and arbitrary proceedings. Government by men whose station and behavior made them appropriate leaders was replaced by a "tumultuous" assembly of "factious persons." They had done this by spreading lies intended to cause division and confusion, the very opposite of good government such as Lord Baltimore's, under which truthful and equitable doings had led to unity, order, and fairness. Coode's actions were not loyalty but rather mutiny against a government duly appointed by William and Mary's predecessors, and those who opposed him were the king and queen's true obedient Protestant subjects.

Such sentiments were not limited to formal addresses. Coode had seen the power of rumor eight years before. He now found himself on the other side, obligated to quash "diverse malicious and evil reports" circulated "by persons popishly inclined and otherwise ill-affected to their majesties." Rumor had it that the assembly intended to make further arrests of delinquent or disaffected individuals and impose "great and extraordinary . . . taxes" on the inhabitants.[38] Letters expressing dismay at Coode's proceedings traveled north and south as well as east. Col. Nicholas Bayard of New York wrote to Edmund Andros in Boston that he had "received some letters from Maryland who [sic] tell me that at St. Mary's was imprisoned twenty Protestants upon pretense that they [were] Papists and traitors."[39] In the spring of 1690 Coode attempted to warn Lieutenant Governor Francis Nicholson of Virginia about the ancient conspiracy of Frenchmen, Indians, and papists, but Nicholson's reply was cool.[40] Coode faced military resistance within Maryland as well. In the summer of 1690 Richard Hill, a Quaker, fled to Virginia after a failed attempt to raise armed opposition to the Associators' government. Hill said that he "was encouraged to do so by a great number of the inhabitants" and counted Coode worse in many ways than "that raging tyrant of France," Louis XIV.[41]

In the face of such wildly differing accounts of what was happening in Maryland, the Privy Council acted cautiously. When they discussed the colony in early January 1689/90, the Associators were referred to not as the legitimate governors of the province, but simply as "those in the present administration of the government of Maryland." Coode and the others had not yet won the argument. But the words in which the council expressed their priorities were telling. They aimed for the "settlement" that would "be most for his majesty's service."[42] What was in William's interest—and, sufficiently patriotic subjects would assume, thus also the interest of England?

William's official justification for invasion had been the replacement of popish French-allied tyranny with lawful authority and the protection of Protestantism and English liberties.[43] The Associators spoke in similar language, and some of what they said was true, not least the failure of Baltimore's regime to proclaim the new monarchs. The war with France was an added incentive. William's invasion of England was part of a larger attempt to contain Louis XIV.[44] Coode and the Associators demonstrated at every opportunity that they could be counted on to be virulently anti-French.[45] They explicitly linked James II, Lord Baltimore, and the French in both Europe and America. Baltimore's council, John Coode and Kenelm Cheseldyn explained in November of 1690, had spoken ill of the new monarchs, and

> daily [broached] lying news (as they pretended sent to the priests and Jesuits from all parts) of the French king's invincible army to conquer England and the late King James his victory in Scotland and Ireland and his great party in England to join with them to subdue the rebels as they termed the Protestants, as also the great strength of the French and Canada Indians if occasion served to invade the province . . . praying publicly in their popish chapels for the Irish and French success against the English and daily drinking healths to the same wishing the arrival of that Golden Day as they termed it.[46]

This breathless statement linked every potential threat to William and his English subjects on both side of the Atlantic—the French, the Irish, James II, the Iroquois—firmly to the Catholic Lord Baltimore. Such an international constellation of enemies was not a fabrication. James II arrived in Ireland in March of 1689 in a French-supported bid to regain his lost kingdom. He failed—hence Coode and Cheseldyn's reference to "lying news"—but the English feared a French invasion even in the summer of 1690. English politics were not merely English, either in the British Isles or in America.[47] Besides, to back up Baltimore William would have needed to send military support, which was expensive, to a Catholic, which might be politically difficult.

At the same time, the Associators' opponents cast them as rebels against legitimate authority. The theme of rebels, rebellions, and coups d'état that overthrew legitimately constituted authority was a ticklish one for William's regime. The debate both within Parliament and out of doors over his new position as monarch had been long and ferocious.[48] And regardless of present circumstances, it was never wise to encourage subjects to decide for themselves when a particular regime was legitimate. Both of these points may have been behind the council's reluctance to give Coode a wholehearted endorsement. The royal letter of February 1, 1689/90, that declared William's "approbation" of the Associators' actions "authorize[d]" Coode to continue in the administration of Maryland, but only "until a full examination" of the case allowed for "a lasting settlement." No promises were made to Coode—and he was reminded to allow Lord Baltimore to continue to collect his customary proprietary revenues.[49]

Coode had several decades of imperial history on his side, however. The Associators leaned heavily on anti-popery to narrate what they had done and argue for the legitimacy of their actions. For those already critical or fearful of the proprietary regime, the language of confessional difference provided the most compelling explanation for the array of troubles the province faced. But anti-popery in the colonial world of 1690 was different from anti-popery in 1630 or 1650. The language was similar but the context had changed. Criticism of the proprietary government on the grounds that it obstructed the power of the king to govern his colonies was more meaningful now than it had been decades before. This critique was entirely consistent with anti-popery and could easily be intertwined with it—but it could also operate on its own. Even anti-popery skeptics among colonial administrators might hesitate to endorse the power and independence Lord Baltimore assumed as his right. And in January 1689/90, an incident occurred in Maryland that suggested such hesitation was well advised.

A royal tax official named John Payne was shot and killed during an attempt to board the *Susanna,* a yacht belonging to Nicholas Sewall, a son-in-law of the proprietor. Payne was linked to the Associators.[50] Those in Payne's party claimed that Sewall was using the yacht to conduct illegal trade between Maryland and Virginia in violation of the Navigation Acts, "cheat[ing] the king of his customs." When Payne identified himself as "King William's collector" and tried to board, those on the boat ordered him to "keep off . . . we do not know you nor King William." Among those on the boat was John Woodcock, a Catholic priest.[51] Those on the boat told a different story. Payne was a maverick who abused an at best doubtful commission. The business of the *Susanna* was lawful—they had tried to show Payne their paperwork—and no one had refused allegiance to the new monarchs.[52]

Several of the men aboard the *Susanna* fled to Virginia, where the authorities apprehended them. They were reluctant to hand the fugitives over to Coode, however, despite his intimations that their refusal might look like countenancing popery.[53] Nevertheless, John Coode milked Payne's death for all it was worth—the drift of royal policy seemed to be moving in his favor in early 1690, but additional evidence of popish plotting in Maryland could hardly hurt his case. He wrote twice that spring to the secretary of state, the Earl of Shrewsbury, to inform him of the murder, which he cast as perpetrated on William himself, by proxy: it had been "committed upon his majesty in his representative Mr. Payne." According to Coode, Payne had been shot without provocation and Sewall had not only deliberately ordered the murder but had freely admitted it afterward. Coode at this point in his letter took the opportunity to remind his correspondent that this was not the first time such a thing had happened in Maryland. "Mr. Christopher Rousby that preceded Mr. Payne in [the] said office of collector had the same tragical end, being barbarously murdered by one Col. George Talbot, an Irish papist and chief governor here, after Lord Baltimore had endeavored by false informations and suggestions before the king and council to deprive him of his life." Coode was exaggerating; Baltimore had merely endeavored to deprive the collector of his job.[54] But the reference was an astute move, given that it was in connection with complaints from Rousby in the early 1680s that the Lords of Trade had fined Baltimore for obstructing royal customs collection.

Payne's family petitioned for justice using much the same language as Coode to describe what had happened. According to Payne's brother William, John had been a loyal subject and participant in "the late Protestant association" who had been "murdered in the execution of his office by . . . papists."[55] The Privy Council advised the king and queen of the matter, and an April 1690 royal letter instructed Chesapeake authorities to prosecute the malefactors with all speed. The language of the royal letter no doubt proved satisfactory to Coode. Payne was described as having been murdered by "papists," and those responsible were to be "conveyed . . . into our . . . province of Maryland" for trial.[56] This was a far cry from the orders back in 1685 to try George Talbot in Virginia because, in essence, no one trusted Baltimore's regime to do it.[57]

To counter such misrepresentations of his officers and his colony, Charles Calvert and his supporters continued to argue that Coode's account of religious and political divisions in Maryland was an utter inversion of the truth. Coode and his allies were those who were abusing the king's and queen's Protestant subjects. "True sons of the Church of England" were at the mercy of "the passions and lusts of . . . factious persons."[58] Lord Baltimore also attempted to play the game of Protestant patriotism. Early in 1690, he suggested to the Privy Council that the best way to restore Maryland to him and secure its obedience to the crown would be to remove Coode and the Associators and put the Protestant Henry Coursey, to be assisted by a council of "professed Protestants and men of good repute, credit and estate," in their place. There were plenty of Protestants in Maryland loyal to Baltimore, the suggestion implied, and these were of far higher quality than those currently running the shop.[59]

In the fall and winter of 1690, Baltimore had an opportunity to argue the matter out with John Coode and Coode's fellow Associator Kenelm Cheseldyn before the Lords of Trade. His own petition to restore his rights was accompanied by documents from several Protestant inhabitants of Maryland, including Henry Coursey, whom Baltimore had earlier proposed as Protestant governor, and Richard Hill, a Quaker who had attempted to overthrow the Associators. Alongside Coursey and Hill, a man named Edward Burford was willing to swear that he had once asked Coode why he had overturned Maryland's government; Coode allegedly replied "God damn me, what I did was in prejudice or revenge to the Lord Baltimore." Coode was also said to have claimed he could "make a popish mass."[60] In response, Coode and Cheseldyn only reiterated the story they had already told. With the exception of an accusation that Richard Hill had said King William "could claim no right neither by descent, law nor justice" and thus it was "treason" to proclaim him, they offered no direct attacks on their Protestant opponents' veracity—after all, by the logic of their own arguments, what Coursey, Hill, and others said, that plenty of Protestants were loyal to Baltimore, was impossible.[61]

In the end, Lord Baltimore lost the argument. Maryland was reorganized as a royal colony.[62] The Associators had not necessarily won, however. At no point did the king or the privy council indicate that they found Coode's account of popish conspiracy in Maryland truly convincing. The part of the Associators' story that gained the most attention was the accusation that the authority of the crown was insufficiently recognized in Baltimore's colony—interference with customs collection was more to the point than ill-substantiated stories of conspiracy with Jesuits. Lionel Copley's commission for the governorship stated only that because of "great neglects and miscarriage in the government" of Maryland, the colony had "fallen into disorder and confusion."[63] Maladministration was consistent with the assumptions of anti-popery—usefully so—but this did not mean that one wanted John Coode in charge. Baltimore was at a disadvantage because although he could argue with justice that Coode's account of the confessional alignments and political troubles in Maryland was a complete and utter fabrication—that the ouster of the proprietary regime had done him, Lord Baltimore, an injury—there was no obvious positive argument for why he should be placed back in charge. Charles and his father Cecil had always drawn heavily on the argument that defense of their privileges was ipso facto defense of monarchy, but by 1690 this argument no longer worked. The relationship between crown and colonies had changed since 1632, and the Catholic Lords Baltimore had become a hindrance to the execution of the crown's power rather than a means of demonstrating it.

EPILOGUE

Much like the revolution in Britain, the consequences of regime change in Maryland took time to work out. Most people's day to day experience with local authority did not change profoundly.[1] Beyond the borders of what was now a royal colony, circumstances peculiar to the Chesapeake and the mid-Atlantic unfolded according to their own logic. Changes in the tobacco economy; the long and slow process of demographic stabilization; the complex system of conflicts and alliances that bound English colonies and their Native American allies—none of these was radically altered by the eclipse of the first proprietary regime.

The formal apparatus of provincial government did change in ways that were more than merely the substitution of one regime for another, however. Although the legal disabilities placed on Catholics were not as onerous in Maryland as they were in England, the proprietors' coreligionists were formally barred from holding office, and the Church of England was established both in law and practice by the early 1700s. There was also a shift in the relations of executive, council, and assembly. Without the former familial ties between the proprietor and the council, not to mention those between the proprietor's personal estate and the province, the relationship among two houses of the assembly and the governor functioned differently. The assembly had more power and operated with more procedural regularity—decades before, for example, the proprietor had refused requests to allow the speaker of the lower house to issue writs for by-elections; Governor Copley allowed it. This did not mean an end to friction, of course. Governor Francis Nicholson complained to the Board of Trade in 1698 that the colonists were all too "willing that his majesty should deliver them from popery and slavery, and protect them in time of war," but now that the provincial government was attempting to "[curb] them in their former atheistical, loose and vicious way of living," not to mention prevent smuggling, they did nothing but connive and complain. That said, Nicholson did not provoke the same deep hostility and suspicion that had been the lot of the proprietors and their representatives in decades past.[2]

These alterations in formal aspects of government were part of a broader shift in imperial politics in the 1690s and early 1700s. These decades did not lack for conflict. King William's War, as the colonists called it, tore through the colonial world in the 1690s and involved a vast array of participants both Native and European; neither did longstanding American conflicts over land, trade, and local power vanish with James II. But the way Anglo-American colonists described conflict and articulated discontent did change. Old narratives of popish subversion in high places were a poor match to the regimes of William and Mary or their successor, Mary's sister, Anne. In Maryland, however dissatisfied one might be with royal officials, one could no longer effectively articulate this in terms of popish conspiracy. Anti-popery was for the most part displaced outward rather than being a crucial part of the internal political conversation of the British state.

More specifically, the constellation of local troubles and constitutional gray areas that had played such an important role in creating and reinforcing the anti-popery narrative so powerful in Maryland no longer existed in the same form after 1689. The confessional antagonism between the proprietary regime and many colonists had been removed by the Revolution. The eclipse of the seventeenth-century personal monarchy of Charles II, James II, and their father and grandfather brought the resolution of questions that had torn the polity apart repeatedly over the past hundred years and which had been crucial to political conflict in Maryland. The question of whether the king was above the law, for example, was resolved in a way that made "the types of experiments in royal absolutism that the Stuarts had engaged in impossible in the future."[3] The points of confessional and constitutional dispute that had opened up a space for the Calverts in the 1630s were no longer so deeply at issue. The revolutionary settlement in Maryland also removed not only Catholic authorities, but key portions of the American version of anti-popery that had rendered them vulnerable. There was "no role for the Potomac nations" in the diplomacy of the post-proprietary regimes of the 1690s and early 1700s, for example. Colonials of those decades found their governors less troubled by diplomatic niceties as far as Indians were concerned.[4] English colonists still feared both French and Native enemies, but the conviction that local Catholic authorities were deeply involved in a conspiracy to destroy the Protestant English with the connivance of these dangerous outsiders was far less tenable in 1700 than it had been in 1680.

The Calvert family regained their charter in the 1710s but on different terms. Most significant in the context of the colony's seventeenth-century history was the decision that preceded the request to the king: Benedict Leonard Calvert, the 4th Lord Baltimore, chose to conform to the state church and convert to Anglicanism. Benedict Leonard died before he could enjoy the restored charter, and was succeeded by his teenaged son Charles. The eighteenth-century empire left no room for a Catholic proprietorship with the vast powers that Cecil and the first Charles Calvert had enjoyed. The prominent Catholic planter Charles Carroll, who had not made himself popular with the new regime in the 1690s, attempted to renegotiate the meaning of the Calverts' "Restoration" in 1715 to return greater political power to Catholics, but failed.[5] As Tim Harris has pointed out in the context of the British Isles, the Anglophone political world changed profoundly between 1680 and 1720, more so than it had between 1630 and 1680;[6] this is true in the colonial world as well. The events of 1688 made a difference.

That 1688 did make a difference points to a separate, but related issue of periodization. This book argues that the religious policy of the Catholic proprietors is key to understanding the history of seventeenth-century Maryland. But the analysis places this policy in a seventeenth-century English context rather than within the long and troubled history of religious liberty in the United States. One effect of such an argument is to cut the idea of "toleration" in Maryland off from a straightforward connection to secularization and modernity—at least if we assume an obvious connection between those two things on the one hand and between them and American national history on the other.

The Revolution of 1688 altered the terms of religious pluralism in Maryland and in the English, soon to be British, empire. As a result, it has long been a focus for debate about modernity, religion, and the state. Historians have moved far beyond the Whig interpretation of 1688 as the last battle between the forces of absolutist Catholic reaction and the modern, Protestant Anglophone tradition of limited constitutional government. There were many modernities in seventeenth-century Europe, and not all of them were tolerant or democratic. English people themselves were deeply divided over what the revolution was intended to achieve and what it meant—central terms like "liberty" or "tyranny" or "popery" had multiple meanings.[7] The Calverts may have been modern—but "modernity" is as slippery as the ecclesiastical policy of Charles I.

The tricky fit between religious pluralism and modernity, however defined, points to an as-yet unstated question of this book, which is what is the relationship between the history of colonial America and the history of the United States?[8] This is not primarily a work of American history in the latter sense. The events of the seventeenth century created the British empire of the eighteenth from which the United States emerged. Connections between the first of those things and the last exist, but they are rarely direct. The religious pluralism of seventeenth-century Maryland is best understood in the context of an early modern political system riven by conflicts sometimes quite foreign to those of the United States after 1783. This system was transformed in the late seventeenth and early eighteenth centuries in both Britain and its empire, whose eighteenth-century ideological flavor was quite distinct from that of the seventeenth century.

Finally, this book is about Maryland, but it is also about the early Chesapeake. Social and economic historians of Maryland and Virginia have described the structures and patterns that the two colonies shared.[9] In some ways, the division between Maryland and Virginia was artificial. Native Americans rarely distinguished the two as much as the English would have liked—looking south or eastward, the Potomac did not seem a particularly meaningful border. But the English persistently expressed a sense that they were very different, and the tension between similarity and difference is central to the Chesapeake's early history. From the perspective of the Virginia Company, Maryland had been carved out of Virginia, and even decades later, some Virginians were still griping about the loss. The two colonies shared an economic system, a staple crop, a social structure, and a set of overlapping regional diplomatic challenges.[10] A seventeenth-century writer, John Hammond, spoke of the two colonies as siblings.[11] Hammond's metaphor was insightful, in that the similarities between the two had a way of highlighting the differences. In the 1660s, a shared problem—the faltering price of tobacco—created a conflict of interest that demonstrated that those involved spoke in a shared political language with a long history, but also that they were more than willing to leverage that language to get the better of their perceived rivals. In the 1670s and 1680s, problems common to the region as a whole seemed primed to create a general rebellion, but the forms in which discontent was articulated and suppressed highlighted the problems of religion and allegiance that differentiated the two colonies. English colonists in Maryland spoke of going to Virginia for help in times of crisis; the proprietary regime feared that malcontents would find ready assistance across the river and that the common planters and servants of Virginia would "come over" and plunder under cover of assistance to oppressed Protestants. The vexed questions of who might politically be trusted, and how best to gauge whether one's leaders (as a Marylander put it in 1689) "espoused the Protestant interest"—whether that interest was best defined as Protestant to begin with—were pushed to the fore by the very things that Maryland and Virginia, both Chesapeake colonies, had in common.

NOTES

ABBREVIATIONS

BL : British Library

C : Chancery records, National Archives, London

CO : Colonial Office papers, National Archives, London

CSP : *Calendar of State Papers*

E : Exchequer records; E 190 are the Port Books of London, National Archives, London

HCA : Admiralty court records, National Archives, London

Md. Arch. Online : Archives of Maryland Online

RVCL : Records of the Virginia Company of London

SP : State Papers Domestic, National Archives, London

INTRODUCTION

1. Carr, Walsh, and Menard, *Robert Cole's World.*

2. On stabilization, stratification, and the eighteenth-century Maryland elite see Burnard, *Creole Gentlemen;* Russo and Russo, *Planting an Empire,* chapters 4 and 5; Breen and Innes, *"Myne Owne Ground";* Walsh, *Motives of Honor, Pleasure, and Profit,* 238–39.

3. According to the Act Concerning Religion of 1649. Before this nothing in Maryland law limited anyone's exercise of religion.

4. Scholarship on Maryland and toleration has tended to read the proprietors' policy and the 1649 Act as rendering religion a "private" affair. Russo and Russo, *Planting an Empire,* 12; Farrelly, *Papist Patriots,* 73. In the most recent detailed study of Maryland's seventeenth-century proprietors, *English and Catholic,* John Krugler sees the Calverts as "[severing] the traditional relationship between secular and religious institutions." He presents them as innovators who believed that colonies would do best "if religion remained a private matter" (6–7).

5. Games, *The Web of Empire,* and "Atlantic Constraints and Global Opportunities."

6. Kupperman, *The Jamestown Project,* chapter 1; Horn, *A Kingdom Strange,* 62–63.

7. Historians of the English Reformation have moved from an assumption that England was uncomplicatedly a "Protestant nation" by the reign of Elizabeth to a more skeptical view of the reach of Protestant "reform" and the appeal of its doctrine. The work of Christopher Haigh and Eamon Duffy is central to this historiographical turn. Haigh, *English Reformations;* Duffy, *The Stripping of the Altars.* Other scholars of Elizabethan England have argued that categories such as "Catholic," "Protestant," or "Puritan" were inherently unstable and subject to revision. The lines between Catholic

recusancy and conformity on the one hand, and Puritanism and conformity on the other, were blurry. Questier, "What Happened to Catholicism after the English Reformation?"; Walsham, *Church Papists;* Marshall, "The Naming of Protestant England"; Collinson, *The Religion of Protestants;* Collinson, "Sects and the Evolution of Puritanism." Collinson sees Puritanism as a stabilizing, establishment force, but others have noted the sometimes uncomfortably close ties between the apparently mainstream and the lunatic fringe. Lake and Como, "Orthodoxy and Its Discontents"; Freeman, "Demons, Deviance and Defiance"; Walsham, "Frantick Hacket." What it meant for the English church to be Protestant was a fraught question, and the relationship between religious authority and the state proved difficult to define. Categories such as Puritan or "papist" were as much polemical devices as descriptions of actual people. There was, however, a rough doctrinal consensus within the Elizabethan church that began to disintegrate after 1590; the disintegration was bound up in a series of interlocked debates over the crown's power, the meaning of conformity (or lack thereof), and the nature of ecclesiastical controversy. Both the highly charged meaning of religious categories and this post-1590 shift within the church informed ongoing debates over Catholics, Puritans, and conformity that shaped the politics of the 1610s through the 1630s—terms like "popularity" that shaped so much of early Stuart political discourse were rooted in the ecclesiastical controversies of the late Elizabethan regime. Thompson, "Sir Francis Knollys's Campaign"; Tyacke, *Anti-Calvinists;* Collinson, "Ecclesiastical Vitriol"; Black, "The Rhetoric of Reaction"; Lake, "Puritanism, Monarchical Republicanism and Monarchy." The ties between Elizabeth and early Stuart overseas activity and Protestantism on the one hand, and the difficulty of pinning down "Protestantism" itself on the other, suggest that there is a mutually constitutive relationship between these two things—which is one of the core contentions of this book.

8. Stern, *The Company-State,* and "Bundles of Hyphens"; Macmillan, *Sovereignty and Possession in the English New World.* On Durham and Maryland specifically, Mullin, "The Palatinate of Durham"; Thornton, "The Palatinate of Durham and the Maryland Charter."

9. Helen Dewar describes this happening in the French imperial context, in "Litigating Empire."

10. Elizabeth Mancke places this question of native rights for British colonists—which was certainly not limited to Maryland—in the context of early modern theories of *imperium* and *dominium.* "Negotiating an Empire." The Maryland charter pushed the confessional aspect of the question by placing the Catholic Lord Baltimore in opposition to such claims. See also Yirush, *Settlers, Liberty and Empire,* which uses this problem of what rights colonists brought with them to reconsider the intellectual origins of the American Revolution.

11. For a discussion of religion and loyalty under the early Stuarts, see chapters 1 and 2. Historians of early Maryland have wrestled at length with the place of anti-popery

in the colony's history. Much of the modern historiography of the early Chesapeake has its roots in the flowering of economic and social history of the region that began in the 1970s and 1980s. Historians of the Chesapeake school and its descendants acknowledge anti-popery's power, but their analyses of early Maryland are naturally centered around other concerns. This body of literature is vast; anti-Catholicism is treated in Carr and Jordan, *Maryland's Revolution;* Carr, "Sources of Political Stability and Upheaval in Seventeenth Century Maryland"; Menard, "Maryland's Time of Troubles"; Carr, Walsh, and Menard, *Robert Cole's World,* passim; Horn, *Adapting to a New World,* 54–55, 370–72. Maryland has also attracted historians interested in the experience and practice of Catholicism in America, including attempts to convert Native Americans. James Axtell connects the failure of the Jesuit mission in Maryland to several factors, including the controversy between the Jesuits and the proprietor, the perhaps characteristically English failure of the missionaries to fully immerse themselves in native culture, and the simple fact that the Piscataways did not necessarily need either the Jesuits or the English in the 1630s and 1640s. "White Legend"; see also Cushner, *Why Have You Come Here?,* chapter 9; Fogarty, "The Origins of the Mission, 1634–1773." The bulk of work on Catholicism in Maryland has focused both on local experiences of religion and Maryland's tradition of religious liberty. This scholarship tends to frame anti-Catholicism as precisely that, rather than anti-popery. Andrews, "Separation of Church and State in Maryland"; Ives, "The Catholic Contribution to Religious Liberty in Colonial America"; Moran, "Anti-Catholicism in Early Maryland Politics"; Hanley, "Church and State in the Maryland Ordinance of 1639," and *Their Rights and Liberties;* Graham, "Lord Baltimore's Pious Enterprise"; Carl N. Everstine, "Maryland's Toleration Act"; Hartsock, "America's First Experiment in Toleration"; Maloney, "Papists and Puritans in Early Maryland"; Meyers, *Common Whores, Vertuous Women, and Loveing Wives;* Krugler, "Lord Baltimore, Roman Catholics, and Toleration," "With Promise of Liberty in Religion," and *English and Catholic.* The distinction between anti-Catholicism and anti-popery is significant, as the former sets the issue up as one of toleration or liberty and its absence, which naturally puts the Calverts' political opponents in the wrong from our point of view, and the latter places it more organically in its seventeenth-century context. Krugler dismisses anti-Catholicism as simple bigotry and those who used it as acting out of "malevolence" in *English and Catholic,* 180–81, 195–97, 237–38. Carr and Jordan provide a more nuanced analysis, but treat anti-popery primarily as an unreasonable popular prejudice. *Maryland's Revolution,* 187–200. The best accounts of Maryland, Catholicism, and anti-popery tend to come from historians interested in transatlantic connections and empire. Hoffman and Mason, *Princes of Ireland, Planters of Maryland;* Stanwood, *The Empire Reformed,* 61–67, 106–14; Pestana, *The English Atlantic in an Age of Revolution,* 34–37, 152–54, and *Protestant Empire.* The Atlantic turn in general has proven fertile for discussions of the way states, empires, and claims about religion mutually constituted one another in the early modern period. See Gregerson and Juster, *Empires of God.* Why the Atlantic or imperial turn is the best framework for understanding the role of anti-popery in the colonial world is suggested by Lauren Benton's argument about legal pluralism and empire. Benton describes the "variegated" and "plural legal spaces" of European empires in the early modern period. There were few obvious legal boundaries—the idea of boundaries or borders as a way of thinking of the American legal landscape is misleading. Many places—and people—were of ambiguous legal status, and it was difficult to ascertain which rules to apply and how to apply them. How then was one to judge the legality of anyone's actions? Benton argues that the concept of treason took on particular force in this context. More often applied to elites than commoners (who could usually be dispatched with charges of mere mutiny) treason offered a way of cutting through the questions of jurisdiction (or lack thereof) posed by new spaces. Treason was a way of charging someone with acting against the interest of the crown or the state. Benton notes that treason in the English context was related to questions of religious conformity, though this is not the focus of her analysis. *A Search for Sovereignty,* 69–103; Benton and Ross, *Legal Pluralism and Empires, 1500–1850,* introduction. In the Chesapeake, and indeed the early English empire as a whole, the idea of loyalty or disloyalty was inevitably refracted through the dense confessional politics of the seventeenth century; claims about sovereignty in the New World were necessarily claims about religion. As this book argues, the process of extending authority into the world beyond Europe required articulation of what the laws were and how they operated and thus almost automatically created conflicts about loyalty, disloyalty, and confessional difference.

12. Maura Jane Farrelly rightly asks why the Protestant Charles would give a colonial charter to a Catholic, but her analysis focuses on the American Catholic experience, which makes it difficult to offer a convincing answer. *Papist Patriots,* 65–68.

13. Armitage, *The Ideological Origins of the British Empire;* Colley, *Britons,* 18–54; Pestana, *Protestant Empire.* Stanwood describes the process by which the English state and imperial administration learned how to make anti-popery work for rather than against both of them. *The Empire Reformed,* parts II–III.

14. Lauren Benton and Ken Macmillan both argue in distinct ways for a shared legal language among European powers in this period. Benton, *A Search for Sovereignty;* Macmillan, *Sovereignty and Possession in the English New World.* Macmillan stresses the Roman roots of English imperial claims; Anthony Pagden argues for shared classical antecedents but explores the significant differences that emerged between Spanish, French, and British theories of empire. Pagden, *Lords of All the World.* Patricia Seed also emphasizes the distinctions among European powers' legal approaches to empire. Seed, *Ceremonies of Possession in Europe's Conquest of the New World.*

15. Mancke, "Empire and State," and "Negotiating an Empire."

16. Greene, "Negotiated Authorities."

17. This raises a question of periodization that historians of the seventeenth-century empire have wrestled with for some time. The 1650s were crucial to the development of the administrative and ideological structures of the later empire. The 1650s and 1660s also saw the beginning of a sharp increase in migration both voluntary and involuntary that profoundly changed the American world (see chapter 5). The economic, diplomatic, social, and even epidemiological world of eastern North America was distinctly different in 1665 or 1670 from what it had been in 1640. But it was not until the later 1670s or even the 1680s that the English empire experienced its transformative political crisis. This book emphasizes these later decades because they reveal in dramatic terms the interplay between the politics of the American continent and the English Atlantic—as well as both the power and the limitations of languages of political order and subversion (see parts II and III).

18. Townsend, "Mutual Appraisals"; Hatfield, *Atlantic Virginia;* Mancall, *The Atlantic World and Virginia, 1550–1624;* Applebaum and Sweet, *Envisioning an English Empire;* for a continental perspective on the Chesapeake, see Rice, *Nature and History in the Potomac Country.* "Atlantic Maryland" is evidently less inspiring a concept than "Atlantic Virginia," although the essays in Quinn, *Early Maryland in a Wider World,* suggest there is no good reason for the deficit of scholarship on the topic. The Atlantic and continental perspectives have the added advantage of integrating the history of the early Chesapeake with the history of the sixteenth century, both in America and in Europe.

19. Bailyn and Morgan, *Strangers within the Realm.* As Nicholas Canny argues, the process of colonization itself is a British creation as well as an American one. "The Ideology of English Colonization," and "Fashioning British Worlds in the Seventeenth Century." As Alison Games has shown, however, even Ireland was influenced by other colonial models available to the English. *Web of Empire,* 256. Amy Turner Bushnell and Michael Witgen have pointed out the Eurocentrism of the Atlantic framework and the problems it poses for historians of Native America. Bushnell, "Indigenous America and the Limits of the Atlantic World, 1493–1825"; Witgen, *Infinity of Nations,* 18, 118–20.

20. David Armitage has offered several subcategories of Atlantic history from which we may choose; Alison Games has accurately described both the possibilities of the concept and the need for careful framing that forays into Atlantic history require. Armitage, "Three Concepts of Atlantic history"; Games, "Atlantic History." For additional background see Bailyn, *Atlantic History;* and Canny, "Writing Atlantic History."

21. Greene and Morgan, *Atlantic History,* part I, "New Atlantic worlds"; Steele, *The English Atlantic, 1675–1740;* Pestana, *The English Atlantic in an Age of Revolution;* Sosin, *English America and the Restoration Monarchy of Charles II;* Games, *Migration and the Origins of the English Atlantic World;* Armitage and Braddick, *The Brit-*

ish Atlantic World, 1500–1800; Rhoden, *English Atlantics Revisited.* April Hatfield has rightly pointed out that different formulations of Atlantic history will be useful for different problems. *Atlantic Virginia,* 227.

22. See chapter 10. Historians of religion in the early Chesapeake have sometimes tried to make the case for religion's significance by arguing that there was genuine piety there. Bond, *Damned Souls in a Tobacco Colony.* There may well have been, but as the work of James Bell suggests, the most compelling framework for the study of religion in the early Chesapeake is one that places it within the shifting structures—and occasionally lack thereof—of administration and empire. Bell, *Empire, Religion and Revolution in Virginia, 1607–1786,* parts II and III. Rhys Isaac's groundbreaking study of eighteenth-century Virginia suggested decades ago the need to separate religion and belief—this is as true for the seventeenth century as it is for the eighteenth. *The Transformation of Virginia, 1740–1790.*

23. The phrase belongs to a Marylander writing in support of Lord Baltimore during the 1650s. John Hammond, *Hammond versus Heamans, or, an Answer to an Audacious Pamphlet,* 1–2. See chapter 4.

1. THE EARLY CHESAPEAKE AND THE POLITICS OF JACOBEAN ENGLAND

1. Fausz, "Merging and Emerging Worlds"; Greenblatt, *Marvelous Possessions.*

2. Games, *The Web of Empire,* 117–46; Kingsbury, *The Records of the Virginia Company of London,* 1: 258.

3. On the Powhatan chiefdom and its late sixteenth- and early seventeenth-century history, see Gallivan, *The James River Chiefdoms,* and "Powhatan's Werowocomoco."

4. Rice, *Nature and History in the Potomac Country,* 13, 101; Rountree, *Pocahontas's People,* especially chapters 2–5, and *Pocahontas, Powhatan, Opechancanough;* Rountree and Davidson, *Eastern Shore Indians of Virginia and Maryland,* 84–123; Merrell, "Cultural Continuity among the Piscataway Indians of Maryland."

5. Games, *The Web of Empire,* 17–20.

6. Kupperman, *Indians and English.*

7. Smith, *A Map of Virginia* (Oxford, 1612), 34; Strachey, *The History of Travell into Virginia Britannia* (1612), 269. Spelling and punctuation have been modernized in quotations throughout.

8. Horn, *A Kingdom Strange.*

9. Ken MacMillan argues that the crown had a consistent policy of colonial oversight, backed by a similarly consistent ideological apparatus, from the beginning of the seventeenth century. Responding to scholars who he says have claimed that the increased administrative oversight of the later seventeenth century was not only innovative but also illegitimate, MacMillan argues for a well-defined "English Atlantic constitution" with legal origins that reached back into the Middle Ages and that never

gave local authorities in the colonial world much independence, even in the early 1600s. MacMillan argues for consistency of legal theory across the century; in practice, however, the sheer amount of dispute that colonial charters engendered, and the claims that subjects made about the nature of the ties that bound them to the center, suggest that whatever the crown may have thought, the situation on the ground was not so clear. The very fact that some colonial subjects clearly believed that some of the things the crown did, whether in the 1630s or in the 1680s, were violations of subjects' liberty, suggests that the ideological consistency of the crown's theory of empire is only part of the story we need to tell. MacMillan, *The Atlantic Imperial Constitution.*

10. Earlier generations of historians cast the political conflicts of late Elizabethan and early Stuart Britain in stark terms. The model was clear-cut ideological conflict over liberty and the powers of the crown. This conflict had roots that went back to Elizabeth's reign; even then, Parliament had been the scene of well-defined arguments over the big issues of the day. There was, in effect, a "high road" to the Civil Wars. Gardiner, *History of England;* Notestein, *The Winning of the Initiative by the House of Commons.* This "Whig view" of English history as a long argument between liberty and tyranny was criticized as early as the 1930s, by Herbert Butterfield in *The Whig Interpretation of History.* However, the basics of the interpretive framework, particularly the idea that the causes of the Civil Wars were long-term and that there were well-defined ideological groups with clear and deep-seated divisions between them, persisted for decades after that. This held true even for historians interested less in ideology than in material circumstances and class conflict. See, for example, Stone, *The Causes of the English Revolution 1529–1642;* Manning, *The English People and the English Revolution.* The revisionists of the 1970s and 1980s dismantled this model of both politics and religion (as well as the link between them). Historians such as Conrad Russell and John Morrill argued that ideological conflict was not the cause of the conflicts of the 1620s or 1640s. Indeed, there was no serious or sustained ideological division in Elizabethan or early Stuart England, and thus no high road to the Civil Wars. Rather than issues of governance or political theory, revisionists stressed the local, the contingent, and the material as causes of (eventual) conflict and motives for entering it. Russell, *Parliaments and English Politics, 1621–1629, The Origins of the English Civil War, The Fall of the British Monarchies,* and "Parliamentary History in Perspective, 1604–1629"; Morrill, *Cheshire 1630–1660,* and *The Revolt of the Provinces.* Others noted that Charles I was far from attempting the sort of "tyranny" his opponents claimed he was—and thus that historians looking for grand ideological conflict might have some difficulty in finding it. Kishlansky, "Tyranny Denied"; Sharpe, *The Personal Rule of Charles I;* Burgess, *Absolute Monarchy and the Stuart Constitution.* The revisionist approach had the advantage of ridding early Stuart history of a series of misleading Cold War–esque assumptions about politics and political conflict. At the same time, it raised the question of how there was a civil war at all in a society so

harmonious. The core contribution of revisionism's best critics has been a sense of how seventeenth-century people tended to parse conflict as well as an awareness of the gaps in their knowledge. Just because Charles I may not have been a closet tyrant out to subvert the liberties of the subject does not mean that many people did not claim that he was—and it certainly does not mean that historians are not obligated to work out why those people thought so. Cogswell, *The Blessed Revolution,* and "A Low Road to Extinction"; Cust, *The Forced Loan and English Politics, 1626–1628,* and *Charles I: A Political Life;* J. P. Sommerville, *Royalists and Patriots;* Milton, "Thomas Wentworth and the Political Thought of the Personal Rule." My own evidence from the colonial world suggests that political divisions in the 1630s were significant—Charles I did not see himself as undermining English law or liberties, but his actions added up to a controversially strong view of royal power that we might as well call absolutism. Sutto, "Lord Baltimore, the Society of Jesus, and Caroline Absolutism in Maryland, 1630–1645."

11. Here and throughout I use "confessional conflict" rather than "religious conflict"; these were at least as much conflicts about competing theories of order and authority as they were conflicts over belief or religious experience.

12. See chapter 2.

13. Walsh, *Motives of Honor, Pleasure, and Profit,* 28–76; Brenner, *Merchants and Revolution,* 93–100.

14. RVCL 4: 58–62, letter of Richard Frethorne to his parents.

15. CO 1/39/44, no. 19.

16. Cogswell, "In the Power of the State."

17. Brenner, *Merchants and Revolution,* 92–102.

18. Ibid., 102.

19. CO 1/39/44, encl. 11, 19; Calvert and Andrews, "Unpublished Letter of the First Lord Baltimore."

20. Craven, *Dissolution of the Virginia Company,* 67–68, 292–336.

21. Cogswell, "The People's Love," 213–14.

22. Cust, "Charles I and Popularity," 235–42; Hammer, "The Smiling Crocodile."

23. Adams, "The Protestant Cause"; Cogswell, *The Blessed Revolution,* "A Low Road to Extinction," "The Politics of Propaganda," and "Phaeton's Chariot." According to James himself, Puritans were "brain-sick and heady preachers." They and "their disciples and followers" had "contempt" for "the civil magistrate" and relied on "their own dreams and revelations" rather than the bible. Puritans turned every doctrinal question into "as great commotion as if the article of the trinity were called in controversy" and "[made] the scriptures to be ruled by their conscience, and not their conscience by the scriptures; and he that denies the least jot of their grounds . . . [is] not worthy to enjoy the benefit of breathing, much less to participate with them in the sacraments";

rather than back down from any of their arguments they would rather "king, people, law and all be trod underfoot." James I, *Political Writings,* 6. On James as Christian peacemaker, see Patterson, *King James VI and I and the Reunion of Christendom.*

24. Craven, *Dissolution of the Virginia Company,* 292–95; Rabb, *Jacobean Gentleman,* 372–81.

25. Cogswell, *The Blessed Revolution,* 148–50, 161–65.

26. Craven, *Dissolution of the Virginia Company,* 145–47.

27. Manchester Papers, 368, quoted ibid., 276–77.

28. Frederick V to the Marquis of Hamilton, 8 May 1621, Scottish RO, GD 406/1/9344, quoted in Cogswell, *The Blessed Revolution,* 84.

29. Craven, *Dissolution of the Virginia Company,* 26, 125–27.

30. CO 1/39/44, encl. 19.

31. RVCL 2: 358–59.

32. RVCL 4: 493.

33. McIlwaine, *Journals of the House of Burgesses of Virginia, 1619–1658/9,* 67.

34. Peckard, *Memoirs of the Life of Mr. Nicholas Ferrar,* 115–17. Peckard was related by marriage to the Ferrars; the *Life* was an edited version of an earlier text by Ferrar's brother John.

35. RCVL 4: 539–40.

36. John Krugler, "Our Trusty and Wellbeloved Councilor."

37. BL Sloane 1828 f. 90v–91.

38. BL Add. 36444 f. 152; Rabb, *Jacobean Gentleman,* 260–69.

39. Krugler, "The Face of a Protestant and the Heart of a Papist," 522.

40. Goodman, *The Court of King James the First,* 1: 376.

41. RVCL 3: 81, 320 (Calvert as investor); RVCL 1: 212, 253, 259, 274–75; 2: 28, 450, 458; 3: 365, 491, 459, 510 (Calvert involved in communications between crown and company); and 4: 494 (Calvert on 1624 commission).

42. BL Add. 48166, f. 151v–152. See also f. 154. James saw himself as a force for moderation in religion and made a point of tolerating both "moderate" nonconformity—though his definition of "moderate" had its limits—and some Catholics. Fincham and Lake, "The Ecclesiastical Policy of James I."

43. BL Ad. 48166, f. 170.

44. Scott, *Vox populi.*

45. BL Sloane 3662, f. 24v.

46. Ibid.

47. CO 1/4/59.

48. See chapter 2.

49. Questier, *Catholicism and Community in Early Modern England,* 342–44. Controversies like that over the oath were part of a long history of Catholics articulat-

ing (sometimes conflicting) versions of Englishness or loyalty in response to a regime that often seemed bent on writing them out of such categories. Highley, *Catholics Writing the Nation in Early Modern Britain and Ireland.*

50. CO 1/5/40.

51. Games, *The Web of Empire,* 152; Stern, "Bundles of Hyphens," 32–37 (corporate government).

52. Benton, *A Search for Sovereignty,* 33, 40–103.

53. Kupperman, *The Jamestown Project,* 257–59.

54. Papenfuse, Md. Arch. Online 1: 7–24.

55. Cust, *Charles I,* 114–21.

2. THE PERSONAL RULE OF LORD BALTIMORE

1. For the politics of the early and middle 1620s, particularly England's entry into the war in Europe, see Cogswell, *The Blessed Revolution;* Adams, "The Protestant Cause."

2. Cogswell, "A Low Road to Extinction."

3. Cogswell, "The Politics of Propaganda"; Richard Cust, "Charles I, the Privy Council, and the Parliament of 1628," and *The Forced Loan and English Politics, 1626–1628.*

4. Millstone, "Evil Counsel."

5. Cust, *Charles I,* chapters 2 and 3.

6. On Charles I and the law, see Burgess, *Absolute Monarchy and the Stuart Constitution,* and *The Politics of the Ancient Constitution;* Cromartie, "The Constitutionalist Revolution," and *The Constitutionalist Revolution;* Milton, "Thomas Wentworth and the Political Thought of the Personal Rule"; Pawlisch, *Sir John Davies and the Conquest of Ireland;* Pocock, *The Ancient Constitution and the Feudal Law;* Sharpe and Brooks, "Debate"; J. P. Sommerville, *Royalists and Patriots.*

7. Cust, *Charles I,* 148–71; Adamson, "Chivalry and Political Culture in Caroline England," 174–75 (quotation); Smutts, *Court Culture and the Origins of a Royalist Tradition in Early Stuart England,* 183–283.

8. Sharpe, *The Personal Rule of Charles I,* 217–35.

9. The scholarship on early modern English Catholicism is bound up in debates about the Reformation. John Bossy posited the creation of a distinctly post-Reformation English Catholicism in the later part of Elizabeth's reign. Bossy, "The Character of Elizabethan Catholicism," and *The English Catholic Community, 1570–1850.* Revisionist historians of the Reformation argued for the continuity of Elizabethan Catholicism with the pre-Reformation past. See for example Haigh, "From Monopoly to Minority," and "The Continuity of Catholicism in the English Reformation." As Alexandra Walsham and Michael Questier have pointed out, the definition of "Catholic" itself was often subject to dispute—the meaning of recusancy or occa-

sional conformity shifted with time, often dramatically so. Walsham, *Church Papists;* Questier, "Conformity, Catholicism and the Law."

10. Lake and Questier, "Agency, Appropriation and Rhetoric under the Gallows." This contest over the meaning of Catholicism—what specific actions or positions meant in terms of one's relation to the state—is the most productive way to understand early Stuart Catholicism too in both the British and Atlantic contexts.

11. Sutto, "Lord Baltimore, the Society of Jesus, and Caroline Absolutism in Maryland, 1630–1645."

12. On anti-popery in seventeenth-century England and Britain, see Clifton, "Fear of Popery," and "Popular Fear of Catholics"; Dolan, *Whores of Babylon;* Shell, *Catholics, Controversy and the English Literary Imagination, 1558–1660* (which highlights many literary tropes of anti-popery that I have found useful in discussing political pamphlets); Haley, "'No popery' in the Reign of Charles II"; Hibbard, *Charles I and the Popish Plot;* Kenyon, *The Popish Plot;* Lake, "Anti-Popery"; Miller, *Popery and Politics in England, 1660–1688;* Scott, "England's Troubles"; Sowerby, "Opposition to Anti-Popery in Restoration England." It is worth emphasizing that the papists of anti-popery narratives did not always map perfectly onto the Catholic neighbors of Protestant English people. Many English Protestants genuinely feared and suspected Catholics—but they could also use the language of anti-popery selectively, inconsistently, or cynically.

The literature on anti-Catholicism in Maryland is less developed. See Carr and Jordan, *Maryland's Revolution of Government, 1689–1692,* 187–88, 194, 226–28; Graham, "Popish Plots"; Krugler, *English and Catholic;* Riordan, *The Plundering Time.* While Graham's article makes the important point that anti-popery provided a framework for integrating a broad variety of grievances in the later seventeenth century, the material on anti-Catholicism in Maryland tends on average to place anti-popery in the context of toleration or lack thereof rather than in the context of early modern claims about order, politics, and the law.

13. On the importance of inversion and binary opposition in early modern thought, see Clark, *Thinking with Demons,* part I. Peter Lake emphasizes that anti-popery was "at least in England, the most obvious and important example of that process of binary opposition, inversion, or the argument from contraries, which . . . played so central a part in both the learned and popular culture of early modern Europe." Lake, "Anti-Popery," 73.

14. Kupperman, *The Jamestown Project,* 12–42.

15. Purchas, *Purchas his pilgrimage,* 631.

16. Allen, *A brief history of the glorious martyrdom of 12 reverend priests,* 41. Allen was likely referring to Humphrey Gilbert's Newfoundland project, which involved a number of Catholic gentlemen. See Quinn, *The Voyages and Colonizing Enterprises of Sir Humphrey Gilbert,* 71–76. In 1646, one writer suggested that English Catholics

either be given toleration or free leave to migrate to Maryland. Anon., *A moderate and safe expedient.* The prospect of Maryland as a dumping ground for Irish Catholics was floated again in the 1650s. SP 25/93/33; SP 25/77, pp. 581–82.

17. Tyacke, *Anti-Calvinists,* and "The Rise of Arminianism Reconsidered"; Ferrell, *Government by Polemic.*

18. Cust, *The Forced Loan and English Politics, 1626–1628,* "Charles I and a Draft Declaration for the Parliament of 1628," "Charles I, the Privy Council, and the Parliament of 1628"; and "Charles I and Popularity"; Tyacke, *Anti-Calvinists;* Lake, "Calvinism and the English Church, 1570–1635." Nicholas Tyacke has recently suggested that Charles's suspicion that Puritans were out to get him may not have been so misplaced after all. Tyacke, "The Puritan Paradigm of English Politics, 1558–1642," esp. 542–50.

19. Fincham and Lake, "Popularity, Prelacy and Puritanism in the 1630s"; Fincham, "Prelacy and Politics," and "The Restoration of the Altars in the 1630s"; Lake, "The Laudian Style"; Milton, *Catholic and Reformed.*

20. Davies, *The Caroline Captivity of the Church,* 206.

21. Hibbard, *Charles I and the Popish Plot,* chapters 2–4; Cust, *Charles I,* 64–82, 190–96; Lake, "The Collection of Ship Money in Cheshire"; Fincham, "The Judges' Decision on Ship Money in February 1637."

22. Cust, *Charles I,* 146.

23. Hibbard, *Charles I and the Popish Plot,* 44.

24. PRO 31/9/17B [transcripts of Panzani correspondence], 22 August 1635 (Old Style), 19 August 1635, 25 August 1635, 9 September 1635, 23 September 1635.

25. Cust, *The Forced Loan and English Politics, 1626–1628,* 248–49.

26. Charles I, *Eikon Basilike,* 89.

27. BL Sloane 3662, f. 25r.

28. Calvert and Andrews, "Unpublished Letter of the First Lord Baltimore."

29. CO 1/6/84; Wentworth, *The Earl of Strafford's Letters and Dispatches,* 178.

30. CO 1/39/44, encl. 19.

31. Ibid., encl. 10. See also Yong, "Extract of a Letter of Captain Thomas Yong to Sir Toby Matthew, 1634." The Spanish had explored the Chesapeake in the mid-1500s. They engaged in trade and around 1560 kidnapped a young man whom they called Don Luís and who was intended to serve as guide and interpreter for a projected Jesuit mission. When the Spanish returned to the area with Don Luís in 1570, the young man escaped and returned to lead an attack on the Spanish that left only one person, a boy, alive. Rountree and Turner, "On the Fringe of the Southeast." The people living in the region had as good reason to beware of the Spanish as they did of the English.

32. CO 1/6/58.

33. Thornton, "The Thrusting out of Governor Harvey," 14–23. See also Kukla, *Political Institutions in Virginia, 1619–1660,* chapters 1–3.

34. Wentworth, *The Earl of Strafford's Letters and Dispatches,* 178; CO 1/6/84.

35. *The Calvert Papers* [MdHS edition], 132–34.

36. Andrew White, *Relation of the Succesful Beginnings of the Lord Baltemore's Plantation in Mary-Land,* 3, 7, and *Voyage to Maryland/Relatio Itineris in Marilandiam,* 34, 35, 40, 68–69, 74.

37. White, *Voyage to Maryland/Relatio Itineris,* 34, 66.

38. White, *Relation of the Succesful Beginnings of the Lord Baltemore's Plantation in Mary-Land,* 2.

39. Cust, *Charles I,* 195.

40. Sutto, "Lord Baltimore, the Society of Jesus, and Caroline Absolutism in Maryland, 1630–1645."

41. Craven, *Dissolution of the Virginia Company,* 326–29.

42. Sir John Harvey renewed Claiborne's commission in early March 1631/2. CO 1/39/44, encls. 3, 6, 7, 8. Claiborne was also engaged in trade with the Dutch. O'Callaghan, *Documents Relative to the Colonial History of the State of New York,* 3: 14–16.

43. Rice, *Nature and History in the Potomac Country,* 92–107; Fausz, "Merging and Emerging Worlds," 58–70.

44. *The Calvert Papers* [MdHS edition], 134, 135–36.

45. CO 1/39/44, encl. 13; C 24/690/14, deposition of Cuthbert Fenwick; Papenfuse, Md. Arch. Online 3: 57–59, and 1: 17–18; CO 1/8/64, and encl. 1.

46. Craven, *Dissolution of the Virginia Company,* 323–29.

47. In 1631/32 the Virginia House of Burgesses petitioned the Privy Council to assure them that "the limits of our plantation, both to the northward and the southward may be preserved against all . . . undertakers" and that they might be given "confirmation of all our lands." McIlwaine, *Journals of the House of Burgesses of Virginia, 1619–1658/9,* 55.

48. Thornton, "The Thrusting out of Governor Harvey," 11–23. See also Kukla, *Political Institutions in Virginia, 1619–1660,* 81–99.

49. CO 1/8/37.

50. *The Calvert Papers* [MdHS edition], 132–34.

51. CO 1/8/25.

52. CO 1/8/26.

53. CO 1/39/44, encl. 13; CO 24/690/14, deposition of Cuthbert Fenwick; Papenfuse, Md. Arch. Online 3: 57–59, and 1: 17–18.

54. CO 1/8/64, and encl. 1.

55. CO 1/39/44 and encls.

56. CO 1/6/76; CO 1/9/87.

57. CO 1/39/44, encl. 11.

58. CO 1/8/27.

59. CO 1/9/120; CO 1/39/44, encl. 16.

60. Pawlisch, *Sir John Davies and the Conquest of Ireland.*

61. CO 1/8/25; CO 1/8/73.

62. CO 1/8/37.

63. CO 1/8/73.

64. CO 1/8/65.

65. CO 1/9/7.

66. CO 1/8/69; CO 1/8/64

67. CO 1/8/84; CO 1/8/85.

68. CO 1/9/42; CO 1/9/45. Charles would soon need the money. Baltimore floated the request to Windebank in February and March 1636/37. The long-simmering resentment over the imposition of the Prayer Book in Scotland came to a head the following summer, leading directly to the war that would require Charles, whether he liked it or not, to summon Parliament to provide funds.

3. ANARCHY AND ALLEGIANCE

1. John Krugler dismisses Ingle as greedy and bigoted, and ascribes his behavior largely to malice against the Calverts and their colony. David Jordan accurately describes the political and confessional tensions laid open by Ingle's actions, although his division of participants into rebels on one hand, and the legitimate government, on the other, is perhaps an oversimplification. The best overview of Ingle's adventures is that of Carla Pestana, who notes in particular the divisions among the governing circle as to how to face the conflict in Britain, as well as the social tensions in the colony that made disorder difficult to contain once initiated. Krugler, *English and Catholic,* 180–82; Jordan, *Foundations of Representative Government in Maryland, 1632–1715,* 47–49; Pestana, *The English Atlantic in an Age of Revolution,* 34–37; see also Riordan, *The Plundering Time;* Fausz, "Merging and Emerging Worlds," 78–79; Menard, "Maryland's Time of Troubles"; Hatfield, *Atlantic Virginia,* 76–77.

2. The mixture of confessional language and opportunistic behavior make Ingle's raid on Maryland difficult to categorize. As Pestana's account suggests, the event is easier to explain if Ingle's own motives are set aside and the conflict is connected to the dilemmas of allegiance that England's civil wars presented to New World colonists. Historians of the British civil wars have wrestled with the problem of how to define a "war of religion." For an overview of that scholarship, see Glenn Burgess, "Introduction." The challenge in wrestling with this question has often been the issue of motives—was religion primarily a way of articulating positions that were not primarily theological or confessional in nature, or did contemporaries understand the conflict as being "about" religion first and foremost? "Religion" is a more convoluted concept than it first appears. Richard Ingle's motives weren't religious in the sense of a disinterested campaign

to extirpate popery for the greater glory of Protestantism, but both the raid itself and its consequences for both Ingle and Lord Baltimore could only have taken the shape they did in a political environment in which problems of allegiance and loyalty were articulated so consistently in confessional terms.

3. The Jesuit presence in Maryland was limited. The mission suffered from chronic shortages of funds as well as the alarming propensity of English Jesuits and lay brothers to succumb to the punishing Chesapeake disease environment. English Jesuits also proved less adept than their French counterparts at learning local languages and making places for themselves in the Native communities they wished to convert. The proprietor's hostility to their legal claims no doubt played a role as well. Their signal success, the conversion of the Piscataway leader Kittamaquund and his family in 1640, complete with formal acknowledgment and ceremonial participation by Maryland's political elite, was a typical early American scene of alliance making via religious conversion. The baptismal names of Kittamaquund and his wife were Charles and Maria, which might suggest a subordinate echo of the English king and queen. Yet the ceremony's usefulness for the English in terms of asserting power over the Piscataways was limited. The mission collapsed in the early 1640s, when Kittamaquund's death, Susquehannock raids, and the transatlantic upheavals of the English Civil Wars forced the Jesuits to abandon it. The Jesuits themselves remained in the colony ministering to English Catholics, although the Protestant perception of their numbers and influence usually far outstripped reality. In 1638, hope was nevertheless still very much alive for future expansion, missionary success among the Native Americans, and perhaps a reconciliation with a proprietor about ecclesiastical privileges. Axtell, "White Legend"; Merrell, "Cultural Continuity among the Piscataway Indians of Colonial Maryland"; Hughes, *History of the Society of Jesus in North America,* Documents vol. 1, part 1, 112–19.

4. Papenfuse, Md. Arch. Online 4: 35–39

5. Ibid.

6. See part III.

7. Papenfuse, Md. Arch. Online 4: 35–39.

8. In the seventeenth century, the year began on 25 March instead of 1 January. The day that we would record as 30 January 1649, for example, would have been written as 30 January 1648. In this book, dates that fall between 1 January and 25 March are written with both years if there is any danger of confusion, e.g., 30 January 1648/9.

9. Papenfuse, Md. Arch. Online 1: 119.

10. The word *Protestant* had a surprisingly fraught history in late Tudor and early Stuart England. Marshall, "The Naming of Protestant England."

11. George Calvert had apparently startled some European Catholic officials in the late 1620s, when he permitted something very similar in his Newfoundland colony—

Catholic masses and Protestant services shared a building. Scritture Originali Referti nei Congressi, Archives of the Congregazione per l'Evangelizzazione dei Popoli (Congregatio de Propaganda Fide), Rome, 1: vol. 259, f. 2v.

12. Graham, "Meetinghouse and Chapel," 258.

13. Krugler and Riordan, "Scandalous and Offensive to the Government," 194–95.

14. The purchase was negotiated between November 1641 and July 1643. Papenfuse, Md. Arch. Online 3: 135–36.

15. Ibid. 135–37. Baltimore seems at this point still to have planned to go to Maryland. In the end, he never did.

16. Or Baltimore may simply have lacked the money. Riordan, *The Plundering Time,* 122.

17. HCA 13/60/K, Cornwaleys v. Ingle, deposition of John Lewgar, 6 August 1645.

18. Papenfuse, Md. Arch. Online 4: 233–34, 237–39.

19. HCA 13/60/H, Ingle v. Looking Glass, deposition of Richard Garrett; SP 16/508, ff. 197v–198v, deposition of William Edrupp; SP 16/508, ff. 151v–153v, deposition of John Durford; SP 16/508, ff. 187r–188v, deposition of Thomas Evans[?].

20. HCA 13/60/H, Ingle v. Looking Glass and SP 16/508 ff. 209v–210r, deposition of Thomas Green; SP 16/508, ff. 193v–194v, deposition of Thomas Evans; SP 16/508, ff. 197v–198v, deposition of William Edrupp; SP 16/508, ff. 151v–153v, deposition of John Durford; C 24/690/14, Cornwaleys v. Ingle, deposition of Cuthbert Fenwick.

21. Papenfuse, Md. Arch. Online 4: 232, 234; C 2/ChasI/C23/15; HCA 13/60/H, Ingle v. Looking Glass, deposition of Richard Garrett; HCA 13/60/H, Ingle v. Looking Glass, and SP 16/508, 210v–211r, depositions of Thomas Green; SP 16/508, f. 188v, deposition of Thomas Evans; SP 16/508, f. 199r, deposition of William Edrupp; HCA 13/119, Cornwaleys v. Ingle, answer of Richard Ingle, 31 July 1645; HCA 13/60/K, Copley v. Ingle, deposition of Thomas Cornwaleys, 8 August 1645; HCA 13/60/K, Copley v. Ingle, deposition of John Lewgar, 6 August 1645.

22. C 24/690/D, Cornwaleys v. Ingle, depositions of John Lewgar and Cuthbert Fenwick. E 190/43/6, f. 150r, show Ingle's ship, the *Richard and Anne,* departing London for Maryland in October of 1640 with Irish servants and various goods for Leonard Calvert; HCA 13/60/L, Cornwaleys v. Ingle, deposition of Richard Ingle, 21 August 1645; Baltimore to Leonard Calvert, Nov. 21–23, 1642, in *The Calvert Papers* [MdHS edition], 211–21.

23. Riordan, *The Plundering Time.*

24. HCA 13/60/H, Ingle v. Looking Glass, deposition of Thomas Green, 10 July 1645.

25. SP 16/508, f. 154rv, deposition of John Durford; SP 16/508, ff. 189r–190r, deposition of Thomas Evans.

26. SP 16/508, f. 178v–181r, deposition of Robert Rawlins.

27. Papenfuse, Md. Arch. Online 3: 92–93.

28. Ibid. 4: 458–59.

29. Ibid. 3: 161.

30. For a detailed overview, see Riordan, *The Plundering Time.*

31. HCA 13/60/K, Ingle v. Looking Glass, deposition of Thomas Green, 10 July 1645.

32. HCA 13/60/H, Ingle v. Looking Glass, deposition of Thomas Green, 10 July 1645; SP 16/508, f. 154rv, deposition of John Durford; SP 16/508, ff. 189r–190r, deposition of Thomas Evans; SP 16/508, f. 178v–181r, deposition of Robert Rawlins.

33. HCA 13/119, Cornwaleys v. Ingle, answer of Richard Ingle, 31 July 1645; HCA 13/119, Copley v. Ingle, answer of Richard Ingle, 29 September 1645; SP 16/508, ff. 54rv.

34. HCA 13/60/H, Ingle v. Looking Glass, deposition of Pascho Panton, 16 July 1645; SP 16/508, f. 146v, deposition of Robert Popley.

35. HCA 13/60/H, Ingle v. Looking Glass, deposition of Thomas Green, 10 July 1645; SP 16/508, f. 227rv, deposition of Richard Garrett; SP 16/508, ff. 146v–47r, deposition of Robert Ropely; HCA 13/60/H, Ingle v. Looking Glass, deposition of Pascho Panton, 16 July 1645

36. Berkeley, *The Papers of Sir William Berkeley, 1605–1677,* 63.

37. C 24/690/13, Cornwaleys v. Ingle, deposition of John Lewgar, 26 September 1645; HCA 13/119, Copley v. Ingle, answer of Richard Ingle, 29 September 1645.

38. Papenfuse, Md. Arch. Online 4: 279.

39. Anti-popery took on a particularly American cast by the end of the seventeenth century. See part III.

40. Papenfuse, Md. Arch. Online 3: 167–71.

41. Gentles, *The English Revolution and the Wars in the Three Kingdoms, 1638–1652,* 270. There were a series of "secret letter" revelations about Charles in the 1640s. See *The Key to the King's Cabinet-Counsell* (London, 1644), and *The Irish Cabinet: Or, His Majesty's Secret Papers, for Establishing the Papal Clergy in Ireland, with Other Matters of High Concernment* (London, 1646). Lord Baltimore got his own "popish cabinet" narrative from Maryland in 1676. Papenfuse, Md. Arch. Online 5: 134–52.

42. Papenfuse, Md. Arch. Online 3: 164–66.

43. Ibid. 181; Brenner, *Merchants and Revolution,* 167–68.

44. Papenfuse, Md. Arch. Online 3: 179–81.

45. SP 25/63, p. 389; SP 25/123, p. 184; SP 25/123, pp. 194–96; SP 25/123, pp. 204, 210, 220, 221, 228, 232.

46. Papenfuse, Md. Arch. Online 3: 201–13.

47. Ibid. 231, 241–42, 243–44; Vol. 1, 313–14, 321.

48. Papenfuse, Md. Arch. Online 1: 292. The only writer in the 1650s to specify the precise religious coloring of the Anne Arundel settlers was John Hammond, who was far from sympathetic to them. He called them "a certain people congregated into

a church, calling themselves Independents." Hammond, *Leah and Rachel, or, the Two Fruitful Sisters Virginia and Mary-Land,* 21.

49. Baltimore's policy succeeded as far as Charles Stuart's son was concerned. After his father's death in 1649, Charles II noted the ease with which Baltimore's loyalties shifted to the Commonwealth and the presence of "schismatics and sectaries" in his colony and granted the governorship of Maryland to William Davenant. Davenant never made it to Maryland—he was captured before he left the English Channel and imprisoned on the Isle of Wight. Cecil Calvert, *The Lord Baltimore's Case Concerning the Province of Maryland, Adjoining to Virginia in America,* 13–20; Campbell, "Notes on D'Avenant's Life."

50. SP 25/63, p. 389; SP 25/123, pp. 184, 194–96, 204, 210, 214, 219, 220, 221, 228, 232, 235, 236, 239, 245, 248, 251, 268, 287, 291, 344; SP 25/64, p.67; SP 25/64, p. 161; SP 25/66, p. 103; Papenfuse, Md. Arch. Online 3: 259.

51. For a general overview of the 1640s and 1650s, see Worden, *The English Civil Wars, 1640–1660;* Gentles, *The English Revolution and the Wars in the Three Kingdoms, 1638–1652;* Kishlansky, *A Monarchy Transformed,* chapters 6 and 7.

4. PAMPHLETS, POLEMIC, AND THE REVOLUTIONARY STATE

1. Pestana, *The English Atlantic in an Age of Revolution*; Games, *The Web of Empire,* 290–93; Stephen Saunders Webb makes a similar point in more exaggerated terms in *The Governors-General.*

2. Pestana notes, correctly, that such plans to "make the state church a central pillar of the British Atlantic" in the later seventeenth century were "doomed." *Protestant Empire,* 8, 99. Part of the process by which early modern states extended their authority both in Europe and in their empires involved grants or delegations of privileges to localities; this created rights or privileges that had not previously existed and with which the state would later have to reckon. Greene, "Negotiated Authorities."

3. Morrill, "Cromwell, Parliament, Ireland and a Commonwealth in Crisis"; Worden, *The Rump Parliament, 1648–1653,* 317–84; Gentles, *The New Model Army in England, Ireland and Scotland, 1645–1653,* 276–85; Kishlansky, *A Monarchy Transformed,* 204–6; Woolrych, *Commonwealth to Protectorate,* 25–102; Pincus, *Protestantism and Patriotism,* 114–18. Sean Kelsey has noted that news of the Rump's dissolution traveled "even as far afield as the American colonies." Kelsey, *Inventing a Republic,* 184.

4. The process of extending English authority throughout the British Isles and abroad was interwoven with misgivings about English character, hopes and fears about God's relationship with England, and arguments about how the English state worked or ought to work—just as Elizabethan and Jacobean explorations had been decades earlier. Carla Pestana explores the questions about English character and God's attitude toward its new regime that the failure of Cromwell's Western Design raised. Pestana, "English Character and the Fiasco of the Western Design." David Armitage

has discussed the influence of 1650s conquests on English republican thought—empires and republics were not incompatible. Armitage, "The Cromwellian Protectorate and the Languages of Empire."

5. SP 25/123, pp. 184, 194–96; Brenner, *Merchants and Revolution,* 123, 147, 588–89; Cecil Calvert, *The Lord Baltimore's Case Concerning the Province of Maryland, Adjoining to Virginia in America,* 8; CO 1/39/44, encl. 19.

6. SP 25/123, p. 213; Brenner, *Merchants and Revolution,* 131–33.

7. Papenfuse, Md. Arch. Online 3: 264–66.

8. Ibid. 1: 209, 220 221, 224, 228–29, 239.

9. Ibid. 3: 219–21.

10. Ibid. 1: 238–44.

11. Ibid. 262–72. His controversy with the Society of Jesus and the political statement that his handling of it made caused Lord Baltimore to speak of the Jesuits in much the same terms as some of his contemporaries used for Puritans. Conflating papists and protestant nonconformists in opposition to loyal Protestants was a staple move for some conforming Protestants (and, later in the century, many Tories) who wished to affirm their loyalty to the king. Baltimore's own Catholicism added a twist to it, but that was part of the point. Throughout the century, the twists and turns of politics often lent an element of truth to such suggestions. James II did woo dissenters in support of a policy of toleration aimed primarily at Catholics; at several points during her husband's reign, the Catholic Henrietta Maria found common cause with Puritans. On Henrietta Maria and Puritans, see Smutts, "Religion, European Politics and Henrietta Maria's Circle, 1625–41," and "The Puritan Followers of Henrietta Maria."

12. Papenfuse, Md. Arch. Online, 1: 259–72.

13. Cecil Calvert, *The Lord Baltimore's Case,* 8–9.

14. Ibid., 9–10.

15. CO 1/11/65.

16. Calvert, *The Lord Baltimore's Case,* 2–4.

17. Ibid., 10.

18. Ibid., 11.

19. Ibid., 7.

20. Papenfuse, Md. Arch. Online 3: 300.

21. Ibid., 259; 1: 327–29. Hammond, *Leah and Rachel or, the Two Fruitful Sisters Virginia and Mary-Land,* 21.

22. See above, n.3.

23. Strong, *Babylon's Fall in Maryland,* 1–4.

24. Roger Heaman, *An Additional Brief Narrative of a Late Bloody Design,* 7. Heaman appears alternately as Heaman and Heamans. I have used the version of his name that appears in the pamphlet attributed to him.

25. [Anon], *Virginia and Maryland, or, the Lord Baltamore's Printed Case, Uncased and Answered,* 17; Heaman, *An Additional Brief Narrative,* 11.

26. Collinson, "Ecclesiastical Vitriol."

27. Hammond, *Hammond Versus Heamans,* 1–2.

28. Langford, *A Just and Cleer Refutation of a False and Scandalous Pamphlet,* 4–5.

29. Strong, *Babylon's Fall in Maryland,* 8.

30. Ibid., 1.

31. On the prerogative and the common law, see Burgess, *The Politics of the Ancient Constitution;* Cromartie, "The Constitutionalist Revolution"; Sharpe and Brooks, "Debate."

32. Burgess, *The Politics of the Ancient Constitution,* 212–31, quote on 230.

33. Anon., *Virginia and Maryland, or, the Lord Baltamore's Printed Case, Uncased and Answered,* 9–10.

34. This point when applied to Maryland implies that the "English nation" was not bound by the geographic limits of England. In general, Lord Baltimore's claims tended to lean more heavily on a distinction between England and "foreign parts," while those of his opponents often conflated the two: what was illegitimate in England must also be so in English colonies. Those versed in the niceties of dominium and imperium might argue that Baltimore's opponents misconstrued the nature of their own polity, but the fact of the difference itself is more interesting: it was not obvious at the time that colonies must necessarily be so legally distinct.

35. Anon., *Virginia and Maryland, or, the Lord Baltamore's Printed Case, Uncased and Answered,* 10–13.

36. Ibid., 13.

37. Ibid., 18.

38. Heaman, *An Additional Brief Narrative,* 8–11.

39. Langford, *A Just and Cleer Refutation of a False and Scandalous Pamphlet,* 3, 5.

40. Hammond, *Leah and Rachel,* 22.

41. Langford, *A Just and Cleer Refutation of a False and Scandalous Pamphlet,* 3–4.

42. Ibid., 5.

43. Ibid.

44. Papenfuse, Md. Arch. Online 3: 332–40; Vol. 1, 369–71.

45. Fendall's confusion is understandable—even for those on the scene in England, it was far from clear what direction things would take. Mayers, *1659.*

46. Sutto, "Built upon Smoke," chapter 8.

47. O'Callaghan, *Documents Relative to the Colonial History of the State of New York,* 2:118.

5. CONFLICTS OF INTEREST

1. Harris, *Restoration;* Hutton, *The Restoration*; Miller, *Popery and Politics in England, 1660–1688,* and *James II;* Scott, "England's Troubles," *Algernon Sidney and the Restoration Crisis, 1677–1683,* and *England's Troubles,* 161–204. Signal reorientations of the historiography of later Stuart England in the past several decades have been a greater emphasis on elements of continuity with the prewar period as well as increased emphasis on the connections between controversies over political order and controversies over religious conformity, uniformity, and dissent. On the related concerns of religion and the state in the decades after 1660, see Knights, "'Meer Religion' and the 'Church-State' of Restoration England," and the essays in Harris, Seaward, and Goldie, *The Politics of Religion in Restoration England.*

2. Walsh shows that the worst period of economic stagnation for the seventeenth-century tobacco economy began around 1680. *Motives of Honor, Pleasure, and Profit,* chapters 2–3. Even before this, however, planters were concerned about the long-term fall in prices. For Chesapeake tobacco prices over the course of the 1600s and early 1700s, see McCusker and Menard, *The Economy of British America, 1607–1789,* chapter 6.

3. This assumption is crucial to understanding the vexed issue of crown finance under James I and Charles I, which played directly into the tensions of the 1620s and 1630s. Like the question of how to manage the tobacco economy, it was a financial question that quickly became a political problem in the broadest possible sense of that term. James I and Charles I were both chronically short of money, in part because their revenues were inadequate for the growing expenses of an early modern court and government, and in part because their subjects, as represented in Parliament, were reluctant to vote supplementary taxation on a regular basis or to change the revenue structure. Their resistance was partly a reluctance to pay taxes, but it also derived from a perception that the problem was not the crown's increasing expenses, or inflation, but rather that the king was wasting money or could not be trusted to spend it properly. Thus, both James and Charles faced a problem that was a question simultaneously of the nuts and bolts of revenue and expense and also of perception and expectation. Crown finance ultimately became a constitutional issue as well. By the late 1620s, much ink and breath had been expended over the extent of Parliament's obligation to vote subsidies for the crown, and whether MPs were allowed to specify (or even discuss) how the money they voted the crown would be used. Questions of finance quickly became questions of trust—were there *arcana imperii,* secrets of state, that required Parliament to finance the crown without information about where that money might go? When the king's subjects did not do as he wished, who or what was at work? When the king resisted the advice of his most loyal subjects, what was the explanation? Peck, "Problems in Jacobean Administration," "Corruption at the Court of James I,"

and *Court Patronage and Corruption in Early Stuart England;* Croft, "A Collection of Several Speeches and Treatises of the Late Treasurer Cecil"; Cuddy, "Reinventing a Monarchy"; Ashton, *The Crown and the Money Market, 1603–1640;* Smith, "Crown, Parliament and Finance"; Thrush, "The Personal Rule of James I."

4. "Interest" later became a key term for early modern theorists of political economy, and it has been the subject of analysis by historians of capitalism, political economy, and related topics. However, although the term eventually came to denote economic interests specifically, it referred during our period to "the totality of human aspirations," both financial and otherwise, and "denoted an element of reflection and calculation with respect to the manner in which those aspirations were to be pursued." Hirschman, *The Passions and the Interests,* 32, 36–37.

5. Morgan, *American Slavery, American Freedom,* 134–35; Walsh, *Motives of Honor, Pleasure, and Profit,* 99–101, 183–85.

6. CO 1/16/63, 64, 65; Sainsbury, *Calendar of State Papers, Colonial Series, America and West Indies, 1661–1668,* 90; Papenfuse, Md. Arch. Online 3: 459–60. The Virginia Company, and later the colony's royal governors, had been attempting to diversify the colony's economy since the 1620s without success.

7. McIlwaine, *Journals of the House of Burgesses of Virginia, 1659/60–1693,* 22.

8. CO 1/16/98; Sainsbury, *CSP, Colonial, 1661–1668,* 106.

9. CO 1/16/103, 104, 105; Sainsbury, *CSP, Colonial, 1661–1668,* 109.

10. Papenfuse, Md. Arch. Online 3: 476–77.

11. Ibid., 477–81.

12. Charles Calvert to Cecil Calvert, 23 July 1663, in *The Calvert Papers* [MdHS edition], 232–34.

13. Papenfuse, Md. Arch. Online 1: 457, 461, 484–85.

14. Ibid. 3: 503–6, 510–12.

15. Ibid.

16. Ibid. 3: 506–10; Berkeley, *The Papers of Sir William Berkeley, 1605–1677,* 164, 187.

17. Papenfuse, Md. Arch. Online 3: 510–12.

18. Ibid. 2: 36–37.

19. Ibid., 37–38.

20. The lower house was increasingly dominated by richer planters as the seventeenth century wore on, but the makeup of the house was not drastically different from the economic profile of Maryland's freemen in general—before 1688, for those members of the house about whom we have information, about half were the middling sort. Falb, *Advice and Ascent,* 98–115.

21. Papenfuse, Md. Arch. Online 2: 39.

22. Ibid. 38.

23. Ibid., 8–10 (for elections to the house), 5: 18; CO 1/21/133.

24. Md. Arch. 2: 38–49, 49–115 passim, 112–15, 143–44;

25. Md. Arch. 3: 547–48, 550–52, 558–60, 561; Md. Arch. 5: 5–9.

26. Papenfuse, Md. Arch. Online 5: 5–9.

27. CO 1/21/133; Papenfuse, Md. Arch. Online 5: 15–20.

28. Hutton, *Charles II,* 195–96, 242; Harris, *Restoration,* 111–12.

29. For the income from tobacco customs, David Lovejoy puts the figure at about a third of the customs revenue by 1670. Lovejoy, *The Glorious Revolution in America,* 8; Coward, *The Stuart Age,* 470; Chandaman, *The English Public Revenue, 1660–1688.* Colonial tax revenues were even more significant after 1671, when the crown stopped farming the customs, but despite the irregularities that went with deputizing collection in the 1660s, the money was sorely needed. Wilson, *England's Apprenticeship, 1603–1763,* 212. For the growth in the re-export trade after 1660, which included tobacco, see Davis, "English Foreign Trade, 1660–1700."

30. Papenfuse, Md. Arch. Online 2: 46–47.

6. War and Peace in the Chesapeake

1. Historians of Native America have urged early Americanists to embrace "continental history" as a way of avoiding the frameworks of language and narrative convention that inadvertently marginalize native people whether the historians employing them intend to or not. Witgen, "Rethinking Colonial History as Continental History," in response to Merrell, "Second Thoughts on Colonial Historians and American Indians." The continental approach also offers a necessary alternative and complement to the Atlantic-oriented view of early America. Witgen, *Infinity of Nations;* Wood, "From Atlantic History to a Continental Approach"; Hinderacker and Horn, "Territorial Crossings." Chesapeake historians have increasingly told the story of seventeenth-century Virginia and Maryland in ways that avoid distinctions between "colonial history" and "the history of Indians." See, for example, Rice, *Nature and History in the Potomac Country,* and *Tales from a Revolution.* My emphasis is on English attempts—and failures—to parse the politics and motives of Native Americans, which draws on the rich historiography of Native Americans in the seventeenth-century Chesapeake and mid-Atlantic, but places English readings of Indian actions within the framework of the politics of the English Atlantic.

2. Rountree and Davidson, *Eastern Shore Indians of Virginia and Maryland,* 93; Menard, "Population, Economy and Society in Seventeenth-Century Maryland"; Fausz, "Merging and Emerging Worlds."

3. Rice, *Nature and History in the Potomac Country,* 108–42.

4. James Merrell, "Cultural Continuity among the Piscataway Indians of Colonial Maryland"; Rountree, *Pocahontas's People,* 89–105; Rountree and Davidson, *Eastern Shore Indians of Virginia and Maryland,* 84–123; Porter, "A Century of Accommodation"; Jennings, "Glory, Death, and Transfiguration."

5. Papenfuse, Md. Arch. Online 2: 15.

6. Anderson, *Creatures of Empire.*

7. Papenfuse, Md. Arch. Online 2: 478, 480.

8. Rountree and Davidson, *Eastern Shore Indians of Virginia and Maryland,* 98. Tension between Maryland and both the Nanticokes and the nearby Wicomiss often appears in the English records. Papenfuse, Md. Arch. Online 5: 11–12, 29–30; 3: 378–81; 2: 196–97.

9. Md. Arch. 2: 488–89, 505–6, 514.

10. In the seventeenth century the Five Nations of the Iroquois Confederacy were the Senecas, Cayugas, Onondagas, Oneidas, and Mohawks. Seventeenth-century English writers often used one or another of these names to refer to the confederacy as a whole. Thus in the Maryland records the Indians referred to as "Cinigos," or "Sinicos," i.e., Senecas, were Iroquois, but not necessarily Senecas.

11. Rice, *Nature and History in the Potomac Country,* 49–50; Rountree and Davidson, *Eastern Shore Indians of Virginia and Maryland,* 84–85; Richter, *The Ordeal of the Longhouse,* 53, 98; Kent, *Susquehanna's Indians,* 7–12, 21.

12. Jennings, *The Ambiguous Iroquois Empire,* 102–3.

13. Rice, *Nature and History in the Potomac Country,* 144–46; Jennings, *The Ambiguous Iroquois Empire,* 127–28.

14. Richter, *The Ordeal of the Longhouse,* 52–53, 58–59.

15. Ibid., 74.

16. Ibid., 98; Merwick, *The Shame and the Sorrow.*

17. Papenfuse, Md. Arch. Online 3: 402–3.

18. Ibid. 1: 406–7; 3: 410–11.

19. Maquamps/Bennett was convicted and hanged. This incident may have been part of the reason the Mattawomans went to speak with the Maryland council in October about whether or not they should move farther away from the settlement. Ibid. 49: 481–84, 489, 491.

20. Ibid. 3: 431–32.

21. Ibid., 412–16.

22. Ibid., 417–18.

23. Ibid., 502–3, 521–26, 530–32, 549–50.

24. Ibid., 487–88.

25. Rice, *Tales from a Revolution,* 20–24.

26. The fear of a "general combination" among the Indians against the English gathered steam in the later 1670s as Bacon's Rebellion coincided with King Philip's War in New England. Governor Berkeley of Virginia, for example, feared this very thing. Berkeley, *The Papers of Sir William Berkeley, 1605–1677,* 498, 507–10. Across the Atlantic, fears of similar dangerous outsiders—Catholics, and the French—created the Popish Plot scare in England. Conspiracies of outsiders convulsed the English-speaking world. The cast of villains was very similar, with the French acting in both

the New and Old world versions, and Native Americans often drawn into the story by way of the French. The pillars of the early modern English polity—its expanding empire, its Protestant identity, and its increasingly powerful state—all shared origins, strengths, and vulnerabilities. Contemporaries understood them to be linked; threats to or crises or weaknesses in one amounted to crises or weaknesses in the whole.

27. Kent, *Susquehanna's Indians,* 23–24, 45–47; Jennings, "Glory, Death, and Transfiguration," 33–34.

28. Papenfuse, Md. Arch. Online 2: 376–78.

29. Ibid., 428–30, 462–63.

30. Ibid., 428–30, Kent, *Susquehanna's Indians,* 47.

31. Craven, *The Southern Colonies in the Seventeenth Century, 1607–1689,* 373–74; Rice, *Tales from a Revolution,* chapter 1; Washburn, *The Governor and the Rebel,* 20–24.

32. Papenfuse, Md. Arch. Online 15: 47–50.

33. Rice, *Tales from a Revolution,* 19–24; Washburn, *The Governor and the Rebel,* 22–24.

34. Rice, *Tales from a Revolution,* 29–53.

35. Papenfuse, Md. Arch. Online. 15: 105–18, 120–26, quote on 124.

36. Carr and Menard, "Wealth and Welfare in Early Maryland"; Menard, "Opportunity and Inequality," and "From Servant to Freeholder"; Lorena S. Walsh argues that the "Age of the Small Planter" extended into the 1670s; by the last decades of the century, hard times had set in. Walsh, *Motives of Honor, Pleasure, and Profit,* 131–37, 198–99.

37. CO 1/39/10; Papenfuse, Md. Arch. Online 5: 152–54. The common planters' grievances in Virginia, as described by Brent Tarter—particularly taxes, and high charges relating to the assembly—are very similar to those voiced in Maryland. Tarter, "Bacon's Rebellion, the Grievances of the People, and the Political Culture of Seventeenth-Century Virginia." William Berkeley concurred with Notley's assessment of the people of both Maryland and Virginia. Berkeley, *The Papers of Sir William Berkeley, 1605–1677,* 567, 569.

38. Morgan, *American Slavery, American Freedom,* Book Three.

9. Papenfuse, Md. Arch. Online 5: 134.

40. Ibid.

41. Ibid. 2: 474–77, 481–83, 485–86, 493–94, 500–501, 503–4, 512–13.

42. Ibid., 354, 357, 359–60, 369, 370, 371, 373.

7. THE PROPRIETARY REGIME AND THE MACHINERY OF EMPIRE

1. Carr and Jordan, *Maryland's Revolution of Government, 1689–1692,* 16–17.

2. Papenfuse, Md. Arch. Online 2: 137–38.

3. Ibid., 392–94.

4. Ibid., 477–78, 532–37.
5. Ibid. 17: 181–86, 244–45, 271.
6. Ibid. 2: 507–8.
7. Ibid. 5: 137–38, 144.
8. Ibid. 7: 333–34.
9. Ibid., 345–46, 354, 355.
10. Ibid., 359–60.
11. Ibid., 377, 380, 385–86, 418.
12. Ibid., 451–53.
13. Ibid., 458–60, 461, 463, 466, 470, 474, 480, 486–89, 491, 494, 505, 530, 533.
14. Ibid. 13: 4.
15. Ibid. 7: 493.
16. Ibid. 13: 39.
17. Charles I agreed to the 1641 Triennial Act only as a concession, and afterwards regretted it deeply as a threat to the basic principles of monarchy. The 1641 act was repealed by the Cavalier Parliament in the early 1660s, and later reinstated in a way that removed any mechanism for enforcing it. Charles II tended to ignore it, especially later in his reign, as he received subsidies from Louis XIV. Hutton, *Charles II,* 167, 211, 422; Cust, *Charles I,* 279; Harris, *Restoration,* 51, 419, 421.
18. Papenfuse, Md. Arch. Online 15: 127–29, 131–32.
19. Ibid. 5: 77–78; 15: 137–42.
20. Ibid. 1: 435–36, 448, 504.
21. Ibid. 2: 347–49, 357, 368–69, 370, 374–75.
22. Ibid., 512.
23. Ibid., 513, 542–51.
24. Colonists' belief in a "fundamental correspondence" between American provincial legislatures and Parliament became a permanent part of colonial American politics during the last decades of the seventeenth century and the first of the eighteenth. Bailyn, *The Origins of American Politics,* 60–64, quote on 60; Greene, *Peripheries and Center,* 30–42, 47.
25. Papenfuse, Md. Arch. Online 2: 159–63.
26. Ibid., 178–79.
27. Ibid. 5: 134–52.
28. Ibid. 2: 161.
29. Ibid. 1: 487–88.
30. Ibid. 2: 168–69.
31. Ibid., 173–77, quote on 176.
32. Ibid., 177–78.
33. Ibid., 179–80.
34. Ibid., 180–81.

35. Ibid., 182–84.

36. Ibid. Online 13: 40.

37. Ibid. 7: 5–6, 9–10.

38. Ibid., 11–12, 13, 15.

39. Some historians have seen little effective restructuring of the empire under the later Stuarts. Sosin, *English America and the Restoration Monarchy of Charles II,* 3–4. Most, however, describe a significant change during the 1670s and 1680s. Stephen Saunders Webb has emphasized the evidence of dysfunction and misrule that emerged from the colonies in the context of Bacon's Rebellion and King Philip's War and has shown in detail the process by which administration changed after 1676. Alison Olson has shown that by the mid-1670s it was evident to the crown that the "right people," i.e., the presumed silent royalist majority, were not in charge in the colonies, and that this was very likely the source of the persistent troubles there. More than that, the lack of adequate tax revenues from Parliament meant that customs revenues from colonial commodities like tobacco were all the more important, and if colonists were tearing one another to shreds—or failing to prevent the Iroquois or the French from doing so—this did not bode well for future revenues. In addition, as Robert Bliss argues, the English state found stronger administrative footing across the board in the 1670s, resulting in a "more purposeful colonial administration." Webb, *1676,* "William Blathwayt, Imperial Fixer," and "The Strange Career of Francis Nicholson"; Olson, *Anglo-American Politics, 1660–1775,* 62–63; Bliss, *Revolution and Empire,* 190; for the Lords of Trade, see Root, "The Lords of Trade and Plantations, 1675–1696." Carla Pestana links this change to the ever more fraught questions of religious affiliation and loyalty in the later Stuart period, noting that it was at this time that "the idea that loyalty to the monarch was best expressed through membership in the Church of England grew stronger." Pestana, *Protestant Empire,* 125. The colonies of New England were troublesome for their confessional irregularities and in particular, as the Navigation Acts stymied their mercantile efforts, for their propensity to flout royal commands. Johnson, *Adjustment to Empire,* 3–70. Maryland posed many of the same difficulties. In both cases, these colonies had been established at a far looser stage of imperial control—1675 represented a turning point in the long process of correcting the unexpected consequences of earlier policies toward and about colonies. Ken Macmillan has argued in *The Atlantic Imperial Constitution* that royal policy did not change over the course of the century, only the scope and vigor of its enforcement—but even if so, by the 1670s and 1680s a quantitative shift proved to be a qualitative one. This turning point in the 1670s was shaped by both the politics of England and its empire and by the very different internal politics of the American continent (see chapter 6). The two came together in the last third of the seventeenth century, creating the sustained period of imperial reorganization (and its many discontents) between about 1675 and 1690.

40. Quoted in Bliss, *Revolution and Empire,* 236. Blathwayt here used "empire" to refer to the strength of the king's power as well as the territorial extent of his dominions. Effingham was hoping to gain the governorship of the entire Chesapeake. He was still hoping in 1687. Howard, *The Papers of Francis Howard, Baron Howard of Effingham, 1643–1695,* 217–18, 283. In the context of anticipated charter revocations, extending the king's empire meant strengthening his power rather than increasing the territorial extent of his colonies.

41. Harris, *Restoration,* 317. Mark Knights has argued persuasively for a multifaceted crisis in the late 1670s and early 1680s comprehending the succession, religion, and constitutional issues. Knights, *Politics and Opinion in Crisis, 1678–1681.* See 205–6 on the Scots rebellion.

42. Hall, *Edward Randolph and the American Colonies, 1676–1703,* chapters 1–4; Johnson, "The Revolution of 1688 in the American Colonies," 218–19.

43. Papenfuse, Md. Arch. Online 5: 134–52. Anticipating the Popish Plot by two years, the document effectively spelled out what English subjects feared from a Catholic ruler. While historians of early Maryland have dismissed this document as pure anti-Catholic invective, or used it as a window into social and economic grievances in the Chesapeake, Stephen Saunders Webb has pointed out that the tract's implied argument was that "imperial dominion" would resolve local conflicts over taxes, defense, and the powers of the proprietary government. Carr and Jordan, *Maryland's Revolution of Government, 1689–1692,* 31–33; Jordan, *Foundations of Representative Government in Maryland, 1632–1715,* 95; Krugler, *English and Catholic,* 237–38; Webb, *1676,* 70–79, quote on 71. Webb is correct insofar as one of the main concerns of the author or authors of the "Complaint" was the nature of monarchical power both in Britain and in the American colonies. The best brief account, however, is that of James Rice, who correctly describes the "Complaint" as an articulation of Chesapeake planters' fears of conspiracy and invasion in the face of regional politics they did not fully understand. Rice, *Nature and History in the Potomac Country,* 151–52. I would also emphasize the relevance of the "Complaint" to transatlantic political debates about confessional identity and political loyalty. The tract can be read as an integration of the politics of the mid-Atlantic with the growing fears in the Anglophone world more generally about the Catholic-friendly policies of Charles II and the probable succession of his Catholic brother James to the British throne—it reveals the evolving connections in the 1670s between the world of the American continent and that of the English Atlantic. As Jonathan Scott has pointed out, the Popish Plot panic of the late 1670s was as much about what Charles was already doing as about what James might do in the future. Scott, "England's Troubles." Maryland's fate might be England's too, argued the authors of the "Complaint," if Catholic rule were not reigned in—it is not an accident that the tract was addressed to Parliament and the City of London rather than the king.

44. CO 1/37/39 encl. 1; Papenfuse, Md. Arch. Online 5: 130–32. That Jesuits and Protestant dissenters were allied—or even one and the same—became a common trope by the late seventeenth century. Jesuits and Quakers were linked in the 1650s. Clifton, "Popular Fear of Catholics during the English Revolution," 34. William Penn was accused of being a Jesuit in disguise in the late 1660s. Wildes, *William Penn,* 48–49. James II offered religious toleration to both Catholics and Protestant dissenters.

45. CO 1/37/38.

46. Papenfuse, Md. Arch. Online 5: 260–61; CO 1/41/27; Md. Arch. Online 5: 261–62, 133–34; CO 1/41/28; Md. Arch. Online 5: 252–54.

47. Papenfuse, Md. Arch. Online 5: 263–69. The inquiries are on 128–30.

48. CO 1/14/59; Sainsbury, *CSP, Colonial, 1661–1668,* 103, 105, 106; nos. 345, 353, 357.

49. Papenfuse, Md. Arch. Online 3: 468, 473; 5: 82–83, 91. See also Antoinette Sutto, "You Dog, Give Me Your Hand."

50. See for example Papenfuse, Md. Arch. Online 5: 82–83. The ship's master was to be tried in a Maryland admiralty court, not by crown officers or in an English court.

51. Papenfuse, Md. Arch. Online 5: 45–47, 113–14, 117–18; 3: 483–85.

52. Sutto, "You Dog, Give Me Your Hand."

53. On the other hand, Effingham also observed that at this point, Maryland's customs paperwork was kept in admirable order. Howard, *The Papers of Francis Howard, Baron Howard of Effingham, 1643–1695,* 259.

54. Ibid., 117, 164, 169, 184. Annexing Maryland to Virginia had been a pet project of Virginia authorities for decades, even after the hopes of the old Company adventurers had been laid to rest—the Virginia Assembly requested it of Charles II in 1660. Berkeley, *The Papers of Sir William Berkeley, 1605–1677,* 131.

55. CO 1/41/143.

56. SP 25/79, p. 163; SP 25/79, p. 646; Papenfuse, Md. Arch. Online 3: 365.

57. Papenfuse, Md. Arch. Online: 1, 399–400, 405, 414–15 (on setting up a mint in Maryland); 3: 383–84.

58. Charles Calvert to Cecil Calvert, 12 April 1672, in *The Calvert Papers* [MdHS edition], 252–76, quote on 265.

8. RUMOR AND POLITICS

1. Anon., *Virginia and Maryland, or, the Lord Baltamore's Printed Case, Uncased and Answered,* 3–4, 8.

2. By the early eighteenth, it helped to hold the empire together. Stanwood, *The Empire Reformed.* To Stanwood's insightful account of the role of anti-popery in building empire, I would add that anti-Catholicism functioned in dialogue with anti-Puritanism or (especially in the early Stuart period) anti-popularity. Anti-popery was a narrative of corruption in high places; it was countered by accounts of corruption or

subversion from below, whether from Puritans or Dissenters specifically or more generalized "factious persons" of low quality. (As Scott Sowerby has noted, there were also specific critiques of anti-popery itself by the 1670s and 1680s, which he playfully calls "anti-anti-popery." Sowerby, "Opposition to Anti-Popery in Restoration England." Anti-popery and anti-Puritanism were political counterweights; anti-popery's power was tied to claims about the nature of Protestant loyalty, whether the key was Protestantism as such, or specifically conformity to the Church of England. The fortunes of the Maryland proprietorship suggest that debates about the nature of Protestant loyalty before 1690 opened up a space for claims about Catholic loyalty—a space for critique of anti-popery, often tied to strong claims about the autonomous power of the crown—which subsequently was not as readily available. Anti-Puritanism allowed for the claim that some Protestants were not loyal; thus loyalty was not tied to Protestantism as such; perhaps there might be room for loyal Catholics. The more diffuse Protestant patriotism and post-Revolution toleration of the eighteenth-century empire adopted "Protestant" as a rough approximation of "good subject" and closed off a rhetorical space previously open to Catholics. The Toleration Act of 1689 excluded Catholics but included Protestant Dissenters, except for non-Trinitarians and atheists.

3. Protestant Associators John Coode, Nehemiah Blakiston, and Kenelm Cheseldyn were all married to daughters of the Catholic Thomas Gerard. Carr and Jordan, *Maryland's Revolution of Government, 1689–1692,* 236–37, 242–43, 245–46.

4. See chapter4.

5. "Dissenters" rather than "Puritans" is a better term for the years after 1660, but both refer to nonconforming Protestants.

6. Their pacifism and refusal to swear oaths provoked him to call them "obstinate" and suggest that they acted only out of a perverse desire "to change the rules of government." Papenfuse, Md. Arch. Online 17: 37–42; 7: 184–85. The boundary conflict with William Penn may also have soured Charles Calvert somewhat on Quakers. Sutto, "The Borders of Absolutism."

7. McIlwaine, *Legislative Journals of the Council of Colonial Virginia,* 1: 468.

8. "Rumor" is a slippery term. It is distinct from news, both in seventeenth-century and in modern usage, but it is not always clear what the distinction is. Rumor often carries a derogatory connotation—rumor is false news, or mistaken news, or the speculations of the vulgar and ill-informed. Rumor can shade into gossip; the distinction for early seventeenth-century people seems to be that rumor is about topics that might be a general threat or public problem, while gossip is confined to the doings or reputation of a person or persons in a private capacity. The terms are gendered—rumor tends to focus more on the actions of men, while gossip is used both to describe and dismiss the actions and concerns of women. And rumor is difficult to distinguish from "report," a word seventeenth-century people often used when talking about accounts of persons or events. "News" tended to be used of fairly brief and concrete statements

about events at home or abroad. "Report" was slightly more amorphous, and often tied to items that might affect, in a good way or a bad, the general reputation of the person or thing reported on. Two other seventeenth-century terms, "advice" and "intelligence," are somewhere between "news" and "report." However, given the near-interchangeability of these words for the people who used them, it is perhaps not best to begin by getting too mired in the distinctions among them.

9. Graham, "Popish Plots." Even those historians more interested in topics other than specifically anti-popery have argued for the significance of religion in helping to create and sustain political alignments in the later seventeenth century. Carr and Jordan, *Maryland's Revolution of Government, 1689–1692,* 200–231.

10. Shibutani, *Improvised News;* Kapferer, *Rumors;* Stoler, "In Cold Blood."

11. Victor, *Satanic Panic,* and "Satanic Cult Rumors as Contemporary Legend"; Hsia, *The Myth of Ritual Murder,* especially chapters 1–2.

12. There were no newspapers published in the North American English colonies until the 1720s. Corantoes or printed news sheets circulated in early Stuart England alongside manuscript news and letters. But price, irregular printing schedules, and limited print runs limited their consumption. As with so many other things, the 1640s and 1650s revolutionized news production, circulation, and consumption in England. By the 1670s and 1680s, despite lingering debates over their legitimacy, regularly printed newspapers were a staple of urban (and in some cases provincial) life. C. John Sommerville, *The News Revolution in England.*

13. CO 1/47/3; Md. Arch Online, 5: 278; CO 1/47/100; CO 1/48/89, encl. 5; Papenfuse, Md. Arch. Online 5: 302–4; 306–8.

14. Howard, *The Papers of Francis Howard, Baron Howard of Effingham, 1643–1695,* 107.

15. CO 1/59/17.

16. Papenfuse, Md. Arch. Online 5: 490–91, 506–12, 532–33.

17. Marvell, *An account of the growth of popery and arbitrary government in England.*

18. Steve Pincus has termed James's strategy "Catholic modernity," a mixture of increased royal power, an enhanced state apparatus, and support for Catholicism—in this, he was not so different from Louis XIV. Pincus, *1688,* 143–78. Pincus calls what James was doing Catholic modernity rather than absolutism, which opens up a space for an alternate Protestant or Whig modernity, but from the perspective of James's subjects in the 1680s this may have been a distinction without a difference. In contrast, John Miller stresses James's desire to encourage Catholicism in England rather than any deliberate tendency toward absolutism. He lost the trust of his subjects because they feared the association of Catholicism and overweening monarchical power, but the king's "abuses of power" were "incidental" rather than "central . . . feature[s] of his rule." Miller, *James II,* 124–28; see also Miller, "The Potential for Absolutism in Later Stuart England." Miller and other revisionists writing in the 1970s and 1980s down-

played the idea of "absolutism" for Charles II and James II much as their early Stuart counterparts did for Charles I; there was a related move to minimize the revolutionary character of both the Revolution in particular and late Stuart English people in general. Speck, *Reluctant Revolutionaries,* 236–40.

19. CO 5/739, pp. 219–20, 227–28; Papenfuse, Md. Arch. Online 8: 77–78, 84–86.

20. Papenfuse, Md. Arch. Online 15: 227.

21. Ibid., 227–28.

22. Ibid., 229–31.

23. Ibid. 1: 420–22.

24. Ibid. 15: 233–34.

25. Danckaerts and Sluyter, *Journal of a Voyage to New York, and a Tour of Several of the American Colonies in 1679–80,* 214–21, quote on 221.

26. CO 1/36/78; Papenfuse, Md. Arch. Online 5: 134–52.

27. Kapferer, *Rumors,* 9; Dowd, "The French King Wakes up in Detroit," and "The Panic of 1751."

28. Victor, *Satanic Panic;* Farge and Revel, *The Vanishing Children of Paris*—the children were to be shipped to America; LeFebvre, *The Great Fear of 1789.* See also Ramsay, *The Ideology of the Great Fear.* LeFebvre assumed that there must have been "agitators" (55, 118), but other accounts indicate no deliberate agitation is necessary to create a rumor panic.

29. Adam Fox has noted that in early modern England to speak of a difference between "oral culture" and "literate culture" is misleading; there was constant interaction between oral communication, the written word, and print. Fox, *Oral and Literate Culture in England, 1500–1700,* chapter 7, 336, 354–63.

30. CO 5/739, pp. 211–13; Papenfuse, Md. Arch. Online 8: 70–72. Darnall, a Catholic, was related by marriage to the proprietor. Carr and Jordan, *Maryland's Revolution of Government, 1689–1692,* 40. For similar rumors during Ingle's invasion, HCA 13/60/H, Ingle v. Looking Glass, deposition of Thomas Green, 10 July 1645; SP 16/508, f. 227rv, deposition of Richard Garrett; SP 16/508, ff. 146v–147r, deposition of Robert Ropely.

31. See chapter 9.

32. CO 5/739, pp. 213–14; Papenfuse, Md. Arch. Online 8: 72.

33. CO 5/739, pp. 212–13; Papenfuse, Md. Arch. Online 8: 71.

34. CO 5/739, pp. 214–16; Papenfuse, Md. Arch. Online 8: 73.

35. Maryland and Virginia negotiated an agreement with the Iroquois in 1682 in which the Five Nations agreed to stay out of Virginia. The agreement was reconfirmed in 1684. O'Callaghan, *Documents Relative to the Colonial History of the State of New York* 3: 321–28; Howard, *The Papers of Francis Howard, Baron Howard of Effingham, 1643–1695,* 142–50 and 142 n.1. This did not close off the prospect of conflict, however. The Iroquois and the English often came away from treaty making with different

understandings of how the agreement would direct Iroquois relations with third parties. If those third parties were native groups in the Chesapeake allied to the English, the effects of the treaty could be limited indeed. Jennings, *The Ambiguous Iroquois Empire,* 162–64.

36. CO 5/739, pp. 217–18; Papenfuse, Md. Arch. Online 8: 75–76.

37. CO 5/739, pp. 218–19; Papenfuse, Md. Arch. Online 8: 76–77.

38. CO 5/739, pp. 214–16; Papenfuse, Md. Arch. Online 8: 73.

39. CO 5/739 pp. 216, 219–20, 227–28; Papenfuse, Md. Arch. Online 8: 74–75, 77–78, 84–86.

40. CO 5/739, pp. 224–25; Papenfuse, Md. Arch. Online 8: 82–84. Bur Harrison and John West and others were later accused of deliberately spreading false rumors. McIlwaine, *Executive Journals of the Council of Colonial Virginia,* 1: 104–6, 519.

41. CO 5/739, pp. 234–35.

42. Ibid., 221; Papenfuse, Md. Arch. Online 8: 79.

43. CO 5/739 pp. 222–24, 225–28; Papenfuse, Md. Arch. Online 8: 79–86;

44. CO 5/739, pp. 235–36.

45. CO 5/718 pt. 1, f. 8rv; CO 5/739 pp. 232–33, 228–29; Md. Arch. 8: 86–94.

46. CO 5/739, p. 234; Papenfuse, Md. Arch. Online 8: 87–94.

9. NEWS, RUMOR, AND REBELLION

1. CO 5/739, pp. 235–36; Papenfuse, Md. Arch. Online 8: 87–94.

2. Quote from Murrin, "The Menacing Shadow of Louis XIV and the Rage of Jacob Leisler." James Rice emphasizes the sheer complexity of the Native American political landscape that colonists were drawn into in the 1670s and 1680s. For the English, the assumption that they simply faced another epicycle of the international Catholic conspiracy was "a comforting alternative to figuring out a terribly complicated situation." More than this, the Native American political tensions that formed so important a part of Bacon's Rebellion did not evaporate with the end of the English rebellion, and "many of the factors that had combined to create a general panic in the summer of 1681 remained in play throughout the 1680s." Rice, *Nature and History in the Potomac Country,* 150, 151, 154, 156. The discreteness of events like Bacon's Rebellion or the almost-uprising of 1681 would have been far more evident to the English than to Indians. The fact that so many of the American factors that created these events were of long standing and created problems the English recognized as crises only at certain points neatly reveals the interplay between continental and English Atlantic concerns as well as the power, for English colonials, of their own narratives of threat and disorder—crises of the sort Maryland experienced were most likely to happen when colonists perceived an intersection between the world of trans-Atlantic European political concerns and that of the American continent.

3. CO 1/39/1.

4. CO 1/40/56 and encl.; Papenfuse, Md. Arch. Online 5: 243–46.

5. Papenfuse, Md. Arch. Online 8: 269–70; 15: 157.

6. Richter, *The Ordeal of the Longhouse,* 145.

7. Jennings, *The Ambiguous Iroquois Empire,* 162–65.

8. Papenfuse, Md. Arch. Online 15: 175–76.

9. Ibid., 236–43

10. Ibid., 175–76.

11. Ibid., 246–53. Whether or not the Piscataways were merely telling the English what they thought they wanted to hear about both the murders and, later, the presence of the French among the Iroquois and Susquehannock raiding parties, is an open question.

12. Ibid., 180–88, 212–13, 217–22, 222–23, 232, 234–35, 236–43.

13. The suspect was apprehended but escaped. In August, the Choptico Indians told the council that he was in Virginia, among the Rappahannock Indians. The sheriff of St. Mary's, Gerrard Slye, was sent down to Virginia to ask the authorities there for permission to bring him back. Ibid., 162–63, 171–72, 190–91.

14. Ibid., 174–75.

15. Ibid., 191–92.

16. Ibid., 274, 277–88.

17. Ibid., 328–31.

18. Ibid., 335–36.

19. Ibid. 17: 3–5.

20. Ibid. 15: 353–55, 373–76.

21. Ibid., 355–56.

22. Ibid., 400.

23. Ibid. 17: 18–21.

24. Ibid., 23–26.

25. Ibid. 15: 356.

26. Ibid., 293–94.

27. Ibid., 244–50.

28. See chapter 8.

29. Ibid. 15: 250.

30. Main, *Tobacco Colony,* 37.

31. Kenyon, *The Popish Plot,* 93–94.

32. Scott, "England's Troubles"; Marvell, *An account of the growth of popery and arbitrary government in England;* Harris, *Restoration,* chapter 3, quote on 165.

33. Papenfuse, Md. Arch. Online 15: 236–43.

34. Ibid., 373–74.

35. Ibid., 348.

36. Canny, "The Ideology of English Colonization"; Ethan Shagan, "Constructing Discord."

37. Papenfuse, Md. Arch. Online 426: 797–98.

38. Ibid. 15: 419–20.

39. CO 1/47/36.

40. Papenfuse, Md. Arch. Online 15: 386–87.

41. Ibid. 392–93.

42. Ibid. 409–11.

43. CO 1/47/43.

44. CO 1/47/33; Md. Arch. Online 5: 280–82.

45. Carr and Jordan, *Maryland's Revolution of Government, 1689–1692,* 245–48.

46. Papenfuse, Md. Arch. Online 15: 388–90.

47. Ibid. 17: 55–56.

48. Ibid. 15: 244–50.

49. Ibid. 17: 31.

50. Ibid. 15: 391.

51. Ibid., 244–50, 390–91; CO 1/48/16, encl. 1

52. Papenfuse, Md. Arch. Online 15: 388–90.

53. Ibid., 389–90.

54. Ibid. 17: 31–32.

55. Ibid.15: 400–405, 407.

56. Ibid. 17: 55–56.

57. Ibid., 55.

58. Ibid. 15: 391–92.

59. CO 1/47/35.

60. Papenfuse, Md. Arch. Online 15: 378–79, 407–8; 7: 114–15, 117–23.

61. CO 1/47/36.

62. Papenfuse, Md. Arch. Online 7: 112–40.

63. Ibid., 115, 123–27. With the reference to a legal distinction between England and its "conquests," Baltimore seems to invoke the contrast between imperium and dominium so familiar to scholars of early modern law. But he did not use those words, and no one involved in disputes about Maryland referenced the terms in arguing about the problem of English rights for Marylanders.

64. CO 1/47/33; Papenfuse, Md. Arch. Online 5: 280–82.

65. CO 1/48/16, encl. 1.

66. CO 1/48/16; CO 1/47/35; CO 1/47/36.

67. Philip Calvert, *A Letter from the Chancellour of Mary-Land to Col. Henry Meese,* 1.

68. CO 5/723, p. 56; Papenfuse, Md. Arch. Online 5: 300–301; CO 1/47/76.

69. CO 391/3, pp. 297–300; Papenfuse, Md. Arch. Online 5: 301.

70. Papenfuse, Md. Arch. Online 5: 343–44, 344–46; Sutto, "You Dog, Give Me Your Hand."

71. Anon., *To the Parliament of England, the Case of the Poor English Protestants in Mary-Land,* 1–2. The reference to the woman turned out naked with her child was related to the dispute over the area the Dutch called Hoerekill and the English Anglicized to Whorekill. The area had originally been settled by the Dutch, and by the 1670s both Maryland and New York claimed it. Baltimore had encouraged Marylanders to take up land in the area. In the early 1670s he dispatched an expedition there to secure his authority, and one of his lieutenants overstepped. Danckaerts discusses this episode at length in Danckaerts and Sluyter, *Journal of a Voyage to New York, and a Tour of Several of the American Colonies in 1679–80.*

72. Anon., *To the Parliament of England, the Case of the Poor English Protestants in Mary-Land,* 1–4.

73. Ibid., 2.

74. Ibid.

75. Philip Calvert, *A Letter from the Chancellour of Mary-Land to Col. Henry Meese,* 1.

76. Ibid., 2.

77. Knights, *Politics and Opinion in Crisis, 1678–1681,* chapter 10.

78. Krugler, *English and Catholic,* 239–43.

10. GLORIOUS REVOLUTIONS

1. Stanwood, *The Empire Reformed,* parts II and III; Pestana, *Protestant Empire,* 159. The question of what 1688 was about for the colonial world has long posed a challenge to historians of early America. Stanwood and Pestana emphasize the role of Protestant culture and the perceived relations between religion and political order. Alison Olson notes that 1688 had the effect of sucking the ideology out of colonial politics, as the more contentious issues were "drawn off to imperial settlement, leaving colonial politics a matter of spoils and interests rather than tenaciously-held beliefs." Olson, *Anglo-American Politics, 1660–1775,* 75–76. Richard Johnson argues for a "synthesis" of the "virtual autonomy of the colonists' founding years" and the centralization of the 1680s; the key contribution of the Revolution was to combine these two things into a "mutually acceptable coagulation." Johnson, "The Revolution of 1688–9 in the American Colonies," 234–35. Whether one focuses on the political culture of religion or the spoils of politics, the same shift is visible—the Revolution removed, or rearranged, key items of contention in colonial politics before 1688. This does not mean that the world was turned upside down (or right-side up). Lois G. Carr has noted that Maryland was remarkably stable on a local level through the revolution. Carr, "Sources of Political Stability and Upheaval in Seventeenth Century Maryland," 50–51, and "County Gov-

ernment in Maryland, 1689–1709." David Lovejoy suggests that the revolution did not necessarily do everything its American participants wished. English colonists in America had a well-developed sense of their place in the empire; they saw themselves as English subjects with the same liberties and privileges as subjects in England. The crown and colonial administrators disagreed, leading colonists to feel increasingly imposed upon in the later seventeenth century. Their success at using the events of 1688 to redefine their relation to the imperial center was mixed. Lovejoy, *The Glorious Revolution in America,* especially 368–70. In Maryland, the events of 1688 removed the Catholic proprietary regime, which had functioned since the 1630s as the intersection of a network of extremely vexed questions about confessional difference, subjecthood, and the English state. Without this particular focus for conflict, local politics could be conducted on far less eschatological terms. The Revolution of 1688 did not remove ideology from politics, but it resolved some longstanding questions and rearranged the terms of debate, with the result that this particular colony no longer had to work out the nature of the English state, over and over again, in order to function. There was a specifically regional aspect to the change, too. Post-revolutionary Maryland governments of the 1690s and early 1700s abandoned policies of alliance with Native peoples. Rice, *Nature and History in the Potomac Country,* 161–62. The charge that popish proprietary authorities were conspiring with Indians and the French had been key to the constellation of fears that motivated panics and revolutions in Maryland—now, not only were the authorities no longer popish, but the diplomatic efforts that promoted the Indian conspiracy charge had also been removed from the matrix.

2. For a full list, see Carr and Jordan, *Maryland's Revolution of Government, 1689–1692,* 232–88.

3. CO 5/718, f. 30; Papenfuse, Md. Arch. Online 8: 155–57.

4. J. M. Sosin's brief account of events after 1689 indicates that much depended on how the Associators made their case, but he does not treat the matter in detail. *English America and the Revolution of 1688,* 171–78. Historians of the Chesapeake have devoted much effort to the causes and course of the political upheaval of 1689–90 in Maryland. Perhaps the best among existing studies is that of Lois Green Carr and David Jordan, who stress the inhabitants' social and financial grievances and the structural problems of Maryland's government. Religion for Carr and Jordan played a role in the conflict, but not the primary one. They argue that anti-popery certainly motivated some, particularly among the poorer sort, but the overthrow of the proprietary regime was not accomplished through Protestant fervor alone. At the same time, neither was 1689–90 a revolution along strict economic lines. Many supported Coode and the Associators who had no financial or career interest in doing so. Carr and Jordan, *Maryland's Revolution of Government, 1689–1692,* especially 187–95, 221–31; Carr, "Sources of Political Stability and Upheaval in Seventeenth Century Maryland"; Jordan, "Maryland's Privy Council." For a sharper denial of religion's role in these events, see Gleissner, "Reli-

gious Causes of the Glorious Revolution in Maryland." Other accounts of Maryland's 1689 revolution have largely followed that of Carr and Jordan. Historians interested in 1688 in America in general rather than Maryland in particular have offered the most convincing brief accounts of what happened there, e.g., Stanwood, *The Empire Reformed* 106–12, 133–35. This reinforces the argument made here that a transatlantic perspective is key to making sense of Maryland's seventeenth-century history.

5. Papenfuse, Md. Arch. Online 13: 147–53.

6. Ibid.

7. Miller, "Charles II and His Parliaments," 16–17.

8. CO 5/723 p. 109; see also CO 5/723, p. 117; CO 5/1/1; CO 391/6, p. 211. Lord Howard of Effingham "wondered at" some of Lord Baltimore's behavior in 1684, given that "quo warrantos are of such force against charters" and those "of Bermuda's [sic] and of Boston will certainly be vacated next term." Howard, *The Papers of Francis Howard, Baron Howard of Effingham, 1643–1695,* 154, 169–70.

9. CO 5/723, p. 117; CO 5/1/1; CO 391/6, p. 211.

10. CO 5/723, p. 119; Md. Arch. 8: 100–101.

11. Sutto, "You Dog, Give Me Your Hand."

12. Papenfuse, Md. Arch. Online 8: 112.

13. Ibid.

14. Fendall had left Maryland in the 1680s and died by 1688, so he never had the opportunity to join with Coode a second time. Papenfuse, Md. Arch. Online 426: 318.

15. CO 5/718, part 1, f. 47r–49v.

16. Papenfuse, Md. Arch. Online 8: 148.

17. Murrin, "The Menacing Shadow of Louis XIV and the Rage of Jacob Leisler"; Balmer, "Traitors and Papists"; Cherry, "Rumor Has It."

18. William and Mary appointed a long list of new bishops after 1688, creating a "largely Whig episcopate" that on average supported comprehension and, effectively toleration—an expansion of both the reach of the Church of England and the English political nation. This position was not uncontroversial, however; the Whig view of religion, the state, and the church was "fragile and contested" in the early 1690s. Pincus, *1688,* 402–34, quotes on 424, 434.

19. Collinson, "The Monarchical Republic of Queen Elizabeth I," 48–50.

20. Collinson, "The Monarchical Republic of Queen Elizabeth I"; Cressy, "Binding the Nation."

21. Cressy, "Binding the Nation," 229.

22. Papenfuse, Md. Arch. Online Vol. 20: 538–46, quote on 538–39. Coode was among the signatories.

23. Coode's knowledge of English history emerged in other ways, too. When Michael Taney, who was loyal to the proprietary regime, demanded to know by what authority John Coode had acted, Coode replied, "What, this is like King Charles, and

you are King Taney," referring to Charles I's demand during his trial to know the legal authority behind those who prosecuted him. CO 5/718, part 1, p. 34.

24. Protestant Association, *The Declaration of the Reasons and Motives for the Present Appearing in Arms;* Md. Arch. 8: 101–7; William III, *Declaration of his Highness William Henry, by the Grace of God Prince of Orange, Of the Reasons Inducing him to appear in Armes in the kingdom of England.*

25. Protestant Association, *The Declaration of the Reasons and Motives for the Present Appearing in Arms,* 1–2. Among the key tropes of anti-popery was the idea of things being hidden, masked, painted deceptively white, or locked up. Shell, *Catholicism, Controversy, and the English Literary Imagination, 1558–1660,* 23–55. The "Complaint from Heaven" in the 1670s referenced cloaks, makeup, masks, paint, covers, veils, and secret chambers. Baltimore used the "country cloak" to cover up plots "hatched" in the "popish chamber"; the reader was asked to "unmask the vizard" to see the plot unfolding; a doubtful military expedition against fellow Protestants was "chalked over with an assembly"; Baltimore's supporters "whitelime[d] [their] false . . . actions over with" their and Baltimore's "glistering paternal care." The "popish chamber" assertion also appears earlier in the tract when the authors spoke of "treachery plainly discovered out of the cabinet of popish Maryland." Papenfuse, Md. Arch. Online 5: 135, 136, 141, 143, 144. As noted earlier with reference to Charles I, the "popish cabinet" narrative was common in Stuart England. The Associators' reference to shrouds and hidden corruption draws from these same literary conventions.

26. Protestant Association, *The Declaration of the Reasons and Motives for the Present Appearing in Arms,* 1–2.

27. Ibid., 3–5, 7.

28. Ibid., 4, 6.

29. Ibid., 7.

30. Papenfuse, Md. Arch. Online 8: 118–21.

31. Ibid. 13: 231–32.

32. Carr and Jordan, *Maryland's Revolution of Government, 1689–1692,* 77; CO 5/718/1, pt. 1, ff. 41r–44r; Papenfuse, Md. Arch. Online 8: 114–18.

33. CO 5/718, ff. 64–75; Papenfuse, Md. Arch. Online 8: 127–49.

34. Papenfuse, Md. Arch. Online 8: 142–43.

35. Ibid., 145–47.

36. Ibid., 144–45.

37. Ibid., 128–29.

38. Ibid. 13: 235–38.

39. CO 5/1081/77.

40. CO 5/713/10; CO 5/713/11; CO 5/713/17; Papenfuse, Md. Arch. Online 8: 179–80, 186–88.

41. CO 5/713/12; CO 5/713/13; Papenfuse, Md. Arch. Online 8: 191–92, 181–82.

42. Papenfuse, Md. Arch. Online 8: 162.

43. William III, *Declaration of his Highness William Henry, by the Grace of God Prince of Orange, Of the Reasons Inducing him to appear in Armes in the kingdom of England.* This text was circulated quickly and effectively throughout both England and its overseas possessions. Israel, *The Anglo-Dutch Moment,* "Introduction," 10–21. Defenders of the Revolution in the 1690s leaned very hard on the threat of France, arbitrary power, and popery, even as events of the 1690s became difficult to place in a strictly confessional framework. Pincus, *1688,* 452–54.

44. Troost, "William III, Brandenburg, and the Construction of the Anti-French Coalition, 1672–88," 332–33.

45. CO 5/713/9; Papenfuse, Md. Arch. Online 8: 177–79.

46. CO 5/713/37; Papenfuse, Md. Arch. Online 8: 225–28.

47. Pincus, *1688,* 268–73.

48. Ibid., 283–86.

49. CO 391/6, pp. 312, 313; Papenfuse, Md. Arch. Online 8: 167–68.

50. Papenfuse, Md. Arch. Online 8: 148

51. CO 5/713/3 [accompanies 5/713/2], encl. 5, ff. 10r–11v.

52. CO 5/713/3, encls.

53. Papenfuse, Md. Arch. Online 8: 168–69, 176–77; CO 5/1305/32; CO 5/723, pp. 164–66.

54. CO 5/713/2; CO 5/713/4; Papenfuse, Md. Arch. Online 8: 169–73.

55. CO 5/713/6; CO 5/713/108; Papenfuse, Md. Arch. Online 8: 173–74.

56. CO 5/713/7; CO 5/723, pp. 169–70, 171–72; CO 391/6, p. 322; Papenfuse, Md. Arch. Online 8: 174–76.

57. Sutto, "You Dog, Give Me Your Hand," 248–53.

58. CO 5/713/15; CO 5/713/18; CO 5/713/20 (quote); Papenfuse, Md. Arch. Online 8: 182–84, 192–93.

59. CO 5/718, f. 56; CO 5/723, pp. 174–75; Papenfuse, Md. Arch. Online 8: 165–66.

60. CO 5/713/32; CO 5/723, pp. 179–80; CO 5/713/30; CO 5/713/38, encl. 5; Papenfuse, Md. Arch. Online 8: 211–14, 210.

61. CO 5/713/37; CO 5/713/38, encls. 2 and 3; Papenfuse, Md. Arch. Online 8: 225–28, 224, 196.

62. The fourth Lord Baltimore, Benedict Calvert, converted to Anglicanism in 1713 just a few years before Charles Calvert's death. When Charles died, Benedict petitioned the crown and regained the proprietorship of Maryland, which at his own death in 1715 passed to his son Charles, also an Anglican.

63. CO 5/713/42. Copley was the former lieutenant governor of Hull and had been instrumental in "securing Kingston-upon-Hull for William"; he was reliably loyal and anti-Catholic. Carr and Jordan, *Maryland's Revolution of Government, 1689–1692,* 153.

EPILOGUE

1. Carr, "County Government in Maryland, 1689–1709."

2. Carr and Jordan, *Maryland's Revolution of Government, 1689–1692,* 202–22; Jordan, *Foundations of Representative Government in Maryland, 1632–1715,* 186–238, quote on 203.

3. Harris, *Revolution,* 353–54.

4. Rice, *Nature and History in the Potomac Country,* 161–62.

5. Hoffman and Mason, *Princes of Ireland, Planters of Maryland,* 78–97.

6. Harris, *Revolution,* 512–18.

7. Ibid.; Pincus, *1688,* 3–10; Israel, *The Anglo-Dutch Moment,* 1–43; Cruickshanks, *By Force or by Default?,* 1–7; Speck, *Reluctant Revolutionaries;* Harris, *Politics under the Later Stuarts,* 117–46, and "Lives, Liberties and Estates"; Knights, *Representation and Misrepresentation in Later Stuart Britain*; Schwoerer, *The Declaration of Rights, 1689;* Pocock, *Three British Revolutions.*

8. Historians of sixteenth-, seventeenth-, and eighteenth-century North America continue to engage with this tricky question. For a discussion and some suggestions as to a way out of the difficulty, see Greene, "Colonial History and National History."

9. Walsh, *Motives of Honor, Pleasure, and Profit;* "Forum. Transformations of Virginia"; Bradburn and Coombs, "Smoke and Mirrors"; Meyers and Perreault, *Colonial Chesapeake;* Carr, "Emigration and the Standard of Living," and *The Chesapeake and Beyond;* Carr and Menard, "Wealth and Welfare in Early Maryland"; Carr, Morgan, and Russo, *Colonial Chesapeake Society;* Carr and Walsh, "The Planter's Wife"; Menard, "Opportunity and Inequality," *Economy and Society in Early Colonial Maryland,* "From Servant to Freeholder," and "Population, Economy, and Society in Seventeenth-Century Maryland"; Menard and Walsh, "Death in the Chesapeake"; Tate and Ammerman, *The Chesapeake in the Seventeenth Century;* Clemens, *The Atlantic Economy and Colonial Maryland's Eastern Shore;* Main, *Tobacco Colony;* Parent, *Foul Means;* Debe and Menard, "The Transition to African Slavery in Maryland"; Deal, *Race and Class in Colonial Virginia;* Breen and Innes, *"Myne Owne Ground."*

10. As the above note indicates, the development of slavery was crucial to the first three of these things. I began this project wondering what connections Maryland colonists might draw between slavery and politics. By the end of the century, the presence of slavery is unmistakable, and slaves and "negroes" are often mentioned alongside servants in the records. Slavery considered in the abstract, however, did not shape seventeenth-century white Marylanders' political thinking to the same extent as, say, the fear of the Five Nations or the French. Slaves, like indentured servants, could be part of the unruly multitude that threatened subversion from below, and particular enslaved individuals appear here and there in the records. "Slavery" in the sense of a

general descriptor of labor relations and racial hierarchy in the Chesapeake, however, did not occupy a central place in seventeenth-century conversations about authority, perhaps because labor relations and racial hierarchy themselves were not yet well defined, and because "slavery" in the sense of threats to white male colonists' liberties was of greater cosmic significance to those in a position to write about it. The "slavery" in the "popery and slavery" formula so close to the hearts of late seventeenth-century Protestants on both sides of the Atlantic did not require a consideration of African chattel slavery in order to be meaningful to those who wielded it—that the term had a political resonance separate from the specifics of American life was part of its power.

11. Hammond, *Leah and Rachel, or, the Two Fruitful Sisters Virginia and Mary-Land.*

BIBLIOGRAPHY

MANUSCRIPT SOURCES

Archives of the Congregazione per l'Evangelizzazione dei Popoli (Congregatio de Propaganda Fide), Rome
Scritture Originali Referti nei Congressi
British Library, London
National Archives, London
Admiralty court records
Chancery records
Colonial Office papers
Exchequer records
State Papers Domestic

PUBLISHED PRIMARY SOURCES

Allen, William. *A brief history of the glorious martyrdom of 12 reverend priests.* [Rheims?], 1582.

Anon. *The Key to the King's Cabinet-Counsell.* London, 1644.

———. *The Irish Cabinet: Or, His Majesty's Secret Papers, for Establishing the Papal Clergy in Ireland, with Other Matters of High Concernment.* London, 1646.

———. *A moderate and safe expedient to remove jealousies and fears of any danger, or prejudice to the state, by the Roman Catholics of this kingdom.* London, 1646.

———. *Virginia and Maryland, or, the Lord Baltamore's Printed Case, Uncased and Answered.* London, 1655.

———. *To the Parliament of England, the Case of the Poor English Protestants in Mary-Land under the Arbitrary Power of Their Popish Governor Lord Baltimore.* London, 1681.

Berkeley, William. *The Papers of Sir William Berkeley, 1605–1677.* Edited by Warren M. Billings. Richmond: Library of Virginia, 2007.

Billings, Warren M., ed. *The Old Dominion in the Seventeenth Century: A Documentary History of Virginia, 1606–1700.* 1975; rev. ed. Chapel Hill: University of North Carolina Press, for Omohundro Institute of Early American History and Culture, Williamsburg, VA, 2007.

Calvert, Cecil. *The Lord Baltimore's Case Concerning the Province of Maryland, Adjoining to Virginia in America.* London, 1653.

Calvert, George, and Matthew Page Andrews. "Unpublished Letter of the First Lord Baltimore." *Maryland Historical Magazine* 40, no. 2 (June 1945): 90–91.

Calvert, Philip. *A Letter from the Chancellour of Mary-Land to Col. Henry Meese, Merchant in London, Concerning the Late Troubles in Mary-Land.* London, 1682.

The Calvert Papers. Vol. 1. Baltimore: Maryland Historical Society, 1889.

Chamberlain, John. *The Letters of John Chamberlain.* Edited by Norman Egbert McClure. 2 vols. Philadelphia: American Philosophical Society, 1939.

Charles I [Charles Stuart]. *Eikon Basilike: The Portraiture of His Sacred Majesty in His Solitudes and Sufferings.* Edited by Philip A. Knachel. Ithaca, NY: Cornell University Press, 1966.

Danckaerts, Jasper, and Peter Sluyter. *Journal of a Voyage to New York, and a Tour of Several of the American Colonies in 1679–80.* Translated by Henry C. Murphy. Brooklyn, NY: Long Island Historical Society, 1867.

Goodman, Godfrey. *The Court of King James the First, by Dr. Godfrey Goodman.* Edited by J. S. Brewer. 2 vols. London, 1839.

Hall, Clayton Colman, ed. *Narratives of Early Maryland, 1633–1684.* Bowie, MD: Heritage Books, 1988.

Hammond, John. *Hammond Versus Heamans, or, an Answer to an Audacious Pamphlet.* London, 1655.

———. *Leah and Rachel, or, the Two Fruitful Sisters Virginia and Mary-Land.* London, 1656.

Heaman, Roger. *An Additional Brief Narrative of a Late Bloody Design.* London, 1655.

Howard, Francis. *The Papers of Francis Howard, Baron Howard of Effingham, 1643–1695.* Edited by Warren M. Billings. Richmond: Virginia State Library and Archives, 1989.

Hughes, Thomas. *History of the Society of Jesus in North America: Colonial and Federal: Documents.* 4 vols. London: Longmans, 1908.

James VI and I [James Stuart]. *Political Writings.* Edited by Johann P. Sommerville. Cambridge: Cambridge University Press, 1994.

Kingsbury, Susan M., ed. *The Records of the Virginia Company of London.* 4 vols. Washington: Government Printing Office, 1906–35.

Langford, John. *A Just and Cleer Refutation of a False and Scandalous Pamphlet, Entitled Babylons Fall in Maryland.* London, 1655.

Marvell, Andrew. *An account of the growth of popery and arbitrary government in England.* Amsterdam, 1677.

McIlwaine, H. R., ed. *Executive Journals of the Council of Colonial Virginia.* 3 vols. Richmond: Virginia State Library, 1925–28.

———. *Journals of the House of Burgesses of Virginia, 1619–1658/9.* Richmond: Virginia State Library, 1915.

———. *Journals of the House of Burgesses of Virginia, 1659/60–1693.* Richmond: Virginia State Library, 1914.

———. *Legislative Journals of the Council of Colonial Virginia.* 3 vols. Richmond: Virginia State Library, 1918–19.

O'Callaghan, E. B., ed. *Documents Relative to the Colonial History of the State of New York.* 4 vols. Albany: Weed, Parsons and Company, 1858.

Papenfuse, Edward C., Jr., ed. *Archives of Maryland Online.* Annapolis: Maryland State Archives. Aomol.msa.maryland.gov.

Peckard, Peter. *Memoirs of the life of Mr. Nicholas Ferrar.* Cambridge, 1790.

Protestant Association. *The Declaration of the Reasons and Motives for the Present Appearing in Arms.* London, 1689.

Purchas, Samuel. *Purchas his pilgrimage: or, relations of the world.* London, 1613.

Sainsbury, Noel, ed. *Calendar of State Papers, Colonial Series, America and West Indies, 1661–1668.* London: Stationery Office, 1860–; reprint, Kraus Reprint Ltd., 1964.

Scott, Thomas. *Vox populi: or newes from Spayne.* London, 1620. Not paginated.

Smith, John. *A Map of Virginia. Oxford,* 1612.

Stock, Leo Francis, ed. *Proceedings and Debates of the British Parliaments Respecting North America,* vol. 1: *1542–1688.* Washington, D.C.: Carnegie Institution of Washington, 1924–41.

Strachey, William. *The History of Travell into Virginia Britannia* (1612). In *The Old Dominion in the Seventeenth Century: A Documentary History of Virginia, 1606–1700.* Edited by Warren M. Billings, 267–70. 1975. Rev. ed. Chapel Hill: University of North Carolina Press, for Omohundro Institute of Early American History and Culture, Williamsburg, VA, 2007.

Strong, Leonard. *Babylon's Fall in Maryland, a Fair Warning to Lord Baltamore.* London, 1655.

Wentworth, Thomas. *The Earl of Strafford's Letters and Dispatches.* Edited by William Knowler. London, 1739.

White, Andrew. *Relation of the Succesful Beginnings of the Lord Baltemore's Plantation in Mary-Land. Being an Extract of Certaine Letters Written from Thence, by Some of the Adventurers, to Their Friends in England.* London, [1634?].

———. *Voyage to Maryland / Relatio Itineris in Marilandiam.* Translated by Barbara Lawatsch-Boomgaarden and Josef Ijsewijn. Wauconda, IL: Bolchazy-Carducci Publishers, 1995.

William III. *Declaration of his Highness William Henry, by the Grace of God Prince of Orange, Of the Reasons Inducing him to appear in Armes in the kingdom of England.* The Hague, 1688.

Yong, Thomas. "Extract of a Letter of Captain Thomas Yong to Sir Toby Matthew, 1634." In Hall, *Narratives of Early Maryland,* 55–57.

SECONDARY WORKS

Adams, Simon. "The Protestant Cause: Religious Alliance with the West European Calvinist Communities as a Political Issue in England, 1585–1630." Ph.D. diss., Oxford University, 1973.

Adamson, J. S. A. "Chivalry and Political Culture in Caroline England." In Sharpe and Lake, *Culture and Politics in Early Stuart England,* 161–97.

Anderson, Virginia DeJohn. *Creatures of Empire: How Domestic Animals Transformed Early America.* Oxford: Oxford University Press, 2004.

Andrews, Matthew Page. "Separation of Church and State in Maryland." *Catholic Historical Review* 21 (1935): 164–76.

Applebaum, Robert, and John Wood Sweet, eds. *Envisioning an English Empire: Jamestown and the Making of the North Atlantic World.* Philadelphia: University of Pennsylvania Press, 2005.

Armitage, David. "The Cromwellian Protectorate and the Languages of Empire." *Historical Journal* 35, no. 3 (Sept. 1992): 531–55.

———. *The Ideological Origins of the British Empire.* Cambridge: Cambridge University Press, 2000.

———. "Three Concepts of Atlantic History." In Armitage and Braddick, *The British Atlantic World,* 11–27.

Armitage, David, and Michael J. Braddick, eds. *The British Atlantic World, 1500–1800.* Houndmills: Palgrave; and New York: Macmillan, 2002.

Ashton, Robert. *The Crown and the Money Market, 1603–1640.* Oxford: Clarendon Press of Oxford University Press, 1960.

Aston, Trevor, ed. *Crisis in Europe, 1560–1660: Essays from Past and Present.* London: Routledge, 1965.

Axtell, James. "White Legend: The Jesuit Missions in Maryland." *Maryland Historical Magazine* 81, no. 1 (1986): 1–7.

Bailyn, Bernard. *Atlantic History: Concept and Contours.* Cambridge, MA: Harvard University Press, 2005.

———. *The Origins of American Politics.* New York: Vintage, 1965.

Bailyn, Bernard, and Philip D. Morgan, eds. *Strangers within the Realm: Cultural Margins of the First British Empire.* Chapel Hill: University of North Carolina Press, for Institute of Early American History and Culture, Williamsburg, VA, 1991.

Balmer, Randall. "Traitors and Papists: The Religious Dimensions of Leisler's Rebellion." *New York History* 70, no. 4 (1989): 341–72.

Bell, James B. *Empire, Religion and Revolution in Early Virginia, 1607–1786.* Houndmills: Palgrave Macmillan, 2013.

Benton, Lauren. *A Search for Sovereignty: Law and Geography in European Empire, 1400–1900.* Cambridge: Cambridge University Press, 2010.

Benton, Lauren, and Richard Ross, eds. *Legal Pluralism and Empires, 1500–1850.* New York: New York University Press, 2013.

Black, Joseph. "The Rhetoric of Reaction: The Martin Marprelate Tracts (1588–89), Anti-Martinism and the Uses of Print in Early Modern England." *Sixteenth Century Journal* 23, no. 3 (1997): 707–25.

Bliss, Robert M. *Revolution and Empire: English Politics and American Colonies in the Seventeenth Century.* Manchester: Manchester University Press, 1990.

Bond, Edward L. *Damned Souls in a Tobacco Colony: Religion in Seventeenth-Century Virginia.* Macon, GA: Mercer University Press, 2000.

Bossy, John. "The Character of Elizabethan Catholicism." In Aston, *Crisis in Europe,* 223–46.

———. *The English Catholic Community, 1570–1850.* London: Darton, Longman and Todd, 1975.

Bradburn, Douglas, and John C. Coombs. "Smoke and Mirrors: Reinterpreting the Society and Economy of the Seventeenth-Century Chesapeake." *Atlantic Studies* 3, no. 2 (2006): 131–57.

———, eds. *Early Modern Virginia: Reconsidering the Old Dominion.* Charlottesville: University of Virginia Press, 2011.

Breen, T. H., and Stephen Innes. *"Myne Owne Ground": Race and Freedom on Virginia's Eastern Shore, 1640–1676.* New York: Oxford University Press, 1980.

Bremer, Francis, ed. *Puritanism: Transatlantic Perspectives on a Seventeenth-Century Anglo-American Faith.* Boston: Massachusetts Historical Society, 1993.

Brenner, Robert. *Merchants and Revolution: Commercial Change, Political Conflict and London's Overseas Traders, 1550–1653.* London and New York: Verso, 2003.

Bromley, J. S., and E. H. Kossmann, eds. *Britain and the Netherlands.* The Hague: Martinus Nijhoff, 1975.

Brown, Kathleen. *Good Wives, Nasty Wenches, and Anxious Patriarchs: Gender, Race and Power in Colonial Virginia.* Chapel Hill: University of North Carolina Press, for Institute of Early American History and Culture, Williamsburg, VA, 1996.

Burgess, Glenn. *Absolute Monarchy and the Stuart Constitution.* New Haven, CT: Yale University Press, 1996.

———. "Introduction: Religion and the Historiography of the English Civil War." In Prior and Burgess, *England's Wars of Religion Revisited,* 1–25.

———. *The Politics of the Ancient Constitution: An Introduction to English Political Thought 1600–1642.* Houndmills: Macmillan, 1992.

Burnard, Trevor. *Creole Gentlemen: The Maryland Elite, 1691–1776.* New York: Routledge, 2002.

Bushnell, Amy Turner. "Indigenous America and the Limits of the Atlantic World, 1493–1825." In Greene and Morgan, *Atlantic History,* 191–221.

Butterfield, Herbert. *The Whig Interpretation of History.* London: G. Bell and Sons, 1931.

Campbell, Killis. "Notes on D'Avenant's Life." *Modern Language Notes* 18, no. 8 (1903): 236–39.

Canny, Nicholas. "Fashioning British Worlds in the Seventeenth Century." *Pennsylvania History* 64, no. 5 (1997): 26–45.

———. "The Ideology of English Colonization: From Ireland to America," *William and Mary Quarterly,* 3rd. ser., 30, no. 4 (1973): 575–98.

———. "Writing Atlantic History; or, Reconfiguring the History of Colonial British America." *Journal of American History* 86, no. 3 (1999): 1093–1114.

Carr, Lois Green. "County Government in Maryland, 1689–1709." Ph.D. thesis, Harvard University, 1967.

———. "Sources of Political Stability and Upheaval in Seventeenth Century Maryland." *Maryland Historical Magazine* 79, no. 1 (1984): 44–70.

———. "Emigration and the Standard of Living: The Seventeenth-Century Chesapeake." *Journal of Economic History* 52, no. 2 (1992): 271–91.

———, ed. *The Chesapeake and Beyond: A Celebration: A Collection of Discussion Papers Presented at a Conference, May 22–23, 1992, University of Maryland, University College Conference Center, College Park, Maryland.* Crownsville, MD: Maryland Historical & Cultural Publications, 1992.

Carr, Lois Green, and David W. Jordan. *Maryland's Revolution of Government, 1689–1692.* Ithaca, NY: Cornell University Press, 1974.

Carr, Lois Green, Aubrey C. Land, and Edward C. Papenfuse, eds. *Law, Society, and Politics in Early Maryland: Proceedings of the First Conference on Maryland History, June 14–15, 1974.* Studies in Maryland History and Culture. Baltimore: Johns Hopkins University Press, 1974.

Carr, Lois Green, and Russell R. Menard. "Wealth and Welfare in Early Maryland: Evidence from St. Mary's County." *William and Mary Quarterly,* 3rd ser., 56, no. 1 (1999): 95–120.

Carr, Lois Green, Philip D. Morgan, and Jean B. Russo, eds. *Colonial Chesapeake Society.* Chapel Hill: University of North Carolina Press, for Institute of Early American History and Culture, Williamsburg, VA, 1988.

Carr, Lois Green, and Lorena Walsh. "The Planter's Wife: The Experience of White Women in Seventeenth-Century Maryland." *William and Mary Quarterly,* 3rd ser., 34, no. 4 (1977): 542–71.

Carr, Lois Green, Lorena Walsh, and Russell R. Menard. *Robert Cole's World: Agriculture and Society in Early Maryland.* Chapel Hill: University of

North Carolina Press, for Institute of Early American History and Culture, Williamsburg, VA, 1991.

Chandaman, C. D. *The English Public Revenue, 1660–1688.* Oxford: Clarendon Press of Oxford University Press, 1975.

Cherry, Megan Lindsay. "Rumor Has It: Rumor as a Political Tool in New York in the 1680s." Paper delivered at the North American Conference on British Studies, Portland, OR, November 8–10, 2013.

Clark, Stuart. *Thinking with Demons: The Idea of Witchcraft in Early Modern Europe.* New York: Oxford University Press, 1997.

Clarke, Peter, A. G. R. Smith, and Nicholas Tyacke, eds. *The English Commonwealth, 1547–1640: Essays in Politics and Society.* New York: Barnes and Noble, 1979.

Clemens, Paul G. E. *The Atlantic Economy and Colonial Maryland's Eastern Shore: From Tobacco to Grain.* Ithaca, NY: Cornell University Press, 1980.

Clifton, Robin. "Fear of Popery." In Russell, *The Origins of the English Civil War,* 144–67.

———. "Popular Fear of Catholics during the English Revolution." *Past & Present* 52 (1971): 23–55.

Coakley, Thomas. "George Calvert, First Lord Baltimore: Family, Status, Arms." *Maryland Historical Magazine* 79, no. 9 (1984): 255–69.

Cogswell, Thomas. *The Blessed Revolution: English Politics and the Coming of War, 1621–1624.* Cambridge: Cambridge University Press, 1989.

———. "'In the Power of the State': Mr. Anys's Project and the Tobacco Colonies, 1626–1628." *English Historical Review* 123, no. 500 (2008): 35–64.

———. "A Low Road to Extinction: Supply and Redress of Grievances in the Parliaments of the 1620s." *Historical Journal* 33, no. 2 (1990): 283–303.

———. "The People's Love: The Duke of Buckingham and Popularity." In Cogswell, Crust, and Lake, *Politics, Religion and Popularity in Early Stuart Britain,* 211–34.

———. "Phaeton's Chariot: The Parliament Men and the Continental Crisis of 1621." In Merritt, *The Political World of Thomas Wentworth,* 24–46.

———. "The Politics of Propaganda: Charles I and the People in the 1620s." *Journal of British Studies* 29, no. 3 (1990): 187–215.

Cogswell, Thomas, Richard Cust, and Peter Lake, eds. *Politics, Religion and Popularity in Early Stuart Britain: Essays in Honour of Conrad Russell.* Cambridge: Cambridge University Press, 2002.

Colley, Linda. *Britons: Forging the Nation, 1707–1837.* New Haven, CT: Yale University Press, 1992.

Collinson, Patrick. "Ecclesiastical Vitriol: Religious Satire in the 1590s and the Invention of Puritanism." In Guy, *The Reign of Elizabeth I,* 150–70.

———. *Elizabethan Essays.* London: Hambledon, 1994.

———. "The Monarchical Republic of Queen Elizabeth I." In Collinson, *Elizabethan Essays,* 31–58.

———. *The Religion of Protestants: The Church in English Society, 1559–1625.* Oxford: Clarendon Press of Oxford University Press, 1982.

Coward, Barry. *The Stuart Age: England, 1603–1714.* London: Routledge, 2014.

Craven, Wesley Frank. *Dissolution of the Virginia Company: The Failure of a Colonial Experiment.* New York: Oxford University Press, 1932; reprint, Gloucester, MA: Peter Smith, 1964.

———. *The Southern Colonies in the Seventeenth Century, 1607–1689.* Baton Rouge: Louisiana State University Press, 1970.

Cressy, David. "Binding the Nation: The Bonds of Association, 1584 and 1696." In Guth and McKenna, *Tudor Rule and Revolution,* 217–36.

Croft, Pauline, ed. "A Collection of Several Speeches and Treatises of the Late Treasurer Cecil." *Camden Miscellany* 29. Camden Society Publications, 4th ser., 34 (1987).

Cromartie, Alan. *The Constitutionalist Revolution: An Essay on the History of England, 1450–1642.* Cambridge: Cambridge University Press, 2006.

———. "The Constitutionalist Revolution: The Transformation of Political Culture in Early Stuart England." *Past & Present* 163 (1999): 76–120.

Cruickshanks, Eveline, ed. *By Force or by Default?: The Revolution of 1688–89.* Edinburgh: John Donald, 1989.

———, ed. *The Stuart Courts.* Stroud: Sutton, 2000.

Cuddy, Neil. "Reinventing a Monarchy: The Changing Structure and Political Function of the Stuart Court, 1603–1688." In Cruickshanks, *The Stuart Courts,* 59–85.

Cushner, Nicholas P. *Why Have You Come Here? The Jesuits and the First Evangelization of Native America.* Oxford: Oxford University Press, 2006.

Cust, Richard. *Charles I: A Political Life.* Harlow: Pearson, 2005.

———. "Charles I, the Privy Council, and the Parliament of 1628." *Transactions of the Royal Historical Society* 6th ser., 2 (1992): 25–50.

———. "Charles I and a Draft Declaration for the Parliament of 1628." *Historical Research* 63, no. 151 (1990): 143–61.

———. "Charles I and Popularity." In Cogswell, Crust, and Lake, *Politics, Religion and Popularity in Early Stuart Britain,* 235–58.

———. *The Forced Loan and English Politics, 1626–1628.* Oxford: Clarendon Press of Oxford University Press; and New York: Oxford University Press, 1987.

Cust, Richard, and Ann Hughes, eds. *Conflict in Early Stuart England: Studies in Religion and Politics, 1603–1642.* New York and London: Longman, 1989.

———. *The English Civil War.* London: Arnold, 1997.

Daniels, Christine, and Michael V. Kennedy, eds. *Negotiated Empires: Center and Peripheries in the Americas, 1500–1820.* New York: Routledge, 2002.

Davies, Julian. *The Caroline Captivity of the Church: Charles I and the Remoulding of Anglicanism, 1625–1642.* Oxford: Oxford University Press, 1992.

Davis, Ralph. "English Foreign Trade, 1660–1700." *Economic History Review* 7, no. 2 (1954): 150–66.

Deal, J. Douglas. *Race and Class in Colonial Virginia: Indians, Englishmen, and Africans on the Eastern Shore during the Seventeenth Century.* New York: Garland, 1993.

Debe, Dimitri, and Russell R. Menard. "The Transition to African Slavery in Maryland: A Note on the Barbados Connection." *Slavery and Abolition* 21, no. 1 (March 2011): 129–41.

Dewar, Helen. "Litigating Empire: The Role of French Courts in Establishing Colonial Sovereignties." In Benton and Ross, *Legal Pluralism and Empires,* 49–79.

Dolan, Frances E. *Whores of Babylon: Catholicism, Gender and Seventeenth-Century Print Culture.* Ithaca, NY: Cornell University Press, 1999.

Dowd, Gregory Evans. "The French King Wakes up in Detroit: 'Pontiac's War' in Rumor and Memory." *Ethnohistory* 37, no. 3 (1990): 254–78.

———. "The Panic of 1751: The Significance of Rumors on the South Carolina–Cherokee Frontier." *William and Mary Quarterly,* 3rd ser., 53, no. 3 (1996): 527–60.

Duffy, Eamon. *The Stripping of the Altars: Traditional Religion in England, 1400–1580.* New Haven, CT: Yale University Press, 1992.

Dugmore, C. W., ed. *Studies in the Reformation: Luther to Hooker.* London: Althone, 1980.

Everstine, Carl N. "Maryland's Toleration Act: An Appraisal." *Maryland Historical Magazine* 79, no. 2 (1984): 99–116.

Falb, Susan Rosenfeld. *Advice and Ascent: The Development of the Maryland Assembly, 1635–1689.* New York: Garland, 1986.

———. "Proxy Voting in Early Maryland Assemblies." *Maryland Historical Magazine* 73, no. 3 (1978): 217–25.

Farge, Arlette, and Jacques Revel. *The Vanishing Children of Paris: Rumor and Politics before the French Revolution.* Translated by Claudia Mieville. Cambridge, MA: Harvard University Press, 1991.

Farrelly, Maura Jane. *Papist Patriots: The Making of an American Catholic Identity.* Oxford: Oxford University Press, 2012.

Fausz, J. Frederick. *"By warre upon our enemies and kinde usage of our friends": The Secular Context of Religious Toleration in Maryland, 1620–1660.* Privately published, 1983.

———. "Merging and Emerging Worlds: Anglo-Indian Interest Groups and the Development of the Seventeenth-Century Chesapeake." In Carr, Morgan, and Russo, *Colonial Chesapeake Society*, 47–98.

———. "Profits, Pets, and Power: English Culture in the Early Chesapeake, 1620–1652." *Maryland Historian* 14, no. 2 (1983): 14–30.

Ferrell, Lori Ann. *Government by Polemic: James I, the King's Preachers, and the Rhetorics of Conformity, 1603–1625*. Stanford, CA: Stanford University Press, 1998.

Fincham, Kenneth. "The Judges' Decision on Ship Money in February 1637: The Reaction of Kent." *Bulletin of the Institute for Historical Research* 57, no. 136 (1984): 230–37.

———. "Prelacy and Politics: Archbishop Abbott's Defense of Protestant Orthodoxy." *Bulletin of the Institute for Historical Research* 61, no. 144 (Feb. 1988): 36–64.

———. "The Restoration of the Altars in the 1630s." *Historical Journal* 44, no. 4 (2001): 919–40.

———, ed. *The Early Stuart Church, 1603–1642*. Houndmills: Macmillan, 1993.

Fincham, Kenneth, and Peter Lake. "The Ecclesiastical Policy of James I." *Journal of British Studies* 24, no. 1 (1985): 169–207.

———. "Popularity, Prelacy and Puritanism in the 1630s: Joseph Hall Explains Himself." *English Historical Review* 111, no. 443 (1996): 856–81.

Fogarty, Gerald P. "The Origins of the Mission, 1634–1773." In *The Maryland Jesuits, 1634–1833*, edited by Robert Emmett Curran, 9–27. Baltimore: Corporation of Roman Catholic Clergymen and Maryland Province of the Society of Jesus, 1976.

"Forum. Transformations of Virginia: Tobacco, Slavery, and Empire." *William and Mary Quarterly*, 3rd ser., 68, no. 3 (July 2011): 327–480.

Fox, Adam. *Oral and Literate Culture in England, 1500–1700*. Oxford: Clarendon Press of Oxford University Press, 2000.

———. "Rumor, News and Popular Political Opinion in Elizabethan and Early Stuart England." *Historical Journal* 40, no. 3 (1997): 597–620.

Fox, Adam, and Daniel Woolf, eds. *The Spoken Word: Oral Culture in Britain, 1500–1850*. Manchester: Manchester University Press, 2002.

Freeman, Thomas. "Demons, Deviance and Defiance: John Darrell and the Politics of Exorcism in Late Elizabethan England." In Lake and Questier, *Conformity and Orthodoxy in the English Church*, 34–63.

Gallivan, Martin D. *The James River Chiefdoms: The Rise of Social Inequality in the Chesapeake*. Lincoln: University of Nebraska Press, 2003.

———"Powhatan's Werowocomoco: Constructing Place, Polity, and Personhood in the Chesapeake, C.E. 1200–C.E. 1609." *American Anthropologist* 109, no. 1 (March 2007): 85–100.

Games, Alison. "Atlantic Constraints and Global Opportunities." *History Compass* 1 (2003): 1–4.

———. "Atlantic History: Definitions, Challenges, and Opportunities." *American Historical Review* 111, no. 3 (June 2006): 741–57.

———. *Migration and the Origins of the English Atlantic World.* Cambridge, MA: Harvard University Press, 1999.

———. *The Web of Empire: English Cosmopolitans in an Age of Expansion, 1560–1660.* Oxford: Oxford University Press, 2008.

Gardiner, Samuel Rawson. *History of England.* 10 vols. London: Longman, 1884–86.

Gentles, Ian. *The English Revolution and the Wars in the Three Kingdoms, 1638–1652.* Harlow: Pearson, 2007.

———. *The New Model Army in England, Ireland and Scotland, 1645–1653.* Oxford: Blackwell, 1992.

Gleissner, Richard A. "Religious Causes of the Glorious Revolution in Maryland." *Maryland Historical Magazine* 64, no. 4 (1969): 327–41.

Graham, Michael James. "Lord Baltimore's Pious Enterprise: Toleration and Community in Colonial Maryland, 1634–1724." Ph.D. diss., University of Michigan, 1983.

———. "Meetinghouse and Chapel: Religion and Community in Seventeenth-Century Maryland." In Carr, Morgan, and Russo, *Colonial Chesapeake Society,* 242–74.

———. "Popish Plots: Protestant Fears in Early Colonial Maryland, 1676–1689." *Catholic Historical Review* 79, no. 2 (1993): 197–216.

Greenblatt, Stephen. *Marvelous Possessions: The Wonder of the New World.* Chicago: University of Chicago Press, 1991.

Greene, Jack P. "Colonial History and National History: Reflections on a Continuing Problem." *William and Mary Quarterly,* 3rd ser., 64, no. 2 (2007): 235–50.

———. "Negotiated Authorities: The Problem of Governance in the Extended Polities of the Early Modern Atlantic World." In Greene, *Negotiated Authorities,* 1–24.

———. *Peripheries and Center: Constitutional Development in the Extended Polities of the British Empire and the United States, 1707–1788.* New York: Norton, 1986.

Greene, Jack P., ed. *Negotiated Authorities: Essays in Colonial Political and Constitutional History.* Charlottesville: University of Virginia Press, 1994.

Greene, Jack. P., and Philip D. Morgan, eds. *Atlantic History: A Critical Appraisal.* Oxford: Oxford University Press, 2009.

Gregerson, Linda, and Susan Juster, eds. *Empires of God: Religious Encounters in the Early Modern Atlantic.* Philadelphia: University of Pennsylvania Press, 2011.

Griffey, Erin, ed. *Henrietta Maria: Piety, Politics and Patronage.* Burlington, VT: Ashgate, 2008.

Guth, Delloyd J., and John W. McKenna, eds. *Tudor Rule and Revolution: Essays for G. R. Elton from his American Friends.* Cambridge: Cambridge University Press, 1982.

Guy, John. *The Reign of Elizabeth I: Court and Culture in the Last Decade.* Cambridge: Cambridge University Press, 1995.

Haigh, Christopher. "The Continuity of Catholicism in the English Reformation." In Haigh, *The English Reformation Revised,* 176–208.

———. *English Reformations.* Oxford: Clarendon Press of Oxford University Press, 1993.

———. "From Monopoly to Minority: Catholicism in Early Modern England." *Transactions of the Royal Historical Society* 31 (Dec. 1981): 129–47.

———, ed. *The English Reformation Revised.* Cambridge: Cambridge University Press, 1997.

Haley, K. D. H. "'No Popery' in the Reign of Charles II." In Bromley and Kossmann, *Britain and the Netherlands,* 102–19.

Hall, Michael G. *Edward Randolph and the American Colonies, 1676–1703.* Chapel Hill: University of North Carolina Press, 1960.

Hammer, Paul. "The Smiling Crocodile: The Earl of Essex and Late-Elizabethan 'Popularity.'" In Lake and Pincus, *The Politics of the Public Sphere in Early Modern England,* 95–115.

Hanley, Thomas O'Brien. "Church and State in the Maryland Ordinance of 1639." *Church History* 26 (1957): 325–41.

———. *Their Rights and Liberties: The Beginnings of Religious and Political Freedom in Maryland.* Chicago: Loyola University Press, 1984.

Harris, Tim. "'Lives, Liberties and Estates': Rhetorics of Liberty in the Reign of Charles II." In Harris, Seward, and Goldie, *The Politics of Religion in Restoration England,* 217–48.

———. *Politics under the Later Stuarts: Party Conflict in a Divided Society, 1660–1715.* London and New York: Longman, 1993.

———. *Restoration: Charles II and His Kingdoms.* New York: Penguin, 2006.

———. *Revolution: The Great Crisis of the British Monarch, 1686–1720.* London: Allen Lane, 2006.

Harris, Tim, Paul Seaward, and Mark Goldie, eds. *The Politics of Religion in Restoration England.* Oxford and Cambridge, MA: Basil Blackwell, 1990.

Hartsock, John. "America's First Experiment in Toleration." *History Today* 43 (1993): 22–28.

Hatfield, April Lee. *Atlantic Virginia: Intercolonial Relations in the Seventeenth Century.* Philadelphia: University of Pennsylvania Press, 2004.

Hibbard, Caroline M. *Charles I and the Popish Plot.* Chapel Hill: University of North Carolina Press, 1981.

Highley, Christopher. *Catholics Writing the Nation in Early Modern Britain and Ireland.* Oxford: Oxford University Press, 2008.

Hinderacker, Eric, and Rebecca Horn. "Territorial Crossings: Histories and Historiographies of the Early Americas." *William and Mary Quarterly,* 3rd ser., 67, no. 3 (July 2010): 395–432.

Hirschman, Albert O. *The Passions and the Interests: Political Arguments for Capitalism before Its Triumph.* Princeton, NJ: Princeton University Press, 1977.

Hoffman, Ronald, and Sally Mason. *Princes of Ireland, Planters of Maryland: A Carroll Saga, 1500–1782.* Chapel Hill: University of North Carolina Press, for Omohundro Institute of Early American History and Culture, Williamsburg, VA, 2000.

Horn, James. *Adapting to a New World: English Society in the Seventeenth-Century Chesapeake.* Chapel Hill: University of North Carolina Press, for Institute of Early American History and Culture, Williamsburg, VA, 1994.

———. *A Kingdom Strange: The Brief and Tragic History of the Lost Colony of Roanoke.* Philadelphia: Basic Books, 2010.

Houston, Alan, and Steve Pincus, eds. *A Nation Transformed: England after the Restoration.* Cambridge: Cambridge University Press, 2001.

Hsia, Ronnie P. *The Myth of Ritual Murder: Jews and Magic in Reformation Germany.* New Haven, CT: Yale University Press, 1988.

Hudson, Charles, and Carmen Chaves Tesser, eds. *The Forgotten Centuries: Indians and Europeans in the American South, 1521–1704.* Athens: University of Georgia Press, 1994.

Hutton, Ronald. *Charles II.* Oxford: Clarendon Press of Oxford University Press, 1989.

———. *The Restoration: A Political and Religious History of England and Wales, 1658–1667.* New York: Oxford University Press, 1985.

Isaac, Rhys. *The Transformation of Virginia, 1740–1790.* Chapel Hill: University of North Carolina Press, for Institute of Early American History and Culture, Williamsburg, VA, 1982.

Israel, Jonathan I., ed. *The Anglo-Dutch Moment.* Cambridge: Cambridge University Press, 1991.

Ives, Joseph Moss. "The Catholic Contribution to Religious Liberty in Colonial America." *Catholic Historical Review* 21 (1935): 283–98.

Jennings, Francis. *The Ambiguous Iroquois Empire: The Covenant Chain Confederation of Indian Tribes with English Colonies from Its Beginnings to the Lancaster Treaty of 1744.* New York: Norton, 1984.

———. "Glory, Death, and Transfiguration: The Susquehannock Indians in the

Seventeenth Century." *Proceedings of the American Philosophical Society* 112, no. 1 (1968): 15–53.

Johnson, Richard R. *Adjustment to Empire: The New England Colonies, 1675–1715.* New Brunswick, NJ: Rutgers University Press, 1981.

———. "The Revolution of 1688–9 in the American Colonies." In Israel, *The Anglo-Dutch Moment,* 215–40.

Jonas, Manfred. "The Claiborne-Calvert Controversy: An Episode in the Colonization of North America." *Jarhbuch fuer Amerikastudien* 11 (1966): 241–50.

Jordan, David W. *Foundations of Representative Government in Maryland, 1632–1715.* Cambridge: Cambridge University Press, 1987.

———. "'God's Candle within Government': Quakers and Politics in Early Maryland." *William and Mary Quarterly,* 3rd ser., 39, no. 4 (1982): 628–54.

———. "John Coode, Perennial Rebel." *Maryland Historical Magazine* 70, no. 1 (1975): 1–28.

———. "Maryland's Privy Council." In Car, Land, and Papenfuse, *Law, Society, and Politics in Early Maryland,* 65–87.

———. "The Miracle of This Age: Maryland's Experiment in Religious Toleration, 1649–1689." *Historian* 47, no. 3 (1985): 338–59.

———. "The Royal Period of Colonial Maryland 1689–1715." Ph.D. diss., Princeton University, 1966.

Kammen, Michael G. "Causes of the Maryland Revolution." *Maryland Historical Magazine* 55, no. 4 (1960): 293–333.

Kapferer, Jean-Noel. *Rumors: Uses, Interpretations, and Images.* Translated by Bruce Fink. New Brunswick, NJ: Transaction Publishers, 1990.

Kelsey, Sean. *Inventing a Republic: The Political Culture of the English Commonwealth, 1649–1653.* Stanford, CA: Stanford University Press, 1997.

Kent, Barry C. *Susquehanna's Indians.* Harrisburg: Pennsylvania Historical and Museum Commission, 1989.

Kenyon, J. P. *The Popish Plot.* London: Heinemann, 1972; Phoenix, 2000.

Kishlansky, Mark. "The Emergence of Adversary Politics in the Long Parliament." *Journal of Modern History* 49, no. 4 (1977): 617–40.

———. *A Monarchy Transformed: Britain 1603–1714.* London: Penguin, 1997.

———. "Tyranny Denied: Charles I, Attorney General Heath, and the Five Knights' Case." *Historical Journal* 42, no. 1 (1999): 53–83.

Knights, Mark. "'Meer Religion' and the 'Church-State' of Restoration England: The Impact and Ideology of James II's Declarations of Indulgence." In Houston and Pincus, *A Nation Transformed,* 41–70.

———. *Politics and Opinion in Crisis, 1678–1681.* Cambridge: Cambridge University Press, 1994.

———. *Representation and Misrepresentation in Later Stuart Britain: Partisanship and Political Culture.* Oxford and New York: Oxford University Press, 2005.

Krugler, John. "The Calvert Family, Catholicism, and Court Politics in Early Seventeenth-Century England." *Historian* 43 (1981): 378–92.

———. *English and Catholic: The Lords Baltimore in the Seventeenth Century.* Baltimore: Johns Hopkins University Press, 2004.

———. "The Face of a Protestant and the Heart of a Papist: A Reexamination of Sir George Calvert's Conversion to Roman Catholicism." *Journal of Church and State* 20 (1978): 507–31.

———. "Lord Baltimore, Roman Catholics, and Toleration: Religious Policy in Maryland during the Early Catholic Years, 1630–1649." *Catholic Historical Review* 65 (1979): 47–95.

———. "'Our Trusty and Wellbeloved Councilor': The Parliamentary Career of Sir George Calvert, 1609–24." *Maryland Historical Magazine* 72 (1977): 470–97.

———. "Sir George Calvert's Resignation as Secretary of State and the Founding of Maryland." *Maryland Historical Magazine* 68 (1973): 239–54.

———. "With Promise of Liberty in Religion: The Catholic Lords Baltimore and Toleration in Seventeenth-Century Maryland." *Maryland Historical Magazine* 79, no. 1 (1984): 21–43.

Krugler, John, and Timothy Riordan. "'Scandalous and Offensive to the Government': The 'Poppish Chapel' at St. Mary's City, 1634–1705." *Mid-America* 73, no. 3 (Oct. 1991): 187–208.

Kukla, John. *Political Institutions in Virginia, 1619–1660.* New York and London: Garland, 1989.

Kupperman, Karen O. *Indians and English: Facing off in Early America.* Ithaca, NY: Cornell University Press, 2003.

———. *The Jamestown Project.* Cambridge, MA: Harvard University Press, 2008.

Lahey, R. J. "The Role of Religion in Lord Baltimore's Colonial Enterprise." *Maryland Historical Magazine* 72 (1977): 491–511.

Lake, Peter. "Anti-Popery: The Structure of a Prejudice." In Cust and Huges, *Conflict in Early Stuart England,* 72–105.

———. "Calvinism and the English Church, 1570–1635." *Past & Present* 114 (1987): 32–76.

———. "The Collection of Ship Money in Cheshire." *Northern History* 17 (1981): 44–71.

———. "The Laudian Style: Order, Uniformity and the Pursuit of Holiness in the 1630s." In Fincham, *The Early Stuart Church,* 161–87.

———. "Puritanism, Arminianism and a Shropshire Axe-Murder." *Midland History* 15 (1990): 37–64.

———. "Puritanism, Monarchical Republicanism and Monarchy; or John Whitgift,

Anti-Puritanism and the 'Invention' of Popularity." *Journal of Medieval and Early Modern Studies* 40, no. 3 (Fall 2010): 463–95.

Lake, Peter, and David Como. "Orthodoxy and Its Discontents: Dispute Settlement and the Production of 'Consensus' in the London (Puritan) Underground." *Journal of British Studies* 39, no. 1 (Jan. 2000): 34–70.

Lake, Peter, and Steven Pincus, eds. *The Politics of the Public Sphere in Early Modern England.* Manchester: Manchester University Press, 2007.

Lake, Peter, and Michael Questier. "Agency, Appropriation and Rhetoric under the Gallows: Puritans, Romanists and the State in Early Modern England." *Past & Present* 153 (Nov. 1996): 64–107.

———, eds. *Conformity and Orthodoxy in the English Church, c. 1560–1660.* Rochester, NY: Boydell Press, 2000.

LeFebvre, George. *The Great Fear of 1789: Rural Panic in Revolutionary France.* Translated by Joan White. New York: Pantheon, 1973.

Lovejoy, David. *The Glorious Revolution in America.* Hanover, NH: Wesleyan University Press, 1987.

MacMillan, Ken. *The Atlantic Imperial Constitution: Center and Periphery in the English Atlantic World.* New York: Palgrave Macmillan, 2011.

———. *Sovereignty and Possession in the English New World: The Legal Foundations of Empire, 1576–1640.* Cambridge: Cambridge University Press, 2006.

Main, Gloria. *Tobacco Colony: Life in Early Maryland, 1650–1720.* Princeton, NJ: Princeton University Press, 1982.

Malomet, B. C. *After the Reformation: Essays in Honor of J. H. Hexter.* Philadelphia: University of Pennsylvania Press, 1980.

Maloney, Eric John. "Papists and Puritans in Early Maryland: Religion in the Forging of Provincial Society, 1632–1665." Ph.D. diss., State University of New York at Stony Brook, 1996.

Mancall, Peter C. *The Atlantic World and Virginia, 1550–1624.* Chapel Hill: University of North Carolina Press, for Omohundro Institute of Early American History and Culture, Williamsburg, VA, 2007.

Mancke, Elizabeth. "Empire and State." In Armitage and Braddick, *The British Atlantic World, 1500–1800,* 175–95.

———. "Negotiating an Empire: Britain and Its Overseas Peripheries, c.1550–1780." In Daniels and Kennedy, *Negotiated Empires,* 235–65.

Manning, Brian. *The English People and the English Revolution.* London: Bookmarks, 1976; 2nd ed., 1991.

Marshall, Peter. "The Naming of Protestant England," *Past & Present* 214 (Feb. 2012): 87–128.

Mayers, Ruth E. *1659: The Crisis of the Commonwealth.* Woodbridge, Suffolk: Boydell, 2004.

McCusker, John J., and Russell R. Menard. *The Economy of British America, 1607–1789*. Chapel Hill: University of North Carolina Press, for Institute of Early American History and Culture, Williamsburg, VA, 1985.

Menard, Russell R. *Economy and Society in Early Colonial Maryland*. New York: Garland, 1985.

———. "From Servant to Freeholder: Status Mobility and Property Accumulation in Seventeenth-Century Maryland." *William and Mary Quarterly*, 3rd ser., 30, no. 1 (1973): 37–64.

———. "Maryland's Time of Troubles: Sources of Political Disorder in Early St. Mary's." *Maryland Historical Magazine* 76, no. 2 (1981): 124–40.

———. "Opportunity and Inequality: The Distribution of Wealth along the Lower Western Shore of Maryland 1638–1705." *Maryland Historical Magazine* 69, no. 2 (1974): 169–84.

———. "Population, Economy, and Society in Seventeenth-Century Maryland." *Maryland Historical Magazine* 79, no. 1 (1984): 71–92.

Menard, Russell R., and Lorena Walsh. "Death in the Chesapeake: Two Life Tables for Men in Early Colonial Maryland." *Maryland Historical Magazine* 69, no. 2 (1974): 211–27.

Merrell, James H. "Cultural Continuity among the Piscataway Indians of Colonial Maryland." *William and Mary Quarterly*, 3rd ser., 36, no. 4 (1979): 548–70.

———. "Second Thoughts on Colonial Historians and American Indians." *William and Mary Quarterly*, 3rd ser., 69, no. 3 (July 2012): 451–512.

Merritt, J. F., ed. *The Political World of Thomas Wentworth, Earl of Strafford 1621–1641*. Cambridge: Cambridge University Press, 1996.

Merwick, Donna. *The Shame and the Sorrow: Dutch-Amerindian Encounters in New Netherland*. Philadelphia: University of Pennsylvania Press, 2006.

Meyers, Debra. *Common Whores, Vertuous Women, and Loveing Wives: Free Will Christian Women in Colonial Maryland*. Bloomington: Indiana University Press, 2003.

Meyers, Debra, and Melanie Perreault, eds. *Colonial Chesapeake: New Perspectives*. Lanham, MD: Lexington Books, 2006.

Miller, John. "Charles II and His Parliaments." *Transactions of the Royal Historical Society* 32 (1982): 1–24.

———. *James II*. New Haven, CT: Yale University Press, 2000.

———. *James II: A Study in Kingship*. Hove: Wayland, 1978.

———. *Popery and Politics in England, 1660–1688*. Cambridge: Cambridge University Press, 1973.

———. "The Potential for Absolutism in Later Stuart England." *History* 69 (1984): 187–207.

Millstone, Noah. "Evil Counsel: The Propositions to Bridle the Impertinency of

Parliament and the Critique of Caroline Government in the Late 1620s." *Journal of British Studies* 50, no. 4 (Oct. 2011): 813–39.

Milton, Anthony. *Catholic and Reformed: The Roman and Protestant Churches in English Protestant Thought, 1600–1640.* Cambridge: Cambridge University Press, 1995.

———. "Thomas Wentworth and the Political Thought of the Personal Rule." In Merritt, *The Political World of Thomas Wentworth,* 133–56.

Moran, Dennis. "Anti-Catholicism in Early Maryland Politics: The Puritan Influence." *Records of the American Catholic Society of Philadelphia* 61 (1950): 139–54.

Morgan, Edmund S. *American Slavery, American Freedom: The Ordeal of Colonial Virginia.* New York: Norton, 1975.

Morrill, John. *Cheshire, 1630–1660: County Government and Society during the English Revolution.* London: Oxford University Press, 1974.

———. "Cromwell, Parliament, Ireland and a Commonwealth in Crisis: 1652 Revisited." *Parliamentary History* 30, no. 2 (2011): 193–214.

———. *The Revolt of the Provinces: Conservatives and Radicals during the English Civil Wars, 1630–1660.* New York: Barnes and Noble, 1976.

Mullin, Francis A. "The Palatinate of Durham." *Catholic Historical Review* 21, no. 2 (1935): 177–89.

Murrin, John. "The Menacing Shadow of Louis XIV and the Rage of Jacob Leisler: The Constitutional Ordeal of Seventeenth-Century New York." In Schechter and Bernstein, *New York and the Union,* 29–71.

Nenner, Howard. *By Color of Law: Legal Culture and Constitutional Politics in England, 1660–1689.* Chicago: University of Chicago Press, 1977.

Notestein, Wallace. *The Winning of the Initiative by the House of Commons.* London: Oxford University Press, 1924.

Olson, Alison. *Anglo-American Politics, 1660–1775: The Relationship between Parties in England and Colonial America.* New York: Oxford University Press, 1973.

Pagden, Anthony. *Lords of All the World: Ideologies of Empire in Spain, Britain, and France, c.1500–c.1800.* New Haven, CT: Yale University Press, 1995.

Parent, Anthony, Jr. *Foul Means: The Formation of a Slave Society in Virginia, 1660–1740.* Chapel Hill: University of North Carolina Press, for Omohundro Institute of Early American History and Culture, Williamsburg, VA, 2003.

Patterson, Brown. *King James VI and I and the Reunion of Christendom.* Cambridge: Cambridge University Press, 1997.

Pawlisch, Hans. *Sir John Davies and the Conquest of Ireland: A Study of Legal Imperialism.* Cambridge and New York: Cambridge University Press, 1985.

Peck, Linda Levy. "Corruption at the Court of James I: The Undermining of Legitimacy." In Maloment, *After the Reformation,* 75–93.

———. *Court Patronage and Corruption in Early Stuart England.* London and Boston: Unwin Hyman, 1990.

———. "Problems in Jacobean Administration: Was Henry Howard, Earl of Northampton, a Reformer?" *Historical Journal* 19, no. 4 (1976): 831–58.

Pestana, Carla Gardina. *The English Atlantic in an Age of Revolution.* Cambridge, MA: Harvard University Press, 2004.

———. "English Character and the Fiasco of the Western Design." *Early American Studies* 3, no. 1 (Spring 2005): 1–31.

———. *Protestant Empire: Religion and the Making of the British Atlantic World.* Philadelphia: University of Pennsylvania Press, 2009.

Pincus, Steven. *Protestantism and Patriotism: Ideologies and the Making of English Foreign Policy, 1650–1668.* Cambridge: Cambridge University Press, 1996.

———. *1688: The First Modern Revolution.* New Haven, CT: Yale University Press, 2009.

Pocock, J. G. A. *The Ancient Constitution and the Feudal Law: A Study of English Historical Thought in the Seventeenth Century.* Cambridge: Cambridge University Press, 1957.

———, ed. *Three British Revolutions: 1641, 1688, 1776.* Princeton, NJ: Princeton University Press, 1980.

Porter, Frank. "A Century of Accommodation: The Nanticoke Indians in Colonial Maryland." *Maryland Historical Magazine* 74, no. 2 (1979): 175–92.

Prior, Charles W. A., and Glenn Burgess, eds. *England's Wars of Religion Revisited.* Burlington, VT: Ashgate, 2011.

Questier, Michael. *Catholicism and Community in Early Modern England: Politics, Aristocratic Patronage and Religion, c. 1550–1640.* Cambridge: Cambridge University Press, 2006.

———. "Conformity, Catholicism and the Law." In Lake and Questier, *Conformity and Orthodoxy in the English Church,* 237–61.

———. "What Happened to Catholicism after the English Reformation?" *History* 85, issue 277 (2000): 28–47.

Quinn, David B. *The Voyages and Colonizing Enterprises of Sir Humphrey Gilbert.* Hakluyt Society, ser. 2, no. 83. London: Hakluyt Society, 1940.

———, ed. *Early Maryland in a Wider World.* Detroit, MI: Wayne State University Press, 1982.

Rabb, T. H. *Jacobean Gentleman: Sir Edwin Sandys, 1561–1629.* Princeton, NJ: Princeton University Press, 1998.

Ramsay, Clay. *The Ideology of the Great Fear: The Soissonnais in 1789.* Baltimore: Johns Hopkins University Press, 1992.

Rhoden, Nancy K., ed. *English Atlantics Revisited: Essays Honouring Professor Ian K. Steele.* Montreal: McGill-Queen's University Press, 2007.

Rice, James. *Nature and History in the Potomac Country: From Hunter-Gatherers to the Age of Jefferson.* Baltimore: Johns Hopkins University Press, 2009.

———. *Tales from a Revolution: Bacon's Rebellion and the Transformation of Early America.* Oxford: Oxford University Press, 2012.

Richter, Daniel K. *Facing East from Indian Country: A Native History of Early America.* Cambridge, MA: Harvard University Press, 2001.

———. *The Ordeal of the Longhouse: The Peoples of the Iroquois League in the Era of European Colonization.* Chapel Hill: University of North Carolina Press, for Institute of Early American History and Culture, Williamsburg, VA, 1992.

Riordan, Timothy B. *The Plundering Time: Maryland and the English Civil War, 1645–1646.* Baltimore: Maryland Historical Society, 2004.

Root, Winfred T. "The Lords of Trade and Plantations, 1675–1696." *American Historical Review* 23, no. 1 (Oct. 1917): 20–41.

Rountree, Helen C. *Pocahontas, Powhatan, Opechancanough: Three Indian Lives Changed by Jamestown.* Charlottesville: University of Virginia Press, 2005.

———. *Pocahontas's People: The Powhatan Indians of Virginia through Four Centuries.* Norman: University of Oklahoma Press, 1990.

Rountree, Helen C., and Thomas E. Davidson. *Eastern Shore Indians of Virginia and Maryland.* Charlottesville and London: University Press of Virginia, 1997.

Rountree, Helen C., and E. Randolph Turner III. *Before and After Jamestown: Virginia's Powhatans and Their Predecessors.* Gainesville: University Press of Florida, 2002.

———. "On the Fringe of the Southeast: The Powhatan Paramount Chiefdom in Virginia." In Hudson and Tesser, *The Forgotten Centuries,* 355–72.

Russell, Conrad. "The British Problem and the English Civil War." *History* 72, no. 236 (1987): 395–415.

———. *The Fall of the British Monarchies.* Oxford: Clarendon Press of Oxford University Press, 1991.

———. "Parliamentary History in Perspective, 1604–1629," *History* 61, no. 201 (Feb. 1976): 1–27.

———. *Parliaments and English Politics, 1621–1629.* Oxford: Clarendon Press of Oxford University Press; New York: Oxford University Press, 1979.

———, ed. *The Origins of the English Civil War.* New York: Barnes and Noble, 1973.

Russo, Jean B., and J. Elliott Russo. *Planting an Empire: The Early Chesapeake in British North America.* Baltimore: Johns Hopkins University Press, 2012.

Schechter, Stephen L., and Richard Bernstein, eds. *New York and the Union: Contributions to the American Constitutional Experience.* Albany: New York State Commission on the Bicentennial of the United States Constitution, 1990.

Schwoerer, Lois. *The Declaration of Rights, 1689.* Baltimore: Johns Hopkins University Press, 1981.

Scott, Jonathan. *Algernon Sidney and the Restoration Crisis, 1677–1683.* Cambridge: Cambridge University Press, 1991.

———. "England's Troubles: Exhuming the Popish Plot." In Harris, Seward, and Goldie, *The Politics of Religion in Restoration England,* 108–31.

———. *England's Troubles: Seventeenth-Century English Political Instability in European Context.* Cambridge: Cambridge University Press, 2000.

Seaward, Paul. *The Cavalier Parliament and the Reconstruction of the Old Regime, 1661–1667.* Cambridge and New York: Cambridge University Press, 1989.

———. *The Restoration, 1660–1688.* Basingstoke: Macmillan, 1991.

Seed, Patricia. *Ceremonies of Possession in Europe's Conquest of the New World, 1492–1640.* Cambridge: Cambridge University Press, 1995.

Shagan, Ethan. "Constructing Discord: Ideology, Propaganda, and English Responses to the Irish Rebellion of 1641." *Journal of British Studies* 63, no. 1 (1997): 4–34.

Sharpe, Kevin. *The Personal Rule of Charles I.* New Haven, CT: Yale University Press, 1992.

Sharpe, Kevin, and Christopher Brooks. "Debate: History, English Law, and the Renaissance." *Past & Present* 72 (1976): 133–46.

Sharpe, Kevin, and Peter Lake, eds. *Culture and Politics in Early Stuart England.* Stanford, CA: Stanford University Press, 1993.

Shell, Alison. *Catholicism, Controversy, and the English Literary Imagination, 1558–1660.* Cambridge: Cambridge University Press, 1999.

Shibutani, Tomotsu. *Improvised News: A Sociological Study of Rumor.* New York: Bobbs-Merrill, 1966.

Smith, A. G. R. "Crown, Parliament and Finance: The Great Contract of 1610." In Clarke, Smith, and Tyacke, *The English Commonwealth,* 111–27.

Smutts, Malcolm. *Court Culture and the Origins of a Royalist Tradition in Early Stuart England.* Philadelphia: University of Pennsylvania Press, 1987.

———. "The Puritan Followers of Henrietta Maria." *English Historical Review* 93 (1978): 26–45.

———. "Religion, European Politics and Henrietta Maria's Circle, 1625–41." In Griffey, *Henrietta Maria,* 13–37.

Sommerville, C. John. *The News Revolution in England: Cultural Dynamics of Daily Information.* New York: Oxford University Press, 1996.

Sommerville, J. P. *Royalists and Patriots: Politics and Ideology in England 1603–1640.* 2nd ed. London: Longman; and New York: Addison Wesley, 1999.

Sosin, J. M. *English America and the Restoration Monarchy of Charles II: Transatlantic Politics, Commerce, and Kinship.* Lincoln: University of Nebraska Press, 1981.

———. *English America and the Revolution of 1688: Royal Administration and the Structure of Provincial Government.* Lincoln: University of Nebraska Press, 1982.

Sowerby, Scott. "Opposition to Anti-Popery in Restoration England." *Journal of British Studies* 51, no. 1 (Jan. 2012): 26–49.

Speck, W. A. *Reluctant Revolutionaries: Englishmen and the Revolution of 1688.* Oxford: Oxford University Press, 1988.

Stanwood, Owen. *The Empire Reformed: English America in the Age of the Glorious Revolution.* Philadelphia: University of Pennsylvania Press, 2011.

Steele, Ian K. *The English Atlantic, 1675–1740: An Exploration of Communication and Community.* New York and Oxford: Oxford University Press, 1986.

Stern, Philip J. "Bundles of Hyphens: Corporations as Legal Communities in the Early Modern British Empire." In Benton and Ross, *Legal Pluralism and Empires,* 21–48.

———. *The Company-State: Corporate Sovereignty and the Early Modern Foundations of the British Empire in India.* Oxford: Oxford University Press, 2011.

Stoler, Ann Laura. "'In Cold Blood': Hierarchies of Credibility and the Politics of Colonial Narratives." *Representations* 37 (Winter 1992): 151–89.

Stone, Lawrence. *The Causes of the English Revolution, 1529–1642.* New York: Harper & Row, 1972.

Sutto, Antoinette. "The Borders of Absolutism: William Penn, Charles Calvert, and the Limits of Royal Authority, 1680–1685." *Pennsylvania History* 76, no. 3 (2009): 276–300.

———. "Built upon Smoke: Politics and Political Culture in Maryland, 1630–1690." Ph.D. diss., Princeton University, 2008.

———. "Lord Baltimore, the Society of Jesus, and Caroline Absolutism in Maryland, 1630–1645." *Journal of British Studies* 48, no. 3 (July 2009): 631–52.

———. "'You Dog, Give Me Your Hand': Lord Baltimore and the Death of Christopher Rousby." *Maryland Historical Magazine* 102, no. 4 (2007): 240–57.

Tarter, Brent. "Bacon's Rebellion, the Grievances of the People, and the Political Culture of Seventeenth-Century Virginia." *Virginia Magazine of History and Biography* 119, no. 1 (2011): 2–41.

Tate, Thad W., and David Ammerman, eds. *The Chesapeake in the Seventeenth Century: Essays on Anglo-American Society and Politics.* Chapel Hill: University of North Carolina Press, for Institute of Early American History and Culture, Williamsburg, VA, 1979.

Terrar, Edward F. "Was There a Separation of Church and State in Mid-Seventeenth Century England and Colonial Maryland?" *Journal of Church and State* 35, no. 1 (1993): 61–82.

Thompson, James Cargill. "Sir Francis Knollys's Campaign against the Jure Divino Theory of Episcopacy." In Dugmore, *Studies in the Reformation,* 101–26.

Thornton, J. Mills. "The Thrusting out of Governor Harvey: A Seventeenth-Century Rebellion." *Virginia Magazine of History and Biography* 76, no. 1 (1968): 11–26.

Thornton, Tim. "The Palatinate of Durham and the Maryland Charter." *American Journal of Legal History* 45, no. 3 (2001): 235–55.

Thrush, Andrew. "The Personal Rule of James I." In Cogswell, Crust, and Lake, *Politics, Religion and Popularity: Essays in Honour of Conrad Russell,* 84–102.

Townsend, Camilla. "Mutual Appraisals: The Shifting Paradigms of the English, Spanish, and Powhatans in Tesnacomoco, 1560–1622." In Bradburn and Coombs, *Early Modern Virginia: Reconsidering the Old Dominion,* 57–89.

Troost, Wouter. "William III, Brandenburg, and the Construction of the Anti-French Coalition, 1672–88." In Israel, *The Anglo-Dutch Moment,* 299–334.

Tyacke, Nicholas. *Anti-Calvinists: The Rise of English Arminianism, c. 1590–1640.* Oxford: Clarendon Press of Oxford University Press, 1987.

———. "The Puritan Paradigm of English Politics, 1558–1642." *Historical Journal* 53, no. 3 (Sept. 2010): 527–50.

———. "The Rise of Arminianism Reconsidered." *Past & Present* 115 (May 1987): 201–16.

Underdown, David. *Pride's Purge: Politics in the Puritan Revolution.* Oxford: Clarendon Press of Oxford University Press, 1971.

Victor, Jeffrey. "Satanic Cult Rumors as Contemporary Legend." *Western Folklore* 49, no. 1 (Jan. 1990): 51–81.

———. *Satanic Panic: The Creation of a Contemporary Legend.* Chicago: Open Court, 1993.

Walsh, Lorena S. *Motives of Honor, Pleasure, and Profit: Plantation Management in the Chesapeake, 1607–1763.* Chapel Hill: University of North Carolina Press, for Omohundro Institute of Early American History and Culture, Williamsburg, VA, 2010.

Walsham, Alexandra. *Church Papists: Catholicism, Conformity and Confessional Polemic in Early Modern England.* Woodbridge, Suffolk: Boydell, 1993.

———. "'Frantick Hacket': Prophecy, Sorcery, Insanity and the Elizabethan Puritan Movement." *Historical Journal* 41, 1 (1998): 27–67.

Washburn, Wilcomb. *The Governor and the Rebel: A History of Bacon's Rebellion in Virginia.* Chapel Hill: University of North Carolina Press, for Institute of Early American History and Culture, Williamsburg, VA, 1957.

Webb, Stephen Saunders. *The Governors-General: The English Army and the Definition of the Empire, 1569–1681.* Chapel Hill: University of North Carolina Press, for Institute of Early American History and Culture, Williamsburg, VA, 1979.

———. *1676: The End of American Independence.* Syracuse, NY: Syracuse University Press, 1995.

———. "The Strange Career of Francis Nicholson." *William and Mary Quarterly,* 3rd ser., 23, no. 4 (Oct. 1966): 513–48.

———. "William Blathwayt, Imperial Fixer: From Popish Plot to Glorious Revolution." *William and Mary Quarterly,* 3rd ser., 25, no. 1 (1968): 3–21.

Wertenbaker, Thomas Jefferson. *Torchbearer of the Revolution: The Story of Bacon's Rebellion and Its Leader.* Princeton, NJ: Princeton University Press, 1940.

Wildes, Harry Emerson. *William Penn.* New York: Macmillan, 1974.

Wilson, Charles. *England's Apprenticeship, 1603–1763.* New York: St. Martin's Press, 1965.

Witgen, Michael. *Infinity of Nations: How the Native New World Shaped Early North America.* Philadelphia: University of Pennsylvania Press, 2012.

———. "Rethinking Colonial History as Continental History." *William and Mary Quarterly,* 3rd ser., 69, no. 3 (July 2012): 527–30.

Wood, Peter. "From Atlantic History to a Continental Approach." In Greene and Morgan, *Atlantic History,* 279–98.

Woolrych, Austin. *Commonwealth to Protectorate.* Oxford: Clarendon Press of Oxford University Press, 1982.

Worden, Blair. *The English Civil Wars: 1640–1660.* London: Weidenfeld and Nicolson, 2009.

———. *The Rump Parliament, 1648–1653.* Cambridge: Cambridge University Press, 1974.

Yirush, Craig. *Settlers, Liberty and Empire: The Roots of Early American Political Theory, 1675–1775.* Cambridge: Cambridge University Press, 2011.

INDEX

Abbot, George (Archbishop of Canterbury), 18, 21, 31
Act Concerning Religion (Maryland, 1649), 72, 111–12, 121, 181n3
Addison, John, 139, 159
Africa, 3, 6, 92
agriculture in Maryland, 92, 93; livestock, 92, 93, 145, 147. *See also* tobacco
Allen, Cardinal William, 30
Anglicanism, 120–22; Benedict Calvert converts to, 177, 220n62. *See also* Church of England
Anne (queen of England), 176
Anne Arundel County, 57, 197–98n48; Indians and, 139, 140, 147; resistance to proprietor in, 67, 68, 69, 115
anti-Catholicism, 73, 91, 120, 129, 137, 142, 155, 159, 183n11, 191n12. *See also* anti-popery
Antichrist, 49, 68, 74
anti-popery, 8, 130, 138, 156, 157, 160, 171, 174, 220n43; American, 10, 120, 129; anti-Catholicism vs., 183–84n11; of Associators, 166–67; British empire and, 159, 176, 209–10n2; English Catholics and, 31, 191n13; Maryland and, 44, 53, 68, 72, 75, 82, 142, 182–84n11, 217n4; narrative of, 92, 131, 191n12; as political language, 30, 129, 219n25
anti-Puritanism, 8, 130, 209–10n2; Charles Calvert and, 160; James I and, 188–89n23; Maryland and, 10, 68, 75, 82, 129; as political language, 30, 129
approbation controversy, 28–29
Archbishop of Canterbury, 18, 21, 31, 120
Arundell, Henry, 148
Arundell, Thomas Arundell, Count, 21
Associators. *See* Protestant Associators

Bacon, Nathaniel, 10, 100, 101, 103, 130; rumor and, 142–43
Baconists, 130, 131; Fendall and Coode as, 153, 158, 160
Bacon's Rebellion, 103, 142, 158, 204n26, 207n39; Indians and, 98, 100, 213n2
Badcock, Nicholas, 155, 166
Baltimore, 1st Baron (George Calvert), 2, 22–23, 29, 176, 182n10, 195n2; career of, 20–21, 200n34; as Catholic, 34; Charles I and, 9, 23, 194n68; charter of 1632 and, 6, 16, 33, 71; conversion of, 21, 22, 24; death of, 35; Newfoundland colony and, 195n11, 196n11; in Virginia, 23–24, 25
Baltimore, 2nd Baron (Cecil Calvert), 7, 8, 23, 24, 44, 45, 47, 56, 57, 67, 87, 106, 123, 124, 174, 176; accusations against, 35, 55–56; Leonard Calvert and, 61; Charles II and, 76, 198n49; Council of State and, 124; death of, 101; as father of Charles, 83, 101, 108, 109, 160; Jesuits and, 51, 52; John Harvey and, 39–44; loyalty and, 32, 34, 36, 47, 60–61, 64, 89; as Maryland proprietor, 9, 35, 104, 177; paranoia of, 35–36; political self-defense of, 43–45, 59; as royalist, 47–48, 53; tobacco policy conflict and, 82–91; Virginia Company and, 37–39. *See also* Maryland proprietors

Baltimore, 3rd Baron (Charles Calvert), 9, 102, 106, 113, 118, 120, 133, 146, 149, 158, 160, 172, 174, 176, 210n6, 218n8, 219n25, 220n62, 251n63; Catholicism of, 160–61; criticism of, 115, 120, 162; James II and, 170; Lords of Trade and, 121–22; Maryland assembly and, 106–8, 124, 153; as Maryland governor, 83–84, 87, 116; Privy Council and, 154–55; as proprietor, 100–101, 106–10, 117, 122–23, 160, 177; Protestant supporters of, 173; Quakers and, 130, 210n6; on religion in Maryland, 121–22; rumors about, 147–48, 150, 152; William and Mary and, 163, 164. *See also* Maryland proprietors

Baltimore, 4th Baron (Benedict Leonard Calvert), 177, 220n62

Baltimore, 5th Baron (Charles Calvert), 177, 220n62

Bargrave, Capt. John, 18, 19

Battle of the Severn (1655), 68, 73

Bayard, Col. Nicholas, 169

Berkeley, Sir William, 57, 85, 91, 94, 99, 205n37; Bacon's Rebellion and, 100; Charles I and, 59; Charles II and, 83, 88–89; as governor of Virginia, 59–60; Indians and, 101, 204n26

Billingsley, John, 103

Blakiston, Nehemiah, 159, 165, 210n3

Bond of Association (1584), 165

Bond of Association (1696), 165

Boreman, William, 139

Brandt, Col. Randolph, 146, 152

Brent, Capt. George, 99, 147

Brent, Giles, 51, 52, 56

British empire, 2, 4, 159, 177, 178, 185n17, 185n19. *See also* English empire

Buckingham, George Villiers, 1st Duke of, 18, 19, 26

Burdett, John, 133

Calvert, Benedict Leonard, 177, 220n62

Calvert, Cecil. *See* Baltimore, 2nd Baron

Calvert, Charles (1637–1715). *See* Baltimore, 3rd Baron

Calvert, Charles (1699–1751), 177, 220n62

Calvert, George. *See* Baltimore, 1st Baron

Calvert, Leonard, 50, 51; as Maryland governor, 36, 52–54, 56, 61, 62

Calvert, Philip, 88, 156–57; as Maryland governor, 76, 96

Calvert County, 98, 110–11, 131, 168

Calvert family, 2, 10, 105, 176, 181n4, 194n1

Calvinism, 31

Canada, 103, 135, 150, 170. *See also* France; New France

Carolinas, 88, 103, 122

Carroll, Charles, 177

Carvile, Robert, 105

Carvile, Thomas, 105

Catholicism, Roman, 20, 69, 72, 183n11, 191n10, 211n12; of Calverts, 21, 22, 91, 105, 160–61; concessions to, 21–22; English Civil Wars and, 47; international conspiracy of, 10, 22, 68, 165; in Maryland, 74; meaning of, 191n10; Protestant view of, 29, 191n12

Catholics, 4, 22, 44, 50, 65, 70, 125, 175, 181n7, 189n42, 190n9, 192n16; crypto-, 15, 148; English state and, 2, 28–29, 32–33, 45, 47, 164; French as, 10, 129; Indians conspire with, 69, 131, 135–40, 142, 148–49, 151–53, 163; loyalty of, 29, 34, 37, 48–49, 51, 54, 56,

189–90n49; Maryland proprietors as, 2, 4, 119, 131; New World and, 30–31; oath of allegiance and, 23–24; Popish Plot and, 204–5n26; priests and, 52, 72, 121, 135, 149, 155, 156, 168, 170, 171; subversion of, 43, 156; toleration for, 32

Cecil, Sir Robert, 20

Charles County, 97, 147, 150

Charles I (king of England), 16, 18, 24, 66, 194n68, 201n3, 206n17, 212n18; anti-Puritanism and, 30, 192n18; authority of, 27–28, 37, 74, 75, 104; Cecil Calvert and, 40, 56; George Calvert and, 9, 22–23; loyalty and, 29; civil war and, 2, 47, 57, 59, 187–88n10; charter of 1632 and, 4, 36, 70; monarchy of, 176; Parliament and, 25, 26–27, 109, 110; personal rule of, 27–28; popery and, 15, 31–32, 51, 54, 55; popularity and, 35; proposed marriage to Spanish infanta, 21; Puritans and, 8, 26, 31, 69; rumored conversion of, 32; trial and execution of, 47, 57, 58, 61, 67, 130, 218–19n23; wife of, 32, 33

Charles II (king of England), 57, 209n54, 212n18; George Calvert and, 76, 198n49; Catholicism and, 77, 91, 208n43; death of, 132; as James II's brother, 119, 148; Maryland proprietary and, 9, 59, 104; monarchy of, 176; Parliament and, 109, 154, 206n17; petitions to, 82–83; Restoration and, 81

charters, 6; quo warranto, 218n8; revocation of, 63, 162, 173, 208n40, 218n8. *See also* Maryland charter of 1632

Chesapeake Bay, xii, 7; natives of, 13, 36, 92–103

Chesapeake colonies, 89, 94, 120, 142, 178, 179, 208n40; Glorious Revolution and, 132–33. *See also* Maryland; Virginia

Cheseldyn, Kenelm, 159, 170, 173, 210n3

Chopticos, 145, 146, 214n13

Church of England, 2, 4, 20, 28, 31–32, 124, 168, 175, 207n39, 218n18; conformity to, 7, 50, 119, 210n2; in Maryland, 37, 120, 122–23; uniformity in, 29, 31. *See also* Anglicanism

Claiborne, William, 34, 43, 60, 193n42; controversy with Maryland proprietors, 7, 39, 40, 52–53, 59, 66–68, 70; Kent Island and, 37–38, 41, 42, 44

Coleman, Edward, 148

colonies, 14, 23, 64, 73, 175, 182n10, 185n19, 211n12, 214n11, 221–22n10; administration of, 3, 77, 119, 121, 158, 206n24; charters of, 6, 63, 119, 162, 173, 208n40, 218n8; crown governance of, 3, 6, 15, 58, 66, 77, 81, 104, 160, 175, 186–87n9; English law and, 25, 66; English liberties in, 3, 49; in Newfoundland, 23, 24; political power and, 114–15; proprietary, 162; Revolution of 1688 and, 216–17n1. *See also* British empire; English empire; *and individual colonies*

Committee of the Admiralty, 60

Commonwealth, 60, 67, 71; authority of, 74, 75; Calverts and, 9, 56, 65

"Complaint from Heaven with a Hue and a Crye," 120, 124, 208n43, 219n25

Compton, Henry (Bishop of London), 121

confessional conflict, 47, 188n11; authority and, 48–49; royal power and, 42

confessional identity, 140, 155; political allegiance and, 4, 22, 49, 64, 119, 208n43
conformity, 119, 182n7, 189–90n9
conspiracies, 82, 102; Indian, 99, 217n1; Indian-Catholic, 69, 101–2, 129, 135–38, 148–49; international Catholic, 10, 22, 160, 165, 213n2; popish, 60–61, 130, 131, 156, 217n1; of popularity, 17, 18; Puritanical, 131
Coode, John, 10, 53, 130, 136, 156, 168, 173, 210n3, 217n4, 218n14, 218–19n23; anti-proprietary movements of, 142, 150–54, 159–61, 163–74; arrest and trial of, 152, 154, 157
Copley, Lionel, 173–74, 175, 220n63
Copley, Thomas, 54–55
Cornwallis, Thomas, 36, 40, 52, 55
Council of State, 59, 60, 124
Coursey, Henry, 88, 143, 146, 173
Covill, Richard, 134
Cromwell, Oliver: authority of, 63, 74, 76, 105; Rump Parliament and, 58–59, 67
crown: authority of, 162; colonial governance by, 3, 104, 119, 186–87n9; loyalty to, 17, 24, 208n43; Massachusetts charter and, 120; nonconformists vs., 17; powers of, 7, 8, 77, 182n7; prerogatives of, 5, 70; subjects of, 64; subversion against, 44; taxation to support, 201n3. *See also* monarchy; royal prerogative
Culpeper of Thoresway, 2nd Baron (Thomas Culpeper), as Virginia governor, 152, 154
customs, 209n53; Lord Baltimore and, 148, 155; officers of, 120, 171, 172; revenue, 122, 173, 203n29; tobacco and, 84, 85, 89, 90, 207n39
Dale, Sir Thomas, 25
Danckaerts, Jasper, 135
Darnall, Col. Henry, 105, 136, 138, 139, 140, 157; on overthrow of proprietary regime, 159, 163
Davenant, William, 74, 198n49
Davies, William, 110–11, 115
Delaware River, 95, 123
Delawares, 97, 145
Dent, John, 150, 151
Dickenson, John, 93
Digges, Col. William, 105, 136–38, 140
diseases, Native Americans and, 93, 95, 98, 103
dissenters, 72, 121, 131, 158, 210n5; British empire and, 4, 120; English Civil Wars and, 129–30
Doegs, 99, 146
Don Luís, 192n31
Dorset commission, 35, 43
Durham palatinate, 3, 71, 75
Dutch, 52, 95, 99, 123, 132, 216n71

Eastern Shore, 93, 136
Effingham, Baron Howard of (Francis Howard), 119, 124, 132, 208n40, 209n53, 218n8
Elizabeth I (queen of England), 28, 149, 165, 182n7
England, 111, 191n13, 200n34, 201n1; news from, 131–32, 151, 152, 211n12; political conflict in, 14–15; as Protestant nation, 3, 181n7; Restoration in, 76–77
English Civil Wars, 56, 57, 187n10; Charles I and, 2, 47; dispute over royal power in, 3, 70; Jesuits and, 51, 195n3; politics of, 51, 58–59
English empire, 3, 6, 9, 58, 159, 184n14, 185n17, 209n2; administration of, 5, 7,

9, 63–64, 82, 104–25, 158; expansion of, 30, 45, 81, 198–99n4. *See also* British empire; colonies
English liberties and rights, 3, 106, 170; English Civil Wars and, 47; Maryland charter and, 8; of Maryland freemen, 85, 110–11, 113–15, 152, 153, 162; Parliament and, 109–10
Englishness, 29–30, 189–90n49
Essex, 2nd Earl of (Robert Devereux), 17
Europe, 142; competing colonial empires of, 5, 6; Thirty Years' War in, 14, 18, 27
Evans, Anthony, 133–34
Exclusion Crisis, 119, 132, 148, 154, 157

faction, 8, 130, 153, 173; interest and, 66, 82, 87
Fendall, Josias, 10, 130, 147, 156, 163; arrest and trial of, 151, 152, 154, 157; death of, 159; revolt of, 76, 142, 150–54, 218n14
Five Nations, 142, 143, 146, 212–13n35, 221n10. *See* Iroquois Confederacy
Forced Loan, 32, 33, 38
France, 142, 170, 184n14; British colonists and, 142, 207n39, 214n11; as Catholics, 10, 101; conspiracies of, 129, 130, 165, 169, 217n1; fears of, 55, 120, 176, 221n10; Indians and, 135, 167; in North America, 92; Popish Plot and, 148, 204–5n26; threatened invasion of, 170; papists linked with, 30, 102; Thirty Years' War and, 32
Frederick V, Protestant Elector Palatine, 17, 18
freemen: in Maryland, 85, 110–11, 113–15, 152, 153, 162; in Maryland assembly, 62, 202n20. *See also* English liberties and rights
fur trade, 92, 95

Gates, Sir Thomas, 25
Gent, William, 110–11
Gerard, Thomas, 50, 210n3
Glorious Revolution, 4, 132–33. *See also* Revolution of 1688
Godfrey, Lt. George, 151, 157
Gondomar, Conde de, 19–20, 21
Green, Thomas, 57, 61
Gunpowder Plot, 23; Guy Fawkes Day and, 156

Hammond, John, 69, 178, 197–98n48
Harrison, Bur, 139, 213n40
Harvey, Sir John, 39–40, 42–44, 48, 193n42
Hasleham, Giles, 110–11
Heaman, Roger, 68–69, 73, 199n24
Hermann, Augustine, 145
Hill, Edward, 61
Hill, Richard, 169, 173
historiography: Chesapeake school and, 183n11, 203n1; of early modern English Catholicism, 190n9; of early modern politics, 178, 216–17n1; of Maryland, 178; of Native Americans, 178, 203n1; of Protestant culture and, 216n1; of religion, 186n22, 216n1; of Revolution of 1688, 177; of Tudor-Stuart England and politics, 187n10, 201n1, 207n39; of Virginia, 178
Hoerekill (Whorekill), 216n71
House of Commons, 17, 20–21, 26, 25, 27, 113, 114, 153. *See also* MPs; Parliament
Hunton, Mordecai, 149

Indians. *See* Native Americans; *and individual nations*
Ingle, Richard, 47, 194n1; charges by, 56,

Ingle, Richard (*continued*) 57, 74, 134; raids Maryland, 52–56, 61, 136, 194–95n2
interest, 202n4; private, 81, 88, 101, 102, 130, 161, 162; Protestant, 140, 164; public, 153, 157, 161; royal vs. proprietary, 84; as term, 82
Ireland, 3, 30, 55, 149, 170, 192n16
Iroquois, 10, 93–94, 130, 135–36, 146, 150, 170, 212–13n35, 217n39; Confederacy of, 94, 120, 204n10; English peace with, 98; French and, 140, 149, 167, 214n11; Susquehannocks vs., 94–103; threat of, 140, 142, 163; war and, 143–44, 147. *See also* Five Nations

James I (king of England), 24, 130, 201n3, 208n43; anti-Puritanism and, 30, 188–89n23; Catholicism and, 22; death of, 16; House of Commons and, 20; loyalty and, 29; monarchy of, 176; popularity and, 17; Puritans and, 8, 15; religious tolerance and, 189n42; Spanish marriage diplomacy of, 16, 21; Virginia charter and, 42; Virginia Company and, 19–20, 33
James II (king of England), 161, 162, 168, 176; absolutism and, 211–12n18; converts to Catholicism, 77, 132; as Duke of York, 119, 132, 148; exclusion of, 119, 132, 148, 154; loyalty and, 4; Maryland proprietary and, 9, 104, 167, 170; monarchy of, 176; policy of toleration and, 72, 199n11, 209n44
Jamestown, Virginia, 13, 15–16
Jesuits (Society of Jesus), 170, 199n11, 209n44; abuses by, 48–49; Cecil Calvert and, 37, 41, 51, 52; George Calvert and, 29, 62, 63, 72; chapel constructed by, 50–51; conversions by, 155–56; executions of, 28; Indians and, 135, 150; Maryland and, 34, 121, 129, 183n11, 195n3; papist conspiracy and, 54–55, 92, 148, 167; tropes of, 209n44
Johnson, Henry, 149
Joseph, William, 136, 137, 161, 162
Jowles, Henry, 136–38, 140, 159, 164, 165, 167

Kent Island, 155–56; dispute over, 7, 37–38, 41, 42, 44, 53
King Philip's War, 120, 204n26, 207n39
kingship, 64; Native Americans and, 14, 97. *See also* monarchy
King William's War, 176
Kittamaquund, 195n3

land sales and disputes, 116, 176; with Indians, 92, 96, 103, 145
Langford, John, 74, 76; pro-proprietor writings of, 69, 75
Laud, William (Archbishop of Canterbury), 29, 31, 35, 57; commission of, 39, 41
law and legal structures, 3, 8, 105, 119; Catholics and, 175; colonies and, 25, 66, 70; common, 27, 42, 70, 71, 73, 115; constitution, 5, 73, 161, 164; ecclesiastical, 72; in England, 112; king and, 161, 176; in Maryland, 37, 61–63, 71, 108, 111–13; in New World, 45; Parliament and, 5; pluralism and, 184n11; praemunire and, 28; property and, 38; religion and, 2; Restoration and, 81; royal prerogative and, 32, 70–71, 115; statute, 70, 115; threats to, 210
letters, 137; as source of news, 131–32, 139
letters patent, 3, 6
Lewis, William, 48–49, 50

liberty of conscience, 72, 74
Llewellyn, John, 133
London, 114, 115, 132, 154; bishop of, 121, 167; merchants of, 16, 60; publications in, 64, 68
Long Parliament, 58, 63, 67
Lookout Point, 146, 147, 150, 151
Lords of Trade, 121–23, 132, 155, 158, 159, 162, 163; Maryland proprietor and, 172, 173
Louis XIV (king of France), 142, 169, 170, 211n18
loyalty to crown, 15, 75, 156, 164, 169; Calverts and, 9, 21, 22, 56, 60–61, 64, 89, 160; "Complaint from Heaven with a Hue and a Crye" and, 208n43; Catholics and, 4, 33; confessional identity and, 119, 133; disputes over, 8, 59; Protestantism and, 24, 199n11; religion and, 2, 47, 207n39; royal power and, 42; Stuarts and, 5
Ludwell, Col. Philip, 150, 152, 154

Maquamps (Bennett), 97, 204n19
Marvell, Andrew, 148
Mary, Queen of Scots, 165
Maryland, 1, 135, 215n63, 216n71; armed protest in, 111, 142–58; anti-papist scare in, 159; anti-popery and, 182–83n11; becomes royal colony, 173, 217n1; borders of, 38; Cecil Calvert and, 23; Chesapeake commission and, 60–62, 76; as Catholic colony, 1–2, 6, 74; Church of England in, 120, 122–23; coinage in, 124; cooperates with Virginia on tobacco policies, 82–85, 87–89; creation of, 25; dissenters in, 121, 158; economic decline in, 101; during English Civil Wars, 59; franchise in, 111–12; Glorious Revolution and, 133, 217–18n4; government in, 61, 175; Indian diplomacy of, 95, 217n1; Iroquois and, 212–13n35; Jesuits in, 34, 121, 183n11; landowners in, 68; law and religion in, 37, 111–13, 181n3; legitimacy and, 71, 82; map of, xii; naming of, 33; patent of, 59, 64–65, 66, 74, 75, 116, 118, 119, 153; planters and freemen in, 62, 107, 108–9, 110–11, 113–14, 122, 165, 202n20; popish conspiracy, 176; Protestants in, 6–7, 155–56, 167, 168, 173; reduction of, 59–67; religious toleration and freedom in, 2, 62, 121, 135, 177, 178, 181n4; revolt of 1660 in, 76; royal authority in, 43, 71, 104–25; taxation in, 104–5, 111, 114, 116, 134; tobacco policy conflict in, 81–91; Virginia and, 1, 37–38, 41, 47, 49, 57–59, 65, 66, 83, 119, 209n54; William and Mary and, 163
Maryland assembly, 113–14, 116, 125, 134, 217n4; Associators summon, 167–68; charter and, 114–15, 117–18; Council and, 107, 108, 114, 115–18; elections of, 108–9, 153; independence of, 86, 108–9; Indian policy and, 96, 99, 102–3; laws and legal procedure and, 61–62, 112–17, 153; number of representatives in, 106–10, 152; proprietor and, 152, 153, 161; proprietor's men in, 124; rights and legitimacy of, 63, 110, 114–15; taxes and, 104–5, 122; tobacco policy and, 86, 87–88
Maryland charter of 1632, 3, 33, 38, 61, 62, 104, 107, 109, 124, 161, 182n10; assembly and, 114–15, 117–18; Charles I and, 4, 70; criticism of, 36–37, 39, 44, 115; debates over, 6, 41–42, 56; Durham palatinate in, 71, 75; English

Maryland charter of 1632 (*continued*)
rights and liberties and, 8, 49, 62–63, 109, 113; English nation and, 71–72; legitimacy of, 75–76, 108; revocation of, 63, 173; Virginia Company and, 16, 33–34, 41–42; war and, 117–18
Maryland Council, 68, 83, 86–87, 112, 117–18, 134, 139, 159, 165; armed revolts and, 111, 137–38; assembly and, 107, 108, 114, 115–18; on charter, 115, 118; Coode's coup and, 170, 171; Indian policy and, 97, 100, 102, 143, 145–47; members of, 136, 137, 149, 161
Maryland governor, 65, 74, 101, 117–18, 134; armed revolt and, 111; authority of, 61–62; defense and, 136; first royal, 173–74; revolt of, 76; tobacco policy and, 86–87
Maryland proprietors, 3, 113, 152, 178–79; assembly and, 152–53, 161; authority of, 115, 162; Calvert family as, 2; as Catholic, 2, 4, 119, 131, 177; Chesapeake commission and, 60–62; confessional antagonism and, 176; criticism of, 158, 171; customs duty of, 123, 171; failure to proclaim William and Mary, 163, 164, 167; Glorious Revolution and, 159–74; imperial administration and, 104–25; oath of fidelity to, 69, 74–75, 106, 124, 134, 166; overthrow of, 159, 174; pamphlet war against, 68–77; privilege of, 174; resentment of, 105; rights and powers of, 62, 67, 106–10, 112, 122–23, 153; rumors and, 142, 151; tobacco policy and, 88; writings in support of, 69
Mary II (queen of England): as daughter of James II, 132; as wife of William of Orange, 10, 132, 162, 218n18. *See also* William and Mary
Massachusetts, 120, 158, 159, 169
Mathena, Daniel, 150
Mattapany, 103, 160
Matthews, Samuel, 43–44
Mattwomans, 94, 97, 145, 146, 147, 204n19
McDermott, Edmund, 149
merchants, 16, 93, 139, 156; tobacco trade and, 60, 89
monarchy: bishops and, 17; Charles I's execution and, 58; criticism of, 5, 36–37; defense of, 174; dissenters and, 129–30; as flawed, 162; loyalty to, 75; new, 170; opponents of, 18–21; Parliament and, 161; proprietors and, 64, 106, 161; Restoration of, 76–77; state and, 5; threats to, 22, 31, 120
Monmouth, 1st Duke of (James Scott), 148; rebellion of, 132, 157
Morecraft, John, 124
Mould, John, 149
MPs (Members of Parliament), 18, 161; George Calvert as, 20–21. *See also* House of Commons; Parliament
murders, 166; by Indians, 97, 98, 99, 100, 145, 146, 147, 151, 157; of Indians, 102–3; of tax collectors, 123, 171–72

Nanjaticos, 139
Nanjemys, 146, 147
Nanticokes, 93–94, 204n8
Native Americans, 10, 36, 133, 162, 204n10, 204–5n26, 213n2; as agents of popish subversion, 69; conflict between Chesapeake colonists and, 92–103, 117–18, 175; conspire with Catholics, 69, 131, 135–40, 142, 148–49, 151–53, 160, 163, 167; defense against, 87, 138; English view of, 14, 55; evangelization of,

30–31, 183n11; fear of, 176; French and, 129, 169; land sales of, 62, 103; livestock disputes with, 92, 93, 145, 147; Maryland and, 1, 37, 156, 217n1; murders by, 146, 147, 157; as prisoners, 94; relations with, 15, 82, 122; rumors about, 135–40; as threat, 97, 101, 104, 138. *See also individual nations*
Navigation Acts, 52, 119, 120, 122, 207n39; evasion of, 123, 171
New England, 120, 130
Newfoundland colony of George Calvert, 23, 24
New Model Army, 58–59; dissolution of Parliament by, 63, 67
New Netherland, 95, 99, 135
news: definition of, 210–11n8; from England, 131–32, 150–51; in letters, 131–32; in news books, 131; in newspapers and news sheets, 211n12. *See also* rumors
New York, 95, 143, 159, 164, 165, 169, 216n71. *See also* New Netherland
Nicholett, Charles, 113–14
Nicholson, Francis, 169, 175
Nicklas, Capt. William, 147–48
nonconformists, 27, 67, 130; Church of England and, 28, 31; James I's dislike of, 17, 22; loyalty and, 4, 8; in Maryland, 2, 73. *See also* dissenters
Notley, Thomas, 88, 104, 111, 124; as Maryland governor, 101, 102, 145

Oates, Titus, 148
oath of allegiance, 23, 24, 124, 189–90n49; Baltimore and, 32, 166
oath of supremacy, 24, 32; Catholics and, 23, 189–90n49
Odber, Capt. John, 97–98
pamphlets: anti-Catholic, 155; anti-popery, 148, 156, 191n12; anti-proprietorary, 59, 63–77
Panzani, Grigorio, 32
papists, 8, 23, 24, 29–30, 54, 151, 182n7; conspiracy of, 92, 167, 169
Parliament, 55, 65, 114, 117, 156, 170, 201n3, 206n17, 206n24; ancient constitution vs., 5; George Calvert in, 20–21; Charles I and, 25, 26–27, 58, 110; Charles II and, 154; colonial governance and, 3, 187n10; James I and, 17, 20, 21; king and, 7, 161; nature of power and, 109–10. *See also* House of Commons; Long Parliament; MPs; Rump Parliament
Pate, John, 110–11, 115
patriots, Protestant, 15, 19, 173; Associators as, 166
Patuxent River, 98, 111, 136, 139–40, 145
Payne, John, 171, 172
Penn, William, 209n44, 210n6
peripheries, 5, 6
Person, William, 133–34
Piscataways, 1, 99, 101, 147, 195n3; early relations between colonists and, 92, 93, 214n11; as Maryland allies, 94, 139, 143, 144
plantations, 33, 34, 40, 48, 65, 112, 121, 147; Thomas Barbary's, 111; Chesapeake, 60, 96; Spesutia, 97–98; in Virginia, 15
planters, 81, 89, 122, 202n20, 205n37, 208n43; English birthright of, 85; intercolonial cooperation of, 82; land hunger of, 93; in Maryland assembly, 87; taxes and, 104; tobacco prices and, 84, 90; Virginian, 179
political allegiance: confessional identity and, 1, 22, 28; religion and, 178

politics, English, 8, 70, 202n4, 211n9, 221–22n10; conflicts in, 187–88n10, 201n1; rumor and, 129–41; Virginia Company dissolution and, 16–20
popery, 31, 176, 222n10; of Cecil Calvert, 55; Charles I and, 15, 31–32, 51; definition of, 177; international Catholic conspiracy and, 22, 30; Maryland proprietors and, 72, 75
popish conspiracy, 60–61
Popish Plot, 119, 151, 154, 157, 204n26, 208n43; Lord Baltimore and, 148
popularity, 27, 36, 182n7; Charles I and, 35; James I and, 8, 17, 18, 19, 20, 21; as term, 130
Potomac River, 101, 138, 140, 159; falls of, 99, 100, 102; mouth of, 146; news crosses, 139
Powhatans, 13, 55
praemunire, 28–29
Privy Council, 23, 35, 41, 120, 121, 123, 162, 172, 193n47; Charles Calvert and, 154–55, 173; George Calvert on, 20, 22; colonial governance and, 3, 5; Coode's coup and, 169–70; tobacco policy and, 83, 84, 85, 88–89, 91
proprietary prerogative, 110, 112, 114; Charles Calvert on, 106, 107, 108; Council on, 115; as defense, 36–37; dissenting power, 116, 117; power of, 124, 158; public grievances and, 116–17; support for, 168. *See also* Maryland proprietors
Protectorate, the, 58, 59, 75
Protestant Associators, 10, 160, 210n3, 217n4, 219n25; opponents of, 168, 170–71; overthrow of proprietary regime by, 150, 159–61, 163–74; published statement of, 136, 166–67
Protestant Catholics, 50
Protestant Cause: Charles I and, 27; James I and, 17
Protestant evangelism, 14
Protestantism: British empire and, 4, 181n7, 198n2; Englishness and, 29–31; government legitimacy and, 67–68; history of term, 195n10; lawfulness and, 70; loyalty to crown and, 24, 47; militant, 160; mission of, in colonies, 3
Protestant patriotism, 15, 19, 166, 173
Protestants, 2, 50, 149, 209n44, 210n3, 210n5; Baconists as, 130; as category, 181n7; Catholic abuses of, 49; Catholicism viewed by, 29, 191n12; forcible baptisms of, 23; liberties of, 47, 49; in Maryland, 155–56, 167, 168, 173; monarchical power and, 27; narrative of heroic, 154; political interest and, 179; radical, 72; as recusants, 65; religious liberty of, 57
Puritanism, 31, 44
Puritans, 25, 181n7, 182n7, 199n11, 210n5; Charles I and, 8, 26, 192n18; conversion narrative of, 73–74; James I and, 8, 15, 17, 18, 21; Jesuits compared to, 29, 199n11; New World and, 30; popular agitation and, 19; as stock character, 69
Pye, Edward, 139

Quakers, 173, 209n43; Charles Calvert and, 130, 210n6; in Maryland, 121, 169

Randolph, Edward, 120
recusancy, 73, 190–91n9; of George Calvert, 65, 72
Reformation, 190n9
religion, 81, 177, 182n7; conflicts of, 188n11, 201n1; freedom of, 2, 24,

36–37, 57, 181n4; in Maryland, 111–12, 181n3, 183n11, 217n4; political allegiance and, 28, 65, 178, 182–84n11, 207n39, 211n9; uniformity of, 119, 121, 160, 164
representative assemblies, in colonies, 16, 17, 193n47. *See also* Maryland assembly
Restoration, 76–77, 81, 130
Revolution of 1688, 3, 176, 177; colonial politics and, 175, 216–17n1; end of Calverts' reign in Maryland and, 4–5, 159–74. *See also* Glorious Revolution
Rich, Nathaniel, 18, 19
Rousby, Christopher, 123, 131, 133–34, 140, 147, 155, 166; murder of, 163, 172
royal prerogative, 115, 160; arguments about, 3, 8, 32, 38, 42, 119; common law and, 70, 73; nature of, 7, 41; Restoration and, 81
royalism, 54; English Civil Wars and, 47, 51
rumors, 142, 144, 151, 152, 163, 213n40; Coode and, 169; definition of, 131, 210–11n8; from England, 147–48; politics and, 129–41; power of, 141
Rump Parliament, 58–59, 67

Sandys, Edwin, 16, 18–21
Scotland, 3, 26, 119, 170, 194n68; Presbyterians in, 17, 149
Scott, Thomas, 22
sedition, 20, 37, 75, 86, 89, 110, 113–18, 154, 162
Senecas (Cingaos, Cinigos, Cinnigos, Sinicos, Sinniquos), 96, 97, 99, 100, 143, 204n10; conspire with Maryland Catholics, 139, 149, 150, 151
servants, 179, 221–22n10
Sewall, Nicholas, 171, 172
Sheldon, Gilbert (Archbishop of Canterbury), 121
Shepard, Capt. Richard, 154–55
Shrewsbury, 12th Earl of (Charles Talbot), 172
slavery, 1, 3, 66, 147, 221–22n10; popery and, 166, 175
Smith, John, 14
Smith, Richard, 28–29, 163
Smith, Thomas, 133
smuggling, 171, 175
social structure: of Chesapeake colonies, 1; of Maryland, 137
Society of Jesus. *See* Jesuits
Southampton, 3rd Earl of (Henry Wriothesley), 20
Spain: ambassador of, 19–20; Chesapeake and, 192n31; colonies of, 14; English Catholics and, 34; English pirates vs., 3; English views of, 55; international Catholic conspiracy and, 22, 149, 165; James I's marriage diplomacy with, 16, 21; naval war against, 18; papists linked with, 30; theories of empire and, 184n14; Thirty Years' War and, 32; Virginia as base against, 13, 16, 19, 22
Spencer, Nicholas, 141, 142, 163
Stafford County, Virginia, 99, 100, 138, 139
state, English, 2; authority of, 38; Church of England and, 4; colonies and, 23, 25, 58, 59, 160; English Catholics and, 32–33, 45, 47; expansion of, 77, 81; internal politics of, 5; loyalty to, 65; Maryland proprietorship and, 59, 68; prerogative power and, 110; Protestants and, 74; reinvention of, 57
St. Mary's City, 50–51, 137, 139, 159, 160, 169, 214n13

St. Mary's County, 34, 133, 146, 147, 157, 168
Stone, William, 68, 69; as Maryland governor, 56–57, 65, 73–74
Stourton, Erasmus, 23, 55
Strachey, William, 14
Strong, Leonard, 74; writings of, 68–69
Stuarts, 1; absolutism and, 176; early overseas activity and, 182n7; loyalty and, 5; nature of royal power under, 3; political culture of, 27, 182n7; restructuring of empire under, 207n39. *See also individual Stuart rulers*
subversion: Catholics accused of, 43, 51, 164; royal power and, 42, 44
Susanna (yacht) incident, 171–72
Susquehannocks, 1, 13, 38, 120, 195n3; fort of, 98, 100, 102, 144; French and, 149; Iroquois vs., 94–103; Maryland and, 92, 94, 96, 97, 98; murder of, 102; raiding parties of, 144, 146, 214n11; Senecas and, 143

Talbot, George, 149, 163, 172
taxes, 119; collection of, 160; episcopal, 28; in Maryland, 104–5, 114, 122, 134; ship money as, 32, 38; planters' grievances and, 104, 111, 116, 205n37; revenues from, 203n29, 207n39; reluctance to vote supplementary and, 201n3
Thirty Years' War, 14, 17, 18, 26–27, 32
tobacco: Chesapeake economy and, 9, 175, 201n2, 201n3; credit and, 87; customs revenue and, 203n29, 207n39; debates over, 81, 82; destroyed by Indians, 147; early cultivation of, 13; as economic mainstay, 1; merchants and, 60; policy conflict over, 82–91; prices of, 1, 81, 82, 84, 90, 101, 178; shipping of, 161; 1620s boom of, 14, 15; trade of, 123, 131, 148
toleration, religious, 122; of Catholics, 22, 32, 191–92n16; in Maryland, 2, 119, 121, 177, 181n4
trade, 3, 122, 176; Indians and, 93, 95, 97, 101, 103, 145; posts for, 7; smuggling and, 171, 175. *See also* fur trade; merchants
treason, 24, 28, 41, 43, 54, 148, 152, 164, 173, 184n11
Triennial Act (1641), 109–10, 206n17
Truman, Thomas, 100, 102–3
Tyrling, John, 150

Utie, Nathaniel, plantation of, 97, 98

Virginia, 22, 25, 39, 101, 111, 120, 121, 123, 135, 153, 163, 165, 171, 179; assembly of, 43, 106–7, 209n54; Bacon's Rebellion and, 100, 157; as base against Spanish, 13, 16, 19, 22; Cecil Calvert and, 45, 47; George Calvert in, 23–24, 25; charter of, 35, 42; cooperates with Maryland on Indian policy, 100, 212–13n35; cooperates with Maryland on tobacco policy, 82–85, 87–89, 90–91; Council of, 44, 130; during English Civil Wars, 59–61; English news in, 132, 133; governor of, 45, 76, 124, 149, 152; Indians in, 55, 99; Indian wars and, 15–16, 138–40, 144, 145; Maryland and, 1, 37–38, 41, 47, 49, 57–59, 65, 66, 119, 138–40, 209n54; royal commissions on, 18–19, 21; taxation in, 104, 134; tobacco and, 14, 15, 82, 101, 161
Virginia Company, 13, 35, 60, 66, 202n6;

Cecil Calvert and, 39; George Calvert and, 21; dissolution of, 8, 16–19, 39, 41; Maryland charter and, 33–34, 41–42; Maryland disputes with, 37, 41–42, 57; troubles of, 15–16, 25

war: common fear of Indian, 104; mourning, 94, 95, 146; Susquehannocks and, 98, 143; threat of, 131, 138
Warwick, 2nd Earl of (Robert Rich), 19
Watts, George, 93
Wentworth, Thomas, 33, 35
West, John, 44, 213n40
White, Andrew, 36
William III (king of England), 139; assassination plots against, 165; declaration of, 166; Glorious Revolution and, 132–33; invades England, 169–70; Kingston-upon-Hull and, 220n63; legitimacy of, 173; Mary and, 10, 162, 176, 218n18. *See also* William and Mary
William and Mary: colonies and, 164; Marylanders support, 168; proprietary fails to proclaim, 163, 164, 167. *See also* Mary II; William III
Windebank, Francis, 39, 40, 43, 44, 194n68
Wolstenholme, Sir John, 43, 44

Yeardley, Argyll, 53
Yeardley, George, 37–38, 39, 53
Yeo, John, 120–21

Zouch, Sir John, 39, 44